STUDIES IN FINANCIAL OPTIMIZATION AND RISK MANAGEMENT

COMPUTATIONAL TECHNIQUES IN ECONOMICS AND FINANCE

STUDIES IN FINANCIAL OPTIMIZATION AND RISK MANAGEMENT

Additional books in this series can be found on Nova's website under the Series tab.

Additional E-books in this series can be found on Nova's website under the E-books tab.

COMPUTER SCIENCE, TECHNOLOGY AND APPLICATIONS

Additional books in this series can be found on Nova's website under the Series tab.

Additional E-books in this series can be found on Nova's website under the E-books tab.

STUDIES IN FINANCIAL OPTIMIZATION AND RISK MANAGEMENT

COMPUTATIONAL TECHNIQUES IN ECONOMICS AND FINANCE

CONSTANTIN ZOPOUNIDIS
EDITOR

Nova Science Publishers, Inc.
New York

For permission to use material from this book please contact us:
Telephone 631-231-7269; Fax 631-231-8175
Web Site: http://www.novapublishers.com

Library of Congress Cataloging-in-Publication Data

Computational techniques in economics and finance / editor, Constantin Zopounidis.
p. cm.
Includes bibliographical references and index.
ISBN 978-1-61324-558-3 (hardcover)
1. Economics, Mathematical. I. Zopounidis, Constantin.
HB135.C6235 2011
330.0285--dc23
2011013659

Published by Nova Science Publishers, Inc. †New York

CONTENTS

PREFACE[*]

The increasing volume of available data, the rapid advances in telecommunications, and the interrelationships of the global markets which are becoming stronger, create new challenges for researchers and practitioners in economics and finance. At the same time, the regulatory authorities are in a continuous attempt to establish effective rules for monitoring and regulating the global markets. As a result, the decision making process in economics and finance becomes more and more complex, thus requiring new advanced and sophisticated analysis methodologies to be developed and implemented. The contents of this volume cover a wide range of topics, including among others portfolio optimization, stock market prediction and trading, auditing, investment decisions, banking management and corporate performance.

Chapter 1 - The goal of this paper is to estimate the hazard function of the contraction of business cycle. The estimation of hazard function is given by the Kaplan – Meier estimator. In order to assess the effects of monetary and fiscal policy in hazard rate, we use the Cox model. We also assess the impact of variables such as election, war, and party in duration of contraction. The sample is referred to the period 1854 – 2001 using data from United States of America. With this paper we conclude: firstly, that the expansionary monetary policy in the period of contraction increases the probability of ending the contraction period. This result is consistent with monetary theory. Secondly, we confirm the theory of Opportunistic Political Business Cycle and, thirdly, we fail to confirm the Partisan Political Business Cycle and Rational Partisan Political Business Cycle theories.

Chapter 2 - The aim of this study is to examine the importance of central bank interest rate as a policy tool for the disinflation process in Brazil, China, India, Indonesia, Philippines, Russia, Korea and Vietnam. First, we test for the number of co-integrated vectors by using the Johansen's methodology. Second, we apply the Granger-Engle approach to test the direction of causality between interest rates and inflation. Lastly, we implement the aggregate GETS model in order to examine whether central bank interest rates have a negative effect on inflation for our sample economies. Our empirical results are mixed but we believe that can be useful for the central bank authorities of the economies analysed.

Chapter 3 - The work we present on this occasion is a step towards a search for basic formal elements in the treatment of uncertain economic phenomena taking into consideration

---

[*] Versions of these chapters were also published in *Journal of Computational Optimization in Economics and Finance*, Volume 1, Issues 1-3, published by Nova Science Publishers, Inc. They were submitted for appropriate modifications in an effort to encourage wider dissemination of research.

the notions of pretopology with their correspondent axiomatics. This is a summary of the results obtained in the theoretical investigation realized during the last years. It contributes a theoretical basis, mainly. A theoretical scheme is proposed and developed in this paper to give scientific solidity to the algorithms used in the process of segmentation, grouping and separation of homogenous objects, products, etc. These algorithms form a part of non-numerical mathematics of uncertainty. An illustrative development of the theoretical concepts is made. The results obtained, which are identical among each other are represented too.

Chapter 4 - The systematic classification of a united space and its distribution according to specific criteria, such as the homogeny, the polarity, the level of development or the degree of problems forms a basic subject of the regional science. Specifically, the regions' formation with united characteristics that are, usually, identified with the definition "homogenic regions" are essential for the implementation of effective regional programs and rational policy for each region, meaning the regional policy. In this framework, and in the current application, the homogeneity of the Greek space is surveyed according to the specific demographic, geographical and economic characteristics of the departments of the country, in order to create a basic supportive tool of a rational regional policy. For the needs of the current study, the method of the Hierarchical Cluster Classification is used, with the GDP, the level of rurality and insularity of the departments as criteria. The homogenic groups of the departments, derived from the application, present, in a large extent, a geographic continuity and a distinguishable geographic character, a fact that proves the dynamic of the "economic area" and, in every occasion, compose geographic units with common geographic, demographic and economic characteristics, the knowledge of which could contribute to the definition of the kind and intensity of measures of the regional policy that has to be applied. The results of the method are expected to contribute to the effort of the examination of the rationality of the regional structuring system and the formation of a modification proposal, based on combined criteria-variables, in order to compose a further discussion on a new regionalization currently developed in Greece.

Chapter 5 - This paper proposes a sophisticated empirical analysis on the presence and the nature of interaction effects between human capital and trade openness in the processes of productivity growth. According to our results, this interaction is not always linear. In particular, we will see how trade openness has a positive impact on productivity growth only above a minimum level of human capital. That is, less developed countries may take advantage of trade liberalization only after having reached a certain level of human capital. Obviously this will imply that it is not indifferent for a less developed country to decide first for a trade liberalization policy or for an education development policy.

Chapter 6 - This paper investigates the impact of outliers on the estimated parameters of the CAPM model. A mixed return process, consisting of a regular and an outlier component, is used to model returns for individual stocks. The regular component of stock returns is estimated using Huber's Robust M estimation (HRM) method. The results show that when positive (negative) outlier returns are matched with high (low) market returns a stock's OLS beta is larger than its respective HRM beta, and when matched with low (high) market returns, a stock's OLS beta is smaller than its respective HRM beta. The impact of outlier returns on a stock's estimated alpha is not as straightforward. (JEL: G11, G12).

Chapter 7 - We propose an integrated multiple-criteria methodological framework to support decisions that concern the selection of common stock portfolios. At the first stage of the methodology, two multiple-criteria methods are employed, within the context of the outranking relations theory, towards the initial appraisal of the stocks that are examined. We then utilize a non-linear optimization model, to generate portfolios that consist of the stocks that are classified as those with the optimal characteristics, during of the first stage. Finally, the portfolios designed at the previous stage are evaluated by using a wide set of well-known sophisticated evaluation criteria.

The preferences and experiences of professionals and experts in the field of portfolio management were taken into consideration, through all the stages of the process. The validity of the above methodology is tested through a large scale illustrative application on the stocks that constitute the FTSE-140 index of the Athens Stock Exchange. The advantages of the proposed model against contextual approaches are finally stressed.

Chapter 8 - This paper presents a combination of technical analysis and neural networks based on genetic algorithms for the purposes of forecasting the stock market trend. Various time frame moving average indexes are used as inputs to a neural network. The model uses genetic algorithms as a learning method. Many tests applying various stocks and indexes were carried out. The results were evaluated by the in sample and out of sample trend accuracy rate. Further evaluation was conducted by simulating the model and the returns were measured and compared with the buy and hold strategy. The results are very significant and are subject to further investigation.

Chapter 9 - In this paper, a new procedure for solving the Feature Subset Selection problem is presented. This procedure utilizes a memetic algorithm, which is based on the concepts of Genetic Algorithms (GA) and Particle Swarm Optimization (PSO). Contrary to genetic algorithms, in the proposed algorithm the evolution of each individual of the population is performed using a PSO algorithm. The proposed memetic-based classification algorithm is combined with a number of nearest neighbour based classifiers and is tested in a very significant financial classification task, involving the identification of qualified audit reports. The algorithm is compared with a classic genetic algorithm and other metaheuristic algorithms, like Ant Colony Optimization and Particle Swarm Optimization.

Chapter 10 - In this work we address investment decisions using real options. A standard numerical approach for valuing real options is dynamic programming. The basic idea is to establish a discrete-valued lattice of possible future values of the underlying stochastic variable (demand in our case). For most approaches in the literature, the stochastic variable is assumed normally distributed and then approximated by a binomial distribution, resulting in a binomial lattice. In this work, we investigate the use of a sparse Markov chain to model such variable. The Markov approach is expected to perform better since it does not assume any type of distribution for the demand variation, the probability of a variation on the demand value is dependent on the current demand value and thus, no longer constant and it generalizes the binomial lattice since the latter can be modelled as a Markov chain. We developed a stochastic dynamic programming model that has been implemented both on binomial and Markov models. A numerical example of a production capacity choice problem has been solved and the results obtained show that the investment decisions are different and, as expected the Markov chain approach leads to a better investment policy.

Chapter 11 - In this paper we estimate a dynamic structural model of capital investment at the firm level. Our dataset consists of a balanced panel of 1419 Greek firms. Two important features are present in our dataset. There are periods in which firms decide not to invest and periods of large investment episodes. This empirical evidence of infrequent and lumpy investment is in favour of irreversibilities and non-convex capital adjustment costs. We consider a dynamic discrete choice model of a general specification of adjustment costs including convex and non-convex components. We also assume total irreversibility of investment. We use an indirect inference procedure to estimate the structural parameters. Our goal is to investigate the nature of the capital adjustment process at the firm level for Greek data.

Chapter 12 - This paper evaluates the performance of a sample of branches of a large commercial bank in Greece by means of data envelopment analysis (DEA). A multi-input multi-output model that is geared towards senior management is considered in this country-wide evaluation. In this model the targets on sales of loans and deposits are proxied by the difference between average values of loans and deposits in two consecutive years. A variable returns to scale DEA input oriented model analyzed here led to valuable results pertaining to the performance of individual branches and moreover, useful information has also been obtained from the examination of the effects of selected branch characteristics and location to branch performance.

Chapter 13 - Cooperatives are considered as a form of business able to survive for many years, due to equal market opportunities and lower production costs for all their members. The main purpose of this research is to estimate the viability of a cooperative union under competitive conditions in the agricultural sector and to evaluate the financial aspects of its activities. Two countries, Russia and Greece, were selected for this study. Their development is still a controversial issue for agri-managers and financiers. The comparative analysis was carried out based on the data for four consecutive years (from 2003 to 2006). For the purpose of this study, ten cooperatives from the largest Greek island, Crete, and ten cooperatives from one of the biggest agricultural areas in Russia, the Krasnodar region, were chosen. Factor analysis and a multicriteria method (PROMETHEE II) were used to analyze the data. The aim was to determine the problems that exist within the cooperative unions and to compare them with each other.

In: Computational Techniques in Economics and Finance ISBN: 978-1-61324-558-3
Editor: Constantine Zopounidis

Chapter 1

DURATION ANALYSIS OF ECONOMIC CYCLES: AN EMPIRICAL ANALYSIS USING DATA FROM USA

Polyxeni Gioti*
Department of Economics, University of Ioannina, Greece.

ABSTRACT

The goal of this paper is to estimate the hazard function of the contraction of business cycle. The estimation of hazard function is given by the Kaplan – Meier estimator. In order to assess the effects of monetary and fiscal policy in hazard rate, we use the Cox model. We also assess the impact of variables such as election, war, and party in duration of contraction. The sample is referred to the period 1854 – 2001 using data from United States of America.

With this paper we conclude: firstly, that the expansionary monetary policy in the period of contraction increases the probability of ending the contraction period. This result is consistent with monetary theory. Secondly, we confirm the theory of Opportunistic Political Business Cycle and, thirdly, we fail to confirm the Partisan Political Business Cycle and Rational Partisan Political Business Cycle theories.

JEL codes: E000, H000, C140
Keywords: Kaplan Meier, Cox model, duration, hazard function, business cycle

1. INTRODUCTION

The classical definition of business cycle which is used in literature is given by Burns and Mitchell (1946): "Business cycles are a type of fluctuation found in the aggregate economic activity of nations that organize their work mainly in business enterprises: a cycle consists of expansions occurring at about the same time in many economic activities, followed by similarly general recessions, contractions, and revivals which merge into the expansion phase of the next cycle; the sequence of changes is recurrent but not periodic; in duration business

* Corresponding author: Polyxeni Gioti, e-mail: polgioti@cc.uoi.gr

cycles vary from more than one year to ten or twelve years; they are not divisible into shorter cycles of similar character with amplitudes approximating their own".

There are many theories about the duration of business cycle phases. According to Nordhaus (1975), Lindbeck (1976) and Tufte (1978) the opportunistic political business cycle model suggests that a business cycle trough (that is the beginning of an expansion phase of the business cycle) is likely in the period before an election as an incumbent attempts to increase the chance of reelection. This model also suggests that a business cycle peak (that is the beginning of the contraction phase of a business cycle) follows soon after an election as the preelection stimulus is reversed.

Partisan political business cycle theories suggest that the likelihood of a peak or trough following a presidential election depends upon which party was victorious. Rational partisan theory according to Alesina (1987) suggests that a business cycle peak marking the end of an expansion is more likely in the wake of Republican presidential victory than at other times and less likely after a Democratic presidential victory than at other times. Conversely, a business cycle trough is less likely after a Republican has won a presidential election than at other times and more likely after Democrat has won than at other times.

In the context of this paper we expand Klein's model (1996) by using not only quantitative variables, as Klein did, but also qualitative variables which represent government policy. We also differentiate our work by means of statistics, using methods in order to specify the distribution of functional form. We believe that this way our paper contributes to literature, because, as far as we know, there is no other paper with similar features.

2. Data

The sample is referred to the period 1854 – 2001 using data from USA and concerns 32 contractions. Duration of contractions is from peak to trough of business cycle and is calculated in months according to the National Bureau of Economic Research. For M1 we derive annual data from Federal Reserve Bank (FED) according to definition that is given by FED. We use the average of two last years of M1 with the rate which is referred to the peak of business cycle, in order to assess its effect on the probability of contraction to end. We assume that, on account of Friedman (1961) who claims that an increase in money increasing the nominal GDP with delay of six to twelve months. In the same way we use the data about deficit/surplus and we derive the data from Department of commerce Bureau of Census and Bureau of Economic Analysis. According to monetary theory, the monetary policy exerts great impact on economic procedure. According to Friedman (1968), the Great Contraction of 1993 in the USA, could have been prevented if monetary authorities had avoided mistakes. For example, from October 1929 to June 1933, money supply decreased by 33% (due to many banks shut down) which led to an increase in unemployment rate of about 25% in 1933. Monetary policy can affect total product only in short term. As for fiscal policy, monetarization of the budget deficit during contraction can be effective.

We also use other variables, namely a) election as binary variable, which according to opportunistic business cycle can affect the turning points of business cycle, b) party in power during contraction as binary variable, which exerts influence on turning points, and c) binary variable war, if war was held during contraction.

3. The Method

According to Kiefer (1988), a useful function of duration analysis is the hazard function which is the rate at which spells will be completed at duration t, given that they last until t. For example, which is the probability for an economy to exit from contraction in the next three months given the duration of contraction until now?

The probability that the duration of contraction (T) is less of some value t is $F(t)=\Pr(T<t)$. The survivor function is:

$$S(t)=1-F(t)=\Pr(T\geq t) \tag{1}$$

which estimates the probability that the duration of contraction will equal or exceed the value t. The rate at which an economy will exit from contraction, given that the economy suffers from contraction until now, is $\lambda(t)$ which is called hazard function in terms of probabilities and is given by the following equation:

$$\lambda(t)=\lim_{h\to 0}\Pr\frac{(t\leq T<t+h\,|\,T\geq t)}{h} \tag{2}$$

The equation (2) gives us the Kaplan – Meier estimator. The estimated survivor function is:

$$\hat{S}(t)=\prod_{t=1}^{T}\left(1-\hat{\lambda}_t\right) \tag{3}$$

which is possible to interpret this estimator as a maximum likelihood estimator because according to Kaplan and Meier (1958) maximizes the likelihood of observations.

The observations of the duration of contraction can be either censored or uncensored. Particularly, if a spell of contraction is completed, which means that we know exactly the time period in which an economy is in contraction, then it is referred as uncensored spell. If, on the other hand, we do not know when an economy enters a contraction phase or when abandons it, then the spell is termed censored. Moffit (1985) highlights the fact that censored spells are a drawback for such kind of analysis, because we can not have information about the distribution of such spell beyond the exhaustion point. According to Meyer (1990) we can characterize a spell as censored given that its duration will last more than another observable variable. For example, we can characterize a spell of contraction as censored given that it lasts more than the duration of countercyclical policy but this is an issue which needs further investigation. For simplicity in the context of this analysis, we assume that the spells of duration of contraction are completed, which means that we know exactly the duration of contractions.

Lawless (1982) says that the Kaplan – Meier estimator is shown to be strongly consistent according to the standard errors. Also, according to Fisher and Van Belle (1993), the life table estimates give unbiased estimates only if the censoring mechanism is independent of the occurrence of the endpoint. Thus, we throw away those periods that are characterized as censored, because they do not offer as accurate information. After that, censored observations affect our estimation only by decreasing the length of our sample.

The hazard function has positive duration dependence when the probability that a spell will end shortly increases as the spell increases in length. For example, the more the contraction lasts, the more chances does the economy have to get in the expansion phase. On the other hand, the hazard function has negative duration dependence when the probability that a spell will end shortly decreases as the spell increases in length. For example, the more the contraction lasts, the less chances does the economy have to get in the expansion phase. In many cases, this probability is affected by different factors such as government policy. Also it can be affected by political conditions such as war, elections, party. All these factors are included in the matrix of independent variables.

In this point it is interesting to examine the effect of the duration of contraction. We will examine different cases according to variables. For example, we use the level of rate of M1 for USA, as quoted mark. More specifically, we use this variable in order to divide the sample into two categories. In the first one, we use the observations for which the level of M1, as a ratio, is higher that the mean of M1, whereas in the second case the level of M1 is lower than the mean. In the same way we use and the rest of explanatory variables which are a) deficit/surplus, b) elections, c) party in power and d) war.

According to Moffit (1985), more formal evidence accrues from least – squares regressions on the Kaplan – Meier survivor estimates. A regression of $\log(S_t)$ on t (without an intercept) will yield a coefficient equal to the hazard (and if the distribution is exactly exponential, the R – squared will be one). The results are given in the table 1

Table 1. Least Square Regressions on the Kaplan – Meier Survivor estimates

M1>4.24%	DS>72.91%	Election	War	Democratic Party	
R^2	0.74	0.85	0.86	0.78	0.92
Coefficient	-0.034	-0.028	-0.030	-0.031	-0.027
Std Error	(0.003)	(0.0014)	(0.0027)	(0.0018)	(0.0014)
M1<4.24%	DS<72.91%	No Election	No War	Republican Party	
R^2	0.91	0.73	0.75	0.78	-2.49
Coefficient	-0.027	-0.036	-0.029	-0.031	-0.054
Std Error	(0.0014)	(0.0054)	(0.0019)	(0.0018)	(0.006)

If the distribution of the duration is exponential, then the duration of contraction does not appear in the expression of the hazard rate; this means that the duration of spells of contraction is of no matter. The knowledge of distribution is important in order to use parametric methods to estimate the vector of parameters which maximize the likelihood function. In case where the distribution of the duration is exponential, then $f(t) = \gamma \exp(-\gamma t)$, where $\gamma = \eta\pi$ namely, the hazard depends on η, which is the constant rate at which an economy has the chance to get out of the contraction. Another way to suggest the functional form is the graphical methods for homogeneous observations. Homogeneity is achieved by grouping on explanatory variables. For example, we restrict our attention to these contractions which begin in June.

Table 2. Survival Function

IVM1	sample	Time	Status	Cumulative Proportion Surviving at the Time		N of Cumulative Events	N of Remaining Cases
				Estimate	Std. Error		
0,00	1	8,000	1,00	0,813	0,098	1	15
	2	8,000	1,00	0,813	0,098	2	14
	3	8,000	1,00	0,813	0,098	3	13
	4	10,000	1,00	0,688	0,116	4	12
	5	10,000	1,00	0,688	0,116	5	11
	6	11,000	1,00	0,625	0,121	6	10
	7	13,000	1,00	0,500	0,125	7	9
	8	13,000	1,00	0,500	0,125	8	8
	9	14,000	1,00	0,438	0,124	9	7
	10	18,000	1,00	0,250	0,108	10	6
	11	18,000	1,00	0,250	0,108	11	5
	12	18,000	1,00	0,250	0,108	12	4
	13	23,000	1,00	0,188	0,098	13	3
	14	32,000	1,00	0,125	0,083	14	2
	15	43,000	1,00	0,063	0,061	15	1
	16	65,000	1,00	0,000	0,000	16	0
1,00	1	6,000	1,00	0,938	0,061	1	15
	2	7,000	1,00	0,875	0,083	2	14
	3	8,000	1,00	0,750	0,108	3	13
	4	8,000	1,00	0,750	0,108	4	12
	5	10,000	1,00	0,688	0,116	5	11
	6	11,000	1,00	0,625	0,121	6	10
	7	13,000	1,00	0,500	0,125	7	9
	8	13,000	1,00	0,500	0,125	8	8
	9	16,000	1,00	0,375	0,121	9	7
	10	16,000	1,00	0,375	0,121	10	6
	11	17,000	1,00	0,313	0,116	11	5
	12	18,000	1,00	0,188	0,098	12	4
	13	18,000	1,00	0,188	0,098	13	3
	14	23,000	1,00	0,125	0,083	14	2
	15	24,000	1,00	0,063	0,061	15	1
	16	38,000	1,00	0,000	0,000	16	0

The standard error is estimated by Greenwood’s formula (1926)

4. Kaplan - Meier Estimators

Using Kaplan - Meier estimator we can compare the hazard rate in different cases. For example, using M1 as quoted mark we observe that monetary policy increases the hazard (the probability the contraction to come to an end) in case the rate is higher than the mean (4.24%). For example, if the duration of contraction lasts 18 months, the probability the contraction to last another five months is 0,188 or 18,8% in case the monetary policy is lower than the mean and 0,125 or 12,5% in case the monetary policy is higher than the mean. The expansionary monetary policy increases the hazard by 6,3%. This result is consistent with monetary theory.

In figure 1 that follows we can see diagrammatically that an expansionary monetary policy with a rate higher than the mean increases the probability a contraction to end. The hazard function shifts leftward.

Also we can see that when government tends to follow surplus budget during the contraction, this decreases the hazard, which means that it increases the probability for contraction to survive. But when the government follows a budget that shows a deficit which is less than the mean (-72.91%) the hazard increases. For example, if the contraction lasts 16 months, the probability to last another two months is 16,7% when the budget shows deficit whereas in case the government tends to follow surplus budget the survival probability is 23,1%. This means that surplus budget during contraction increases the probability for contraction to last by 6,4%.

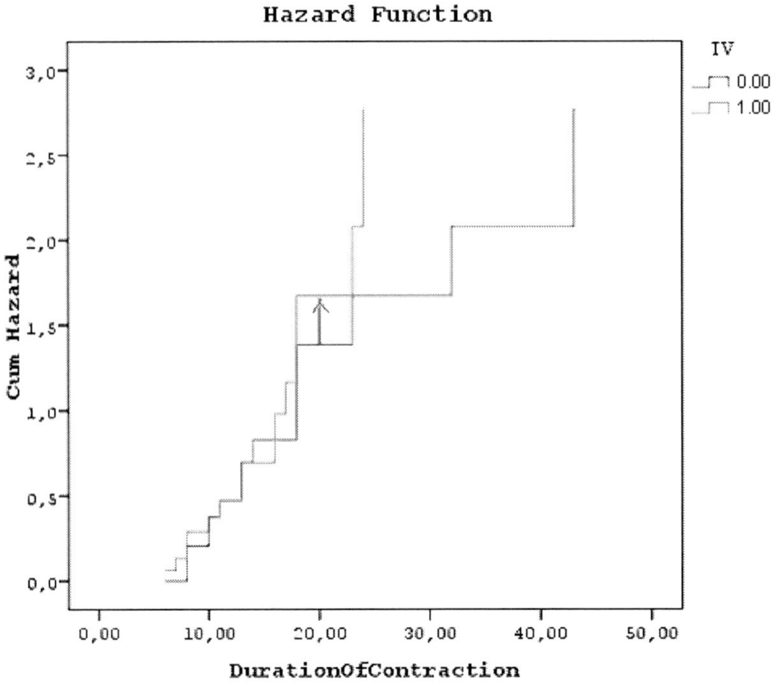

Figure 1. Hazard function.

In case where elections are held, this increases the probability for contraction to last longer. For example, if the contraction lasts 8 months, the probability the contraction to last another two months is 0,667 or 66,7% in case no elections are held and 0,750 or 75% in case elections are held. Which means the probability for contraction to last another two months is higher at a rate of 0,083 or 8.3%. This result is consistent with the theory of opportunistic political business cycle model and we agree with Klein (1996), although he uses the variable of election as time – varying in order to avoid spurious results (in case we use it as dummy variable – as we did).

Also, should a war is held, the probability for contraction to last longer decreases. For example, if the contraction lasts 8 months, the probability the contraction to last another two months is 0,760 or 76% when no war is held and 0,429 or 42,9% in case of a war. In other words, the probability for contraction to last another two months is lower in case of a war and this decrease rates is 0,331 or 33,1%.

Finally, in case the Republicans are in power, the probability for contraction to last longer increases. For example, if the contraction lasts 8 months, the probability the contraction to last another two months, in case the Republicans are in power, is 0.684 or 68.4% and 0.692 or 69.2% in case the Democratic Party is in power. This means that the probability for contraction to last another two months is higher when Republicans are in power, an increase of 0.008 or 8%. This is consistent with Rational Partisan Theory. All the statistical results are available upon request.

In order to assess the impact of independent variable into dependent variable we use Cox model. The advantage of this model is that it gives us the chance to estimate the impact of independent variables into dependent variable, which can be either binary or not.

5. Cox Model

According to Kiefer (1988) the explanatory variables can affect the distribution of the depended variable by moving its mean around. The way to estimate these effects is the proportional hazard models. The sign of the coefficient indicates the direction of the effect of the explanatory variable on the conditional probability of completing spell and are interpreted in the same way as coefficients in the linear model.

Cox (1972) suggests the partial likelihood approach according to which we can estimate the vector of coefficients β in the proportional hazard model without specifying the form of the baseline hazard function λ_0. The fact that we do not know or we do not want to take into account the form of the distribution, it is not a serious problem according to Cox, because, even if we lose some information about the coefficients, he demonstrates that his method of analysis has sensible properties, whatever the form of the function of the baseline hazard function is.

We can interpret the information of the Cox model in the follow way; the contribution to likelihood is the ratio of the hazard for the individual whose spell was completed at duration t divided by the sum of the hazards for individuals whose spells where still in progress just prior to time t. The proportional hazard function is:

$$\lambda(t;z) = \exp(z\beta)\lambda_0(t) \quad (4)$$

where $\lambda_0(t)$ is the baseline hazard function for the standard set of explanatory variables $z = 0$ and β is a $p \times 1$ vector of unknown parameters.

We estimate the equation (4) using Cox model. We can see that variables M1 and Election are statistically important. In particular, the effect of M1 in hazard function is 100*(exp(0.077)-1)=8%. The effect of election is -1.240 which means that decreases the hazard rate by 100*(exp(-1.240)-1)=71.06%.

We can use Chi – Square distribution with one degree of freedom in order to test the statistical significance of independent variables. We reject the null hypothesis $H_0 : \beta_i = 0$ because the Wald test value is greater than critical value $X^2_{1,0.05} = 3.84$.

Table 3. Cox model estimation

	B	SE	Wald	Df	Sig.	Exp(B)
M1	0,077	0,035	4,909	1	0,027	1,080
Election	-1,240	0,525	5,567	1	0,018	0,289

We can also assess the hypothesis $\beta_1 = \beta_2 = \ldots = \beta_k = 0$ using chi – square distribution in this case $X^2_{2,0.05} = 9.606 > 5.99$, thus, we reject the null hypothesis which means that at least one coefficient exerts significant impact on the dependent variable, which is the duration of contraction.

A basic drawback in this analysis is the small sample. A common method to face off this problem is the bootstrap method which is proposed by Efron (1979). Bootstrapping is a general approach to statistical inference based on building a sampling distribution for a statistic by resampling from the data at hand. The term "bootstrapping" is an allusion to the expression "pulling oneself up by one's bootstrap" in this case using the sample data as a population from which repeated samples are drawn.

According to bootstrap method, the results have as follows, when the estimations relied on 30.000 samples and the model has the form:

$$\ln\frac{haz_i(t)}{h_0(t)} = \underset{0.007}{0.054}{*}\,M1 + \underset{0.0002}{0.0004}{*}\,Def/Surp - \underset{0.125}{1.018}{*}\,Election + \underset{0.076}{0.468}{*}\,War \quad (5)$$

where $\ln\frac{haz_i(t)}{h_0(t)}$ is the logarithm of relative risk (relative hazard) if the independent variable is increased by one unit. For one more time, we can observe that not only money supply and elections are statistically important but also war seems now to exert influence on duration of contraction. The variable deficit/ surplus is marginally accepted, but the influence on duration is extremely low.

The results are consistent with monetary theory as far as M1 and deficit are concerned and with the theory of opportunistic political business cycle in case of election. The theory of Rational Partisan Theory is not confirmed by Cox model. We would like to notice that Klein (1996) reaches the same results as far as election and party are concerned.

Table 4. Parameter Estimates

	Parameter	Estimate	Std. Error	95% Confidence Interval		$X^2_{1,\alpha}$
				Lower Bound	Upper Bound	
Asymptotic	m	0.054	0.007	0.041	0.068	59.51
	d	0.0004	0.0001	3.43E-005	0.001	16.00
	e	-1.018	0.093	-1.210	-0.827	119.82
	w	0.468	0.097	0.268	0.667	23.28
	p	0.073	0.082	-0.096	0.241	0.79
Bootstrap (a,b)	m	0.054	0.008	0.039	0.070	45.56
	d	0.0004	0.0002	-9.04E-005	0.001	4.00
	e	-1.018	0.125	-1.263	-0.773	66.38
	w	0.468	0.076	0.318	0.617	37.92
	p	0.073	0.093	-0.110	0.256	0.62

CONCLUSIONS

In the context of this paper we try to estimate the probability a contraction to end and to assess the impact of independent variables on this probability. In order to do so we use the Kaplan – Meier estimator and the Cox model. Thus with this paper we conclude: firstly, that the expansionary monetary policy in the period of contraction increases the probability of ending the contraction period. This result is consistent with monetary theory. Secondly, we confirm the theory of Opportunistic Political Business Cycle and, thirdly, we fail to confirm the Partisan Political Business Cycle and Rational Partisan Political Business Cycle theories.

REFERENCES

Alesina, A. (1987) “Macroeconomic policy in a two – party system as repeated game”, *Quarterly Journal of Economics*, 102(3), 651 – 678.

Burns, A. F. and Mitchell, W. C. (1946) “Measuring Business Cycles”, *National Bureau of Economic Research,* New York.

Cox, D. R. (1972) “Regression Models and Life – Tables”, *Journal of the Royal Statistical Society.* Series B (Methodological), 34 (2), 187 – 220.

Efron, B. (1979) “Bootstrap methods: Another Look at the Jackknife”, *The Annals of Statistics,* 7(1), 1-26.

Fisher, D.L. and Van Belle, G. (1993) “*Biostatistics. A methodology for the health sciences*”, John Wiley and Sons, New York.

Friedman, M. (1961) "The lag in effect of monetary policy". Journal of Political Economy. 69(5), 447-466.

Friedman, M. (1968) "The role of monetary policy", *The American Economic Review*, 58 (1), 1 – 17.

Kaplan, E. L. and Meier, P. (1958) "Nonparametric estimation from incomplete observations", *Journal of the American Statistical Association*, 53(282), 457 – 481.

Kiefer, N. (1988) "Economic duration data and hazard function", *Journal of Economic Literature,* 26(2), 646 – 679.

Klein, W. Michael (1996) "Timing Is All: Elections and the Duration of United States Business Cycles", *Journal of Money, Credit, and Banking*, 28(1), 84 – 101.

Lawless, J. (1982) "*Statistical models and methods for life time data*", (2nd edition) Wiley, New York.

Lindbeck, A. (1976) "Stabilization Policies in Open Economies with endogenous Politicians", *American Economic Review Papers and Proceedings*, 66, 1-19.

Meyer, B. D. (1990) "Unemployment insurance and unemployment spells", *Econometrica*, 58(4), 757 – 782.

Moffit, R. (1985) "Unemployment insurance and the distribution of unemployment spells", *Journal of Econometrics*, 28, 85 – 101.

Nordhaus, W. (1975) "The Political Business Cycle", *Review of Economic Studies*, 42, 169-190.

Tufte, E. R. (1978) "*Political Control of the Economy*", Princeton, N. J.: Princeton University Press.

In: Computational Techniques in Economics and Finance
Editor: Constantine Zopounidis
ISBN: 978-1-61324-558-3

Chapter 2

Is Central Bank Interest Rate a Policy Tool for Disinflation? Evidence from Developing Economies

Stelios Karagiannis [*a] **, *Yannis Panagopoulos*** [b] ***and Prodromos Vlamis*** [c]
[a]Centre for Planning and Economic Research, Athens, Greece
[b]Centre for Planning and Economic Research, and
Athens University of Economics & Business, Athens, Greece
[c]Centre for Planning and Economic Research, Athens, Greece, and
University of Cambridge, UK

Abstract

The aim of this study is to examine the importance of central bank interest rate as a policy tool for the disinflation process in Brazil, China, India, Indonesia, Philippines, Russia, Korea and Vietnam. First, we test for the number of co-integrated vectors by using the Johansen's methodology. Second, we apply the Granger-Engle approach to test the direction of causality between interest rates and inflation. Lastly, we implement the aggregate GETS model in order to examine whether central bank interest rates have a negative effect on inflation for our sample economies. Our empirical results are mixed but we believe that can be useful for the central bank authorities of the economies analyzed.

J.E.L. Classification: E52, E43, C22.
Keywords: Central Bank Interest Rate, Aggregate General-to-Specific Model, Developing Economies.

* Corresponding Author: Centre for Planning and Economic Research (KEPE), 11 Amerikis Str, 106 72, Athens, Greece. E-mail: stkatag@kepe.gr

1. Introduction

Mainstream economic theory describes central bank interest rate (CB hereafter) as one of the tools -probably the most important one- that monetary authorities can use to influence inflation in any economy. As it is argued by the Monetarist school of thought, inflation is always a monetary phenomenon (see Meltzer, 1998, p.13). The CB rate can be considered as a vehicle policy variable, which is related to central bank's choices regarding monetary policy effectiveness on inflation. In this paper, we focus on the interest rate channel of monetary policy that is how the central bank rates are affecting inflation. More specifically, we are interested in unveiling the existence and importance of CB interest rate behaviour for exercising effective monetary policy with respect to inflation.

We are concentrating in analyzing a group of developing economies, namely Brazil, China, India, Indonesia, Philippines, Russia, Korea and Vietnam. These countries although not geographically homogenous, they belong to a group of rapidly growing economies (see Graph 1 below). Having said that, their level of income and size in terms of population, differ substantially (see Graph 2 below and Table 1 in the Appendix).

Graph 1.
Developing Economies, GDP (%)
(Average 1997-2007)

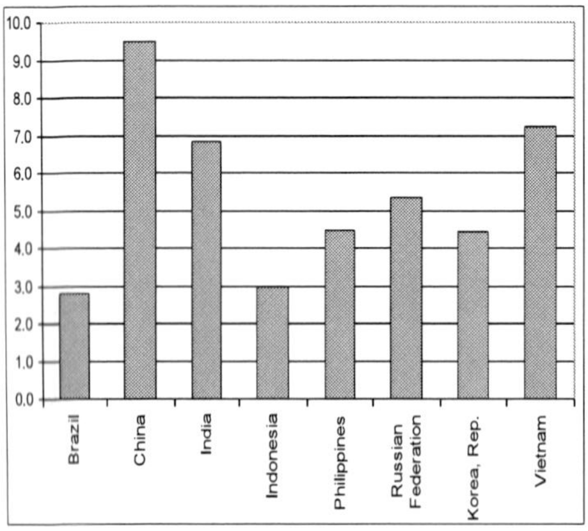

Graph 2.
Developing Economies, GDP per capita
(Average 1990-2007)

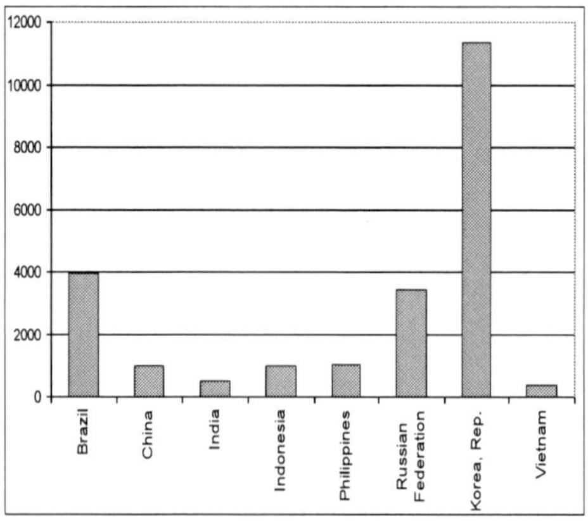

Source: World Economic Outlook Database, International Monetary Fund

We address the question whether the CB interest rate can be a tool for combating inflation. This is particularly important in the context of these developing economies as the majority of them experienced relatively high inflation rates during the 1990s (Figures 1-8 in the Appendix). We employ the aggregate LSE-Hendry general-to-specific model (hereafter GETS, see Hendry Pagan, Saragan, 1984; Hendry, 1987) to examine the relationship between the CB interest rates and inflation.

Related empirical literature is focusing on the examination of the Fisher's equation i.e. the nominal short rates are decomposed into ex ante real rates and expected inflation. Results are rather mixed, were some studies (e.g. Nelson and Schwert, 1977; Kinal and Lahiri, 1988) present evidence that real interest rates behave like a random walk (see also Garbade and Wachtel, 1978; Fama and Gibbons, 1982; Antoncic, 1986 for similar findings). Other studies show evidence that a time-varying term premium might explain the econometric failures of the expectations hypothesis of the term structure, without addressing the relationship of inflation and real interest rate (see Engle and Ng, 1993; Mayfeld and Murphy, 1996; Tzavalis and Wickens, 1997).

There are two main reasons that lead us to believe that our paper contributes to the existing literature on CB interest rate policy. First, we employ an econometric model, the aggregate GETS, which allows us to estimate and make inferences about the CB's interest rate elasticities. This model has not been used before in the relevant literature. Second, to the best of our knowledge it is the first attempt to make a comparative study between a number of developing economies regarding the relationship between CB's interest rate and inflation in the new era characterized by financial market deregulation. Our empirical results are mixed. Regarding India, Indonesia, Philippines, Russia and Korea, our empirical results do not support our prior theoretical hypothesis with respect to the long-run effect from the interest rate to inflation. As far as it concerns Brazil and China, there is a negative long-run effect from the interest rates to inflation, although not statistically significant.

The paper is structured as follows. Section 2 presents data, the theoretical framework and the econometric methodology. The empirical results and the estimates of the speed of adjustment are given in Section 3. Section 4 concludes the paper.

2. Data, Theoretical Framework and Econometric Methodology

2.1. Data

Data used for the developing countries are collected from the International Financial Statistics produced by the International Monetary Fund. We use monthly data for all the economies analysed but the examined time period is not identical1. Fluctuations of the key variables used, that is inflation and CB interest rate are shown in Figures 1-8 in the Appendix.

2.2. Theoretical Framework

The simple model of monetary policy from the CB interest rate to the inflation rate takes the following algebraic form:

$$\dot{P}_t = c + \sum_{j=1}^{n} k * \dot{P}_{t-j} + \sum_{i=1}^{n} \phi * i_{CB,t-i} + e_t \tag{1a}$$

where:

ϕ , is the long-run coefficient of the CB interest rate

[1] More specifically, periods of analysis for the SEE economics are: for Brazil (1997M1-2007M12), for China (1990M6-2007M12), for India (1990M6-2007M12), for Indonesia (1990M8-2007M12), for Philippines (1990M5-2007M12), for Russia (1997M2-2007M12), for Korea (1990M8-2007M12) and finally for Vietnam (1996M1-2006M12).

k, is the long-run coefficient of the lagged dependent variable.

In addition

$$\Delta \dot{P}_t = c + \sum_{j=1}^{n} \rho * \Delta \dot{P}_{t-j} + \sum_{i=1}^{n} \lambda * \Delta i_{CB,t-i} - \theta * e_{t-1} + u_t \quad (1b)$$

is a simple dynamic error correction model (ECM) where:

λ, is the short-run coefficient of the CB interest rate

ρ, is the short-run coefficient of the lagged dependent variable

θ, is the speed of adjustment initiated from the CB interest rate changes

There are two main theoretical issues which are worth examining. First, the speed of adjustment initiated from the CB interest rate changes (the θ coefficient of the error correction term in equation 1b) and second, the long-run and short-run interest rate elasticities ((the φ's and the $\lambda's$ coefficients in equations (1a) and (1b), respectively)) from the CB to the inflation rate. In our empirical part we estimate and present all three coefficients (the φ's, the $\lambda's$ and θ's) but we interpret only φ's and θ's coefficients since only those two coefficients are critical to our research question.

2.3 Econometric Methodology: The LSE-Hendry General to Specific (GETS) Model

We know from the relevant literature that a simple aggregate dynamic Granger–Engle Vector Error Correction model has the following form:

$$\Delta \dot{P}_t = c + \sum_{i=1}^{n} \beta \, \Delta \dot{P}_{t-i} + \sum_{i=0}^{n} \delta \, \Delta i_{CB,t-i} - \theta \, e_{t-1} + u_t \quad (2)$$

where: $i_{CB,t}$, stands for the CB interest rate while the, $\dot{P}_t$, stands for the inflation rate. The e_{t-1} is the error correction term. Moving a step forward, the GETS model could be presented in the following form[2]:

$$\Delta \dot{P}_t = \sum_{i=1}^{n} \beta \, \Delta \dot{P}_{t-i} + \sum_{i=0}^{n} \delta \Delta i_{CB,t-i} - \theta \, (\dot{P}_t - \varphi 0 - \varphi 1 \, i_{CB,t} - \varphi 2 \, T)_{t-1} + u_t \quad (3a)$$

[2] This model is estimated with the Non-Linear Least Squares method.

or alternatively

$$\Delta \dot{P}_t = \gamma_0 + \sum_{i=1}^{n} \beta \, \Delta \dot{P}_{t-i} + \sum_{i=0}^{n} \delta \, \Delta i_{CB,t-i} - \theta \, (\dot{P}_t - \varphi 1 \, i_{CB,t} - \varphi 2 \, T \,)_{t-1} + u_t \quad (3b)$$

where: θ is the speed of adjustment coefficient in the GETS model and T is the time trend. The choice between the two GETS models (3a) and (3b) depends on the performance and plausibility of the estimation results.

3. Results

As it is standard in empirical time series analysis, we test for the number of co-integrated vectors (r) between the dependent and the independent variable by using the Johansen's methodology (Johansen, 1995). Since the number of existing co-integrating vectors from the Johansen's process is sensitive to the number of lagged variables of the initial vector (Karfakis, 2004), we implement five different lag selection criteria. These are the modified Likelihood Ratio test statistic (LR), the Final Prediction Error test (FPE), the Akaike Information Criterion (AIC), the Schwarz Information Criterion (SC) and finally the Hannan-Quinn information criterion (HQ).

The aforementioned selection criteria regarding the optimal lag length do not all concur in the majority of the examined cases3. Thus, the majority rule is applied as a sub-optimal solution. According to the Eigenvalue and Trace tests there is a unique co-integrated vector of order 1 (r=1) for all the examined economies with the exception of Indonesia and Vietnam (r=0). This supports the hypothesis that CB interest rate and inflation tend to co-integrate pairwise (see Table 2 in the Appendix).

We also implement Granger-Engle (1987) approach to test the direction of causality among interest rates and inflation for the economies analyzed. From Table 3, column 2 and 3, we infer that for India, Indonesia, Philippines, Russia and Korea CB interest rate Granger causes inflation. Additionally, in the case of Vietnam a feedback outcome is observed. Finally, for Brazil and China the causality outcome is reversed, as it seems that inflation Granger causes CB's interest rate movements. Therefore, in line with the standard monetary theory, we use inflation as the dependent variable in our GETS model for India, Indonesia, Philippines, Russia and Korea.

Then, we implement the aggregate GETS model in order to examine whether CB interest rates have a negative effect on inflation. The coefficients of the error correction term, θ's, have the expected negative sign and are statistically significant in all the examined cases (Table 4, columns 1-8). This implies that there is a long-run relationship between inflation and interest rates. Coefficient ϕ_1 (in eq. 3a) indicates whether there is a long-run effect from the CB interest rate to inflation. It seems from our results that there is not such a negative relationship for India, Indonesia, Philippines, Russia and Korea. Nevertheless, the positive relationship is statistically significant only for Indonesia and Russia.

[3] Results for the five different lag selection criteria are available from the authors upon request.

As for Brazil and China, despite the reversed causality result (see ECVAR causality tests in Table 3) we also implement the aggregate GETS model with inflation as the dependent variable. Although not econometrically justified, we proceed with this kind of modeling in order to test our prior theoretical hypothesis that CB interest is the key policy-target variable to fight inflation. Results for these two countries indicate that although their coefficients of the error correction term, θ's, have the expected negative sign, they are statistically insignificant. Also, ϕ_1 coefficient is not statistically significant but it has the appropriate sign which implies that CB interest rate might be employed as an anti-inflationary policy tool.

Conclusions

Policy interest rates (the official central bank rate) play an important role in any economy and are crucial for Governments, commercial banks and investors' decision making. This study examines the importance of central bank interest rate policy for the disinflation process in a group of developing economies.

We test for the number of co-integrated vectors (r) by using the Johansen's methodology and then we apply the Granger-Engle approach to test the direction of causality among interest rates and inflation. Lastly, we implement the aggregate GETS model in order to examine whether CB interest rates have a negative effect on inflation in the economies analysed. Regarding India, Indonesia, Philippines, Russia and Korea, our empirical results do not support our prior theoretical hypothesis with respect to the long-run effect from the interest rate to inflation. As far as it concerns Brazil and China, there is a negative long-run effect from the interest rates to inflation, although not statistically significant.

Our results provide an answer to the question set out at the outset, namely whether there is an effect of CB interest rates on inflation in the developing economies. More specifically, it turns out that the interest rate policy designed and run by the Central Bank does not have a negative effect on inflation as expected by standard economic theory. This might be explained by the fact that the majority of these economies have only recently integrated the market mechanism into their economic systems.

Moreover, they might have possibly used alternative policy instruments to stabilise prices, like contractionary income and fiscal policy. The analysis of the effect of these other policy instruments on inflation is beyond the scope of this paper. We believe that our results can be useful for the central bank authorities of these countries in their attempt to monitor the competitiveness of their economies and, therefore, reinforce their macroeconomic stability.

APPENDIX

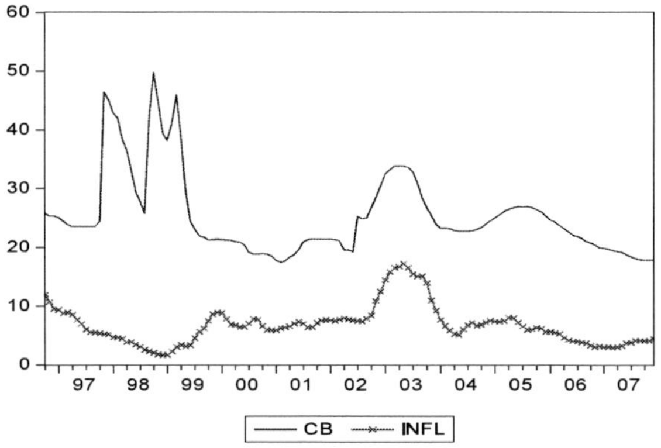

Figure 1. Inflation & CB Interest Rate in Brazil.

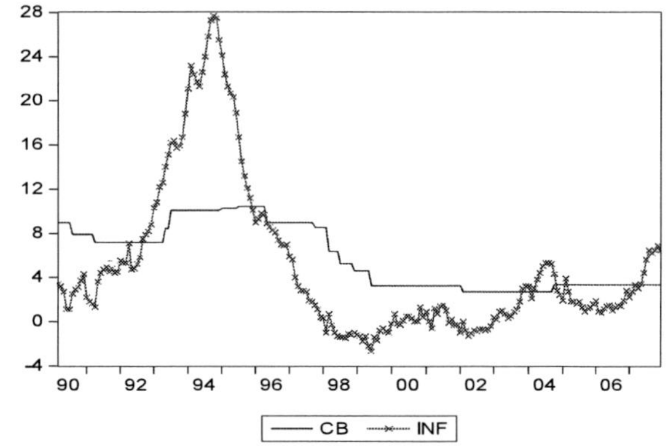

Figure 2. Inflation & CB Interest Rate in China.

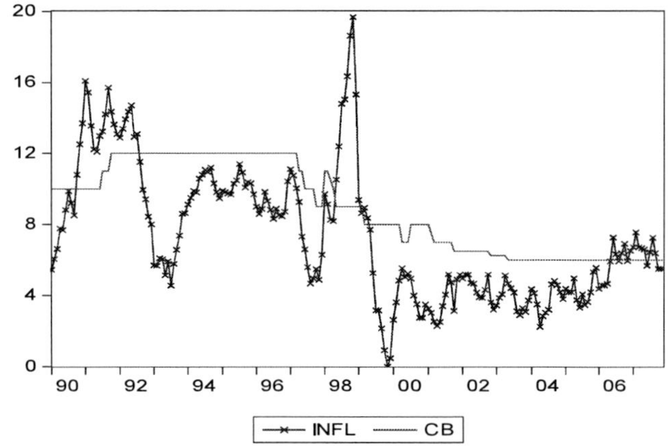

Figure 3. Inflation & CB Interest Rate in India.

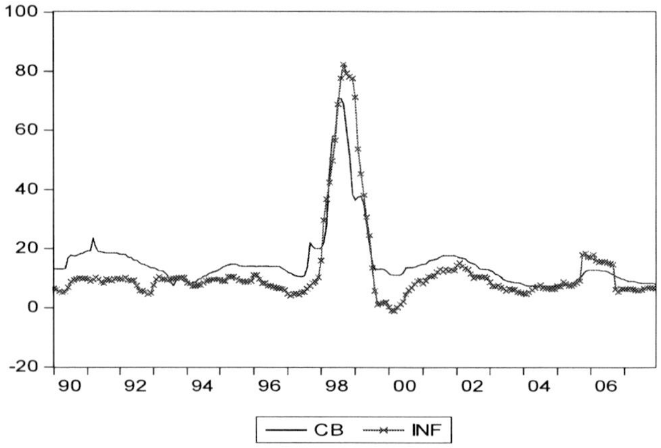

Figure 4. Inflation & CB Interest Rate in Indonesia.

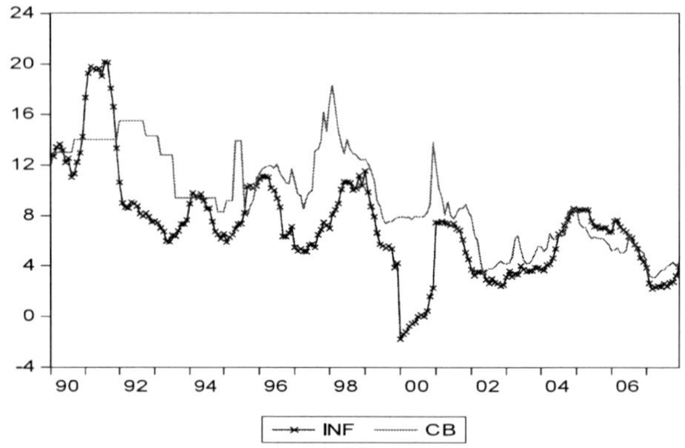

Figure 5. Inflation & CB Int. Rate in Philippines.

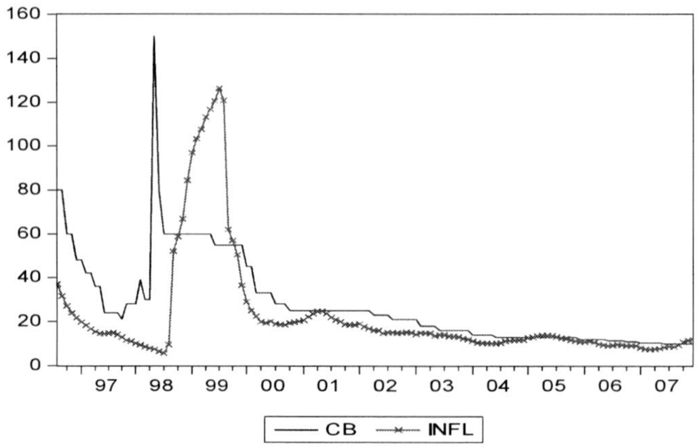

Figure 6. Inflation & CB Interest Rate in Russia.

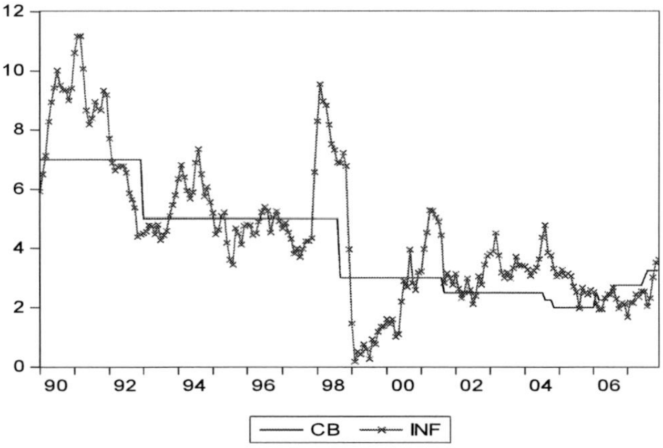

Figure 7. Inflation & CB Interest Rate in Korea.

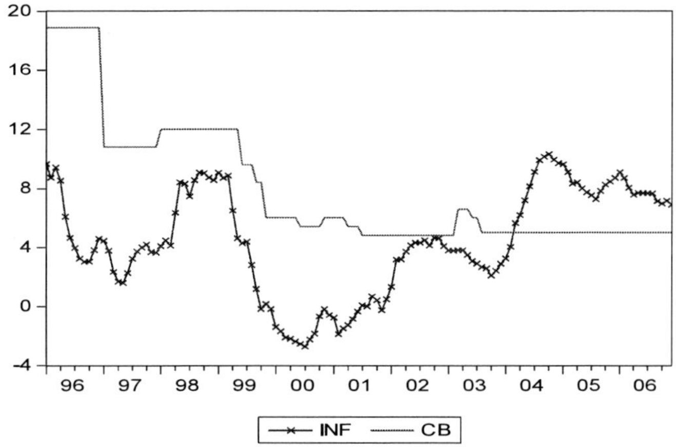

Figure 8. Inflation & CB Interest Rate in Vietnam.

Table 1. Economy & Income, (Average 1990 – 2007)

	GDP (million $)	GDP (per capita)	GDP (% growth)	Population (million)
Brazil	685,459.4	3975.1	2.4	170.5
China	1,251,119.9	985.0	10.0	1239.2
India	505,216.8	496.2	6.3	989.5
Indonesia	205,238.4	997.8	4.9	202.3
Philippines	77,372.7	1025.6	3.8	74.2
Russian Fed.	497,595.2	3422.9	0.4	146.2
Korea, Rep.	530,435.7	11370.6	5.8	46.2
Vietnam	30,700.1	388.5	7.5	76.3

Table 2. The Johansen Pairwise Co-intregration Tests

Causality test	No. of Lags	Rank	Max. Eigenvalue	Trace	No. of Co-integrating Vectors (of r order)
Brazil					
i_{CB} vs. $\dot{P}$	(2)	r=0	50.9	54.1	r=1
		r≤1	3.2	3.2	
China					
i_{CB} vs. $\dot{P}$	(2)	r=0	16.2	17.9	r=1
		r≤1	1.7	1.7	
India					
i_{CB} vs. $\dot{P}$	(4)	r=0	17.4	17.4	r=1
		r≤1	0.06	0.06	
Indonesia					
i_{CB} vs. $\dot{P}$	(6)	r=0	49.1	59.8	r=0
		r≤1	10.7	10.7	
Philippines					
i_{CB} vs. $\dot{P}$	(3)	r=0	15.8	18.9	r=1
		r≤1	3.0	3.0	
Russia					
i_{CB} vs. $\dot{P}$	(5)	r=0	23.7	23.9	r=1
		r≤1	0.18	0.18	
Korea					
i_{CB} vs. $\dot{P}$	(6)	r=0	36.3	38.4	r=1
		r≤1	2.0	2.0	
Vietnam					
i_{CB} vs. $\dot{P}$	(2)	r=0	10.2	15.5	r=0
		r≤1	5.3	5.3	

The critical value for accepting that r=1 at the 5% level for both the Maximum Eigenvalue test and the Trace test is 3.84. The lag selection has been done according to the *Final Prediction Error* test (*FPE*), the *Akaike* Information Criterion (*AIC*), the *Lagrange Ratio Criterion* (LR), the *Schwarz* Information Criterion (*SC*) and the *Hannan-Quinn* information criterion (*HQ*).

Table 3. The EC.VAR Causality tests

Variables	γ - coefficient & (t- ratio)	Long - run causality direction	No of lags
Brazil			
$\Delta\dot{P}$ vs. Δi_{CB}	-0.25 (-7.65)	$i_{CB} \Leftarrow \dot{P}$	2
Δi_{CB} vs. $\Delta\dot{P}$	-0.003 (-0.11)		
China			
$\Delta\dot{P}$ vs. Δi_{CB}	-0.03 (-4.01)	$i_{CB} \Leftarrow \dot{P}$	2
Δi_{CB} vs. $\Delta\dot{P}$	-0.01 (-0.82)		
India			
$\Delta\dot{P}$ vs. Δi_{CB}	-0.01 (-1.70)	$i_{CB} \Rightarrow \dot{P}$	4
Δi_{CB} vs. $\Delta\dot{P}$	-0.09 (-3.63)		
Indonesia			
$\Delta\dot{P}$ vs. Δi_{CB}	0.02 (1.11)	$i_{CB} \Rightarrow \dot{P}$	6
Δi_{CB} vs. $\Delta\dot{P}$	-0.10 (-4.92)		

Variables	γ - coefficient & (t- ratio)	Long - run causality direction	No of lags
Philippines			
$\Delta\dot{P}$ vs. Δi_{CB}	-0.02 (-1.22)	$i_{CB} \Rightarrow \dot{P}$	3
Δi_{CB} vs. $\Delta\dot{P}$	-0.07 (-3.79)		
Russia			
$\Delta\dot{P}$ vs. Δi_{CB}	-0.14 (-1.07)	$i_{CB} \Rightarrow \dot{P}$	5
Δi_{CB} vs. $\Delta\dot{P}$	-0.10 (-4.33)		
Korea			
$\Delta\dot{P}$ vs. Δi_{CB}	-0.01 (-1.28)	$i_{CB} \Rightarrow \dot{P}$	6
Δi_{CB} vs. $\Delta\dot{P}$	-0.34 (-5.90)		
Vietnam			
$\Delta\dot{P}$ vs. Δi_{CB}	-0.01 (-2.15)	$i_{CB} \Leftrightarrow \dot{P}$	2
Δi_{CB} vs. $\Delta\dot{P}$	-0.01 (-2.32)		

The EC.VAR formula has the following form : $\Delta y_t = \text{const.} + \sum_{i=1}^{n}\alpha\Delta y_{t-1} + \sum_{j=1}^{n}\beta\Delta x_{t-1} - \gamma\, ECT_{-1} + e_{t.}$

Table 4. The LSE/Hendry GETS results

Dependent variable	Inflation Rate ($\Delta \dot{P}$)							
	Brazil*	China	India*	Indonesia*	Korea*	Vietnam	Philippines	Russia*
Regressor	(1)	(2)	(3)	(4)	(5)	(6)	(7)	(8)
$\Delta \dot{P}_{t-1}$	-0.06 (-0.08)	-0.05 (-0.51)	0.43 (6.32)	0.50 (7.04)	0.01 (0.28)	0.49 (5.72)	0.23 (3.51)	0.29 (3.37)
$\Delta \dot{P}_{t-2}$	-0.006 (-0.08)	-0.004 (-0.04)	-0.12 (-1.70)	-0.09 (-1.22)	0.12 (2.12)	-0.05 (-0.58)	0.23 (3.38)	0.18 (2.39)
$\Delta \dot{P}_{t-3}$	-	-	0.12 (1.68)	0.03 (0.36)	0.06 (1.04)	-	0.07 (1.06)	0.20 (2.89)
$\Delta \dot{P}_{t-4}$	-	-	0.002 (0.02)	0.04 (0.58)	-0.02 (-0.42)	-	-	0.11 (1.83)
$\Delta \dot{P}_{t-5}$	-	-	-	0.07 (0.94)	0.27 (4.85)	-	-	0.07 (1.12)
$\Delta \dot{P}_{t-6}$	-	-	-	0.03 (0.44)	0.003 (0.06)	-	-	-
$\Delta i_{CB,t-1}$	0.68 (7.84)	-0.61 (-0.73)	0.07 (0.28)	0.01 (0.21)	-0.38 (-1.31)	0.06 (0.98)	0.12 (2.00)	-0.46 (-5.17)
$\Delta i_{CB,t-2}$	-0.06 (-0.71)	0.14 (0.17)	-0.32 (-1.22)	0.16 (2.18)	-0.14 (-0.50)	0.15 (2.16)	-0.05 (-0.82)	-0.39 (-4.10)
$\Delta i_{CB,t-3}$	-	-	-0.23 (-0.88)	-0.01 (-0.26)	0.46 (1.58)	-	0.05 (0.86)	-0.06 (-0.70)
$\Delta i_{CB,t-4}$	-	-	0.47 (1.78)	0.16 (2.20)	0.69 (2.25)	-	-	0.63 (9.08)
$\Delta i_{CB,t-5}$	-	-	-	0.08 (1.23)	1.92 (6.28)	-	-	0.05 (0.64)
$\Delta i_{CB,t-6}$	-	-	-	-0.01 (-0.17)	-0.23 (-0.70)	-	-	-
θ (ECT $_{-1}$)	-0.02 (-1.34)	-0.07 (-1.38)	-0.10 (-3.88)	-0.18 (-4.99)	-0.15 (-6.36)	-0.04 (-1.85)	-0.07 (-3.82)	-0.16 (-4.45)
ϕ_0 (or γ_0)	0.09 (0.82)	-0.11 (-0.13)	1.08 (1.33)	0.20 (0.30)	0.70 (3.09)	0.03 (0.08)	0.26 (0.58)	-0.36 (-1.81)
ϕ_1	-0.81 (-0.43)	-4.03 (-0.89)	0.13 (0.23)	0.49 (2.51)	0.09 (0.32)	0.008 (0.01)	0.50 (1.30)	1.42 (5.96)
T (time)	0.00002 (0.14)	0.007 (2.11)	-0.003 (-1.49)	0.003 (1.35)	-0.001 (-2.69)	0.002 (0.59)	-0.0008 (-0.51)	0.001 (2.10)
R^2	0.45	0.07	0.23	0.67	0.46	0.32	0.21	0.77

* A dummy is included for the following time periods (Brazil, 1997M11-1998M3 & 1998M9-1999M4), India (1999M10-1999M12), Indonesia (1998M4-1999M4), Korea (1999M1-2000M6), Russia (1998M9-1999M2)).

REFERENCES

Antonic, M. (1986), "High and volatile real interest rates.", *Journal of Money, Credit and Banking*, 18, pp. 18-27.

Engle, F.R. and Ng, V.K. (1993), "Time varying volatility and the dynamic behaviour of the term structure.", *Journal of Money, Credit and Banking*, 25, pp. 336-49.

Fama, E.F. and Gibbons, M.R. (1982), "Inflation, real returns and capital investments.", *Journal of Monetary Economics,* 9, pp. 279-323.

Garbade, K.D. and Wachtel, P. (1978), "Time variation in the relationship between inflation and interest rates.", *Journal of Monetary Economics,* 4, pp. 755-65.

Hendry, D., Pagan, A. and Saragan, D., (1984), "Dynamic Specification", in *Handbook of Econometrics Vol. 2,*(eds.) Grilliches, Z. and Intriligator, M., Amsterdam: North-Holland, pp. 1023-1100.

Hendry, D., (1987), "Econometrics Methodology: A Personal Perspective", in T.F. Bewley (ed.) *Advances in Econometrics Fifth World Congress*, Vol. 2, Cambridge: Cambridge University Press.

Johansen, S., (1995), *Likelihood Based Inference in Cointegrated Vector Autoregressive Models*, Oxford: Oxford University Press.

Karfakis, C. (2004), "Testing the quantity theory of money in Greece: Reply to Özmen", *Applied Economic Letters*, 11, pp. 541-43.

Kinal, T. and Lahiri, K. (1988), "A model for ex ante real interest rates and derived inflation forecasts.", *Journal of the American Statistical association,* 8, pp. 665-73.

Mayfield, E.S. and Murphy, R.G. (1996), "Explaining the term structure of interest rates: A panel data approach.", *Journal of Economics and Business,* 48, pp. 11-21.

Meltzer, A. (1998), "Monetarism : The issues and the outcome", *Atlantic Economic Journal*, pp. 8-31.

Nelson, C.R. and Schwert, G. W. (1977), "Short term interest rates as predictors of inflation: on testing the hypothesis that the real rate of interest is constant.", *American Economic Review*, 67 , pp. 477-86.

Tzavalis, E. and Wickens, M.R., (1997), "Explaining the failures of the term spread models of the rational expectations hypothesis of the term structure.", *Journal of Money, Credit and Banking*, 29, pp. 364-80.

In: Computational Techniques in Economics and Finance
Editor: Constantine Zopounidis
ISBN: 978-1-61324-558-3

Chapter 3

THE OPTIMIZATION OF THE ECONOMIC SEGMENTATION BY MEANS OF FUZZY ALGORITHMS

Jaime Gil–Aluja*[1], *Ana Maria Gil– Lafuente*[2] and *Anna Klimova*

University of Barcelona, Av. Diagonal 690,
08034 Barcelona, Spain

ABSTRACT

The work we present on this occasion is a step towards a search for basic formal elements in the treatment of uncertain economic phenomena taking into consideration the notions of pretopology with their correspondent axiomatics. This is a summary of the results obtained in the theoretical investigation realized during the last years. It contributes a theoretical basis, mainly.

A theoretical scheme is proposed and developed in this paper to give scientific solidity to the algorithms used in the process of segmentation, grouping and separation of homogenous objects, products, etc. These algorithms form a part of non-numerical mathematics of uncertainty.

An illustrative development of the theoretical concepts is made. The results obtained, which are identical among each other are represented too.

Keywords: Economics; Decision analysis; Segmentation process; Fuzzy sets; Pretopology.

[1] Tel.: +34.93.402.19.62 Fax: +34.93.201.80.47; gilaluja@fuzzyeconomics.com (Jaime Gil-Aluja)
[2] Tel.: +34.93.201.61.55 Fax: +34.93.201.80.47; amgil@ub.edu (Ana Maria Gil-Lafuente)
*Corresponding author. Tel.: +34.679.42.81.44 Fax: +34.93.201.80.47; Email addresses: klimova4919@hotmail.com (Anna Klimova).

1. Introduction

The use of pretopological studies in economy was sporadic and was made by applying different aspects of combinatorics mainly. Despite this, its presentation in scientific foro was encouraging and deserved acknowledgement from certain circles eager to have new formal structures with a high level of generality. But, these contributions did not satisfy our needs in the process of searching for a set of tools capable to dealing with the new phenomena and economic structures immersed in uncertain environments.

During the last decade we have been using some theoretical and technical elements compiled from different sources that had a connection with certain axioms of pretopologic spaces. But there was no "structure" sufficiently solid to represent all connections between existing studies in this field. So we decided to collect all fragments to form a whole body that could fill the void.

To reach this objective we considered an interesting precedent, thanks to Arnold Kaufmann [27], published in one of his "work notes". The study of his proposal led us to think about the meaning that has to be given to the elements that form a referential set.

2. Preliminaries

In our study, we consider a finite referential *E* as a point of departure. The first thinking has to do with the nature of the elements of *E*. In this sense, a referential could have two contents: referentials of fuzzy subsets or the fuzzy subsets themselves. The interest in using one or another appears when the process starts for determining a set over which a mapping Γ will be established in the pretopologies. We refer to it as either *K*(*E*) or *P*(*E*).

This initial consideration is a starting point for taking a position in the task of "fuzzyfying" the corresponding spaces, see [2-5,8,11,26,42-44,47-50]. Each approach is referred to as either *a* or *b*.

a There are two referentials: $E = \{\chi_j / j = 1,2,...,m\}$ and $P = \{P_k / k = 1,2,...,n\}$.

Let us describe each element of referential *P* by means of the fuzzy subset $\underset{\sim}{A}_k$ with the referential of the elements of *E*. So, the relation between $\underset{\sim}{A}_k$ and P_k is established when for $\chi_j \in E$, P_k has a level μ_j and it is presented as follows:

$$\mu_{\underset{\sim}{A}_k}(\chi_j) = \mu_j, \quad \mu_j \in [0,1]. \tag{1}$$

This yields the following set:

$$K(E) = \{\underset{\sim}{A}_k / k = 1,2,...,n\}, \quad \underset{\sim}{A}_1 = \varnothing, \quad \underset{\sim}{A}_n = E. \tag{2}$$

Let us determine set $K(E)$ through $P(E)$ for the purpose of unifying terminology in the process of comparison it with the second approach. In this conception, $P(E)$ could be infinite because L^E already is.

b We start out from the following referential of the fuzzy subsets: $E = \{\underset{\sim}{P}_i / i = 1, 2, ..., n\}$,

with the help of which we obtain the set formed of its own parts or "power set", and it is referred to as $P(E)$. In this approach $P(E)$ is finite:

$$P(E) = \{\varnothing,\ \{\underset{\sim}{P}_1\},\ \{\underset{\sim}{P}_2\}, ..., \{\underset{\sim}{P}_n\},\ \{\underset{\sim}{P}_1, \underset{\sim}{P}_2\}, ...,\ \{\underset{\sim}{P}_{n-1}, \underset{\sim}{P}_n\}, ..., E\}. \quad (3)$$

To clarify our explanation and obtain better results in the comparison process we will express 2^n elements of "power set" as follows:

$$P(E) = \{\underset{\sim}{A}_k / k = 1, 2, ..., 2^n\},\ \ \underset{\sim}{A}_1 = \varnothing,\ \ \underset{\sim}{A}_{2^n} = E. \quad (4)$$

Having seen the sense that the referential E and the set $P(E)$ could have in each of the approaches we proceed, first of all, to present the axiomatics of the pretopology in uncertainty.

3. Axioms for an Uncertain Pretopology

In the two approaches described above there is both a referential E and set $P(E)$ but they have a different nature. Let us define uncertain pretopology, developed in [13, 27, 28, 39, 40, 42].

Definition 1. A mapping Γ of $P(E)$ in $P(E)$ is uncertain pretopology of E if, and only if, the following axioms are given:

$$\Gamma\varnothing = \varnothing.$$
$$\forall \underset{\sim}{A}_k \in P(E):\ \ \underset{\sim}{A}_k \subset \Gamma\underset{\sim}{A}_k \text{ (where } \Gamma E = E\text{)}.$$

Using the same terms as usual in determinism, a mapping Γ for all elements of $P(E)$ will be called as an "adherent mapping" or "adherence". It is also possible to associate Γ with an "inner mapping" or "inner" δ, defined by:

$$\forall \underset{\sim}{A}_k \in P(E):\ \ \delta\underset{\sim}{A}_k = \overline{\Gamma\overline{\underset{\sim}{A}}_k} \text{ (where } \overline{\underset{\sim}{A}}_k \text{ is a complement of } \underset{\sim}{A}_k\text{)}. \quad (5)$$

Definition 2. $\underset{\sim}{A}_k$ is closed set for an uncertain pretopology if $\underset{\sim}{A}_k = \Gamma\underset{\sim}{A}_k$.

Definition 3. $\underset{\sim}{A}_k$ is open set for an uncertain pretopology if $\underset{\sim}{A}_k = \delta\underset{\sim}{A}_k$.

We considered the widest notion of uncertain pretopology. If new axioms are added then new uncertain pretopological spaces appear with characteristics and properties of special interest for the description and treatment of the problems of economic systems.

Definition 4. A mapping Γ of $P(E)$ in $P(E)$ is uncertain isotone pretopology of E if, and only if, the following axioms are carried out:

$$\Gamma\varnothing = \varnothing.$$
$$\forall \underset{\sim}{A}_k \in P(E): \quad \underset{\sim}{A}_k \subset \Gamma \underset{\sim}{A}_k, \text{ extensivity.}$$

$$\forall \underset{\sim}{A}_k, \underset{\sim}{A}_l \in P(E): \quad \left(\underset{\sim}{A}_k \subset \underset{\sim}{A}_l\right) \Rightarrow \left(\Gamma \underset{\sim}{A}_k \subset \Gamma \underset{\sim}{A}_l\right), \text{ isotony.}$$

Let us pay special attention to one of the uncertain isotone pretopologies that satisfies the property, which is idempotency, and can be represented as the fourth axiom.

$$\Gamma\left(\Gamma \underset{\sim}{A}_k\right) = \Gamma \underset{\sim}{A}_k, \text{ idempotency.}$$

with these four axioms, we get Moore's closure which, moreover, has the property $\Gamma\varnothing = \varnothing$, not required in the axiomatic of this closure.

Moore's closure is of special importance in the development of the algorithms capable of dealing with segmentation problems which is demonstrated below. So, it is necessary to establish ways for obtaining Moore's closures on the basis of the concepts (data) that could easily be found in the information supported by companies and institutions.

4. Obtaining a Moore's Closure

On the basis of previous practice, we have found two concepts that seem to adapt well to the exposed necessities. These are the notion of a family (Moore's family) and a graph or fuzzy relation, see [2,26,28,49].

- Axiomatic of Moore's family.

Definition 5. Let one family be determined through $F(E) \subset P(E)$. If there are two axioms:

$$E \in F(E).$$
$$(\underset{\sim}{A}_k, \underset{\sim}{A}_l \in F(E)) \Rightarrow (\underset{\sim}{A}_k \cap \underset{\sim}{A}_l \in F(E)).$$

then this is Moore's family.

Moore's closure is obtained by the following way:

a Once the family *F*(*E*) is available it is necessary for each element $\underset{\sim}{A}_k \in P(E)$ to find a subset of elements of *F*(*E*) that contain $\underset{\sim}{A}_k$ and will be referred to as $F_{\underset{\sim}{A}_k}(E)$.

b For each $F_{\underset{\sim}{A}_k}(E)$ its intersection $\bigcap_{F \in F_{\underset{\sim}{A}_k}(E)} F$ is obtained.

c A mapping $M\underset{\sim}{A}_k$ is determined by the mode that $\bigcap_{F \in F_{\underset{\sim}{A}_k}(E)} F$ will be corresponded to each element $\underset{\sim}{A}_k$, that is to say: $M\underset{\sim}{A}_k = \bigcap_{F \in F_{\underset{\sim}{A}_k}(E)} F$.

So, Moore's closure was found using one family. There is only one closure for each family.

- The concept of relation is at the basis of a majority of algorithms of non-numerical mathematics of uncertainty, considered by Zadeh [48] and Kaufmann [26]. To formalize this relation there are two graphs that can be used represented either in matrix form or arrowlines.

Let us consider a fuzzy relation $[\underset{\sim}{R}]$ between the elements of a referential $E = \{y_1, y_2, ..., y_n\}$, such as $[\underset{\sim}{R}] \subset E \text{ x } E$.

a With this information a Boolean graph is determined, taking a threshold α as follows:

$$[R_\alpha] = \{(y_i, y_j) \subset E \text{ x } E / \ \ \mu_{\underset{\sim}{R}}(y_i, y_j) \geq \alpha\}, \ \ \alpha \in [0,1]. \qquad (6)$$

b Predecessors and successors of y_i limited to the level α are determined as:

$$\left.\begin{array}{l} y_j \text{ is a sucessor of } y_i \\ y_i \text{ is a predecessor of } y_j \end{array}\right\} \text{ if: } (y_i, y_j) \in [R_\alpha]. \qquad (7)$$

These concepts allow us to find the connection to the right $R_\alpha^+ \underset{\sim}{A}_k$ and to the left $R_\alpha^- \underset{\sim}{A}_k$.

Definition 6. A connection to the right $R_\alpha^+ \underset{\sim}{A}_k$ or, a mapping R_α^+ of *P*(*E*) in *P*(*E*) such that for all $\underset{\sim}{A}_k \in P(E)$, R_α^+ is a subset of elements of *E* that are successors, limited to the level α, of all element that belong to $\underset{\sim}{A}_k$. It is written as:

$$R_{\alpha}^{+}\underset{\sim}{A}_{k} = \{y_j \in E \,/\, (y_i, y_j) \in [R_{\alpha}], \forall\, y_i \in \underset{\sim}{A}_{\alpha}\}, \quad \text{with } R_{\alpha}^{+}\varnothing = E. \tag{8}$$

Definition 7. A left connection $R_{\alpha}^{-}\underset{\sim}{A}_{k}$ or, a mapping R_{α}^{-} of $P(E)$ in $P(E)$ such that for all $\underset{\sim}{A}_{k} \in P(E)$, R_{α}^{-} is a subset of the elements of E that are predecessors, limited to the level α, of all elements that belong to $\underset{\sim}{A}_{k}$. It is expressed as:

$$R_{\alpha}^{-}\underset{\sim}{A}_{k} = \{y_i \in E \,/\, (y_i, y_j) \in [R_{\alpha}], \forall\, y_j \in \underset{\sim}{A}_{k}\}, \quad \text{with } R_{\alpha}^{-}\varnothing = E. \tag{9}$$

c The right connection $R_{\alpha}^{+}\underset{\sim}{A}_{k}$ and the left one $R_{\alpha}^{-}\underset{\sim}{A}_{k}$ can be found directly by simple reading of the relation $[R_{\alpha}]$, in the following way:

$$\forall\, y_i \subset \underset{\sim}{A}_{k} \in P(E): \qquad R_{\alpha}^{+}\underset{\sim}{A}_{k} = \bigcap_{y_i \subset \underset{\sim}{A}_{k}} R_{\alpha}^{+}\{y_i\}. \tag{10}$$

$$R_{\alpha}^{-}\underset{\sim}{A}_{k} = \bigcap_{y_i \subset \underset{\sim}{A}_{k}} R_{\alpha}^{-}\{y_i\}. \tag{11}$$

d Two Moore's closures corresponding to the fuzzy relation $[R_{\alpha}]$ or to the graph, limited to level α, are obtained by the maxmin convolution R_{α}^{-} with R_{α}^{+} and R_{α}^{+} with R_{α}^{-}. It is written:

$$M_{\alpha}^{(1)} = R_{\alpha}^{-} \bullet R_{\alpha}^{+}. \tag{12}$$

$$M_{\alpha}^{(2)} = R_{\alpha}^{+} \bullet R_{\alpha}^{-}. \tag{13}$$

where $M_{\alpha}^{(1)}$ and $M_{\alpha}^{(2)}$ are the two Moore's closures.

Two concepts, such as a family and a graph, can be used to obtain Moore's closures which are considered to be important for a wide rang of economic approaches.

5. Moore's Closed Sets as Maximum Groups

As for any pretopology, a set of Moore's closed sets is formed by the elements that comply with the following condition:

$$\forall\, \underset{\sim}{A}_{k} \in P(E): \underset{\sim}{A}_{k} = M\underset{\sim}{A}_{k}. \tag{14}$$

Let us determine a subset of closed sets of *P*(*E*) corresponding to Moore's closure $M_\alpha^{(2)}$ as $C(E, M_\alpha^{(2)})$. As $R_\alpha^- \underset{\sim}{A}_k$ is a closed of *P*(*E*) for $M_\alpha^{(2)}$, which can be written as follows:

$$C(E, M_\alpha^{(2)}) = \bigcup_{\underset{\sim}{A}_k \in P(E)} R_\alpha^- \underset{\sim}{A}_k . \tag{15}$$

and, $R_\alpha^+ A_k$ is a closed for $M_\alpha^{(1)}$ and we determine the subset of closed sets of *P*(*E*) corresponding to Moore's closure $M_\alpha^{(1)}$ as $C(E, M_\alpha^{(1)})$, we get:

$$C(E, M_\alpha^{(1)}) = \bigcup_{\underset{\sim}{A}_k \in P(E)} R_\alpha^+ \underset{\sim}{A}_k . \tag{16}$$

Both families $C(E, M_\alpha^{(1)})$ and $C(E, M_\alpha^{(2)})$ are isomorphic and dual for each other. They are also antitone. Therefore, so we get:

$$\underset{\sim}{A}_k \in C(E, M_\alpha^{(1)}) \Rightarrow \ (\underset{\sim}{A}_l = R_\alpha^- \underset{\sim}{A}_k \in C(E, M_\alpha^{(2)}) \ \text{and} \ \ R_\alpha^+ \underset{\sim}{A}_l = \underset{\sim}{A}_k). \tag{17}$$

$$\underset{\sim}{A}_l \in C(E, M_\alpha^{(2)}) \Rightarrow \ (\underset{\sim}{A}_k = R_\alpha^+ \underset{\sim}{A}_l \in C(E, M_\alpha^{(1)}) \ \text{and} \ \ R_\alpha^- \underset{\sim}{A}_k = \underset{\sim}{A}_l). \tag{18}$$

These families of closed sets can be associated to each other and each of the families forms a finite lattice [26]. As a result of the maxmin convolution, both families of closed sets provide the groupings with the greatest possible number of elements of the referential *E*. In the formation of groups, the groupings of the elements of one family of the closed sets are accompanied by the other groupings of the other family of closed sets related to them. This is very important in the developing the algorithm.

6. Algorithms Generalized by Means of Rectangular Matrices

Our objective is to find a way to generalize with the help of rectangular matrices. Two referentials E_1 and E_2 are considered. There is a fuzzy rectangular relation $[\underset{\sim}{R}] \subset E_1 \times E_2$. As demonstrated by Gil Aluja [14] in this case the necessary properties obtained for only one referential are kept (dual families of antitone nature with the property of isomorphism of their lattices). Only one lattice is obtained after two lattices were joined and where each vertex represents the relation of the groupings of elements of set E_1 with the groupings of elements of set E_2 taking into consideration a previously established level α. If this happens then there is affinity between the groups of the elements limited to the correspondent level. This lattice determines an order and structure for these relations, and depending on the movement from the lower vertex to the upper vertex, or on the contrary, a number of the associated elements of one referential increases and a number of the associated elements of the other referential decreases.

If, when the upper end of the lattice is different to $(E_2, \varnothing)$ and the lower end is different to $(\varnothing, E_1)$, we add these vertices, then we have a Galois lattice that shows up two sets of Moore's closed sets that have the previous relations $(E_2, \varnothing)$ and $(\varnothing, E_1)$ as the upper and lower ends.

Practical developments realized on the basis of this scientific achievement were decisive. They opened new ways to solve the problems of human resources management [16], finance analysis [17], organization, commercial and sports management [21,22], etc. The possibilities of formal structures based on uncertain pretopology increases [15]. Some algorithms were developed which gave an adequate solution to the problems. Two algorithms such as the maximum inverse correspondence algorithm and the maximum complete sub-matrices algorithm are described:

i. Algorithm of the maximum inverse correspondence.

a It is stared out from a Boolean relation $[R_\alpha]$ obtained as the result of limiting the fuzzy relation $[\underset{\sim}{R}]$ to a certain level of acceptable homogeneity.
b The set with the lowest number of elements is chosen between two sets E_1 and E_2.
c We create a set $P(E_1)$ where E_1 is the set with the lowest number of elements selected as established in the previous step.
d "Right connection" R_α^+ is obtained, that is to say, for all $\underset{\sim}{A}_k \in P(E_1)$, $R_\alpha^+ \underset{\sim}{A}_k$ compiles the successors of all the elements that belong to $\underset{\sim}{A}_k$.
e For each non-empty set of $R_\alpha^+ \underset{\sim}{A}_k$ we select the set corresponding to $\underset{\sim}{A}_k$ which has the greatest number of elements of referential E_1.
f The relations obtained form a lattice. If we add the empty-referential and the referential-empty vertices, we obtain a Galois lattice.

ii. Algorithm of the maximum complete sub-matrices.

a It is started out from a Boolean matrix $[R_\alpha]$ obtained as the result of making a "cut" of the fuzzy relation $[\underset{\sim}{R}]$ at level α.
b "Right connection" R_α^+ and "left" one R_α^- are obtained.
c We form two families $C(E_1, M_\alpha^{(2)})$ and $C(E_2, M_\alpha^{(1)})$ using the elements of images on R_α^+ and R_α^-, respectively.
d We obtain a Cartesian product of all elements of $C(E_1, M_\alpha^{(2)})$ and all elements of $C(E_2, M_\alpha^{(1)})$, and obtaining, thus, complete and incomplete matrices.
e All incomplete matrices are eliminated.
f All matrices which are situated inside the other ones are eliminated, too.
g As a result of the previous steps we obtained complete and maximum matrices.

h The relations obtained form a lattice. If we add the empty-referential and the referential-empty vertices, we have a Galois lattice.

The generalization that implies adopting a fuzzy rectangular relation instead of a fuzzy square matrix, introduced by Pichat [29,38], as an initial element, made it possible to construct the algorithms with the possibilities for future development.

It is useful to make a reference to a hierarchical cluster analysis based on fuzzy set theory [9,19,34] that has a similarity with the methods described. A general explication follows.

Hierarchical cluster analysis is a method of classification using a measure of similarity or distance for an arbitrary pair of objects. In this analysis it is not necessary to specify the number of groups, classes or clusters as a part of the inputs. Hierarchical cluster analysis involves two important decisions [9]. The first decision is the selection of an appropriate distance measure and the second stage to the clustering process is choosing the clustering or linkage algorithms, i.e. the rules which govern how distances are measured between clusters and then used to fuse clusters. As with the distance measures, there are many methods available [34]. There are two major classes. Divisive method begins with all of the cases in one cluster which is broken down into sub-clusters until all cases are separated [7,30,46]. The agglomerative approach works in the opposite direction as single-member clusters are increasingly fused until all cases are in one cluster [10,18,25,35,36].

Hierarchical algorithms can be expressed in terms of either graph theory (fuzzy graph theory) or matrix algebra [24,32]. A dendrogram is often used to visualize a hierarchical clustering.

Hierarchical cluster algorithms and the algorithms described in this paper fulfill the same objectives, such as: development of a good scheme for classification, search for a structure hidden in the data, understanding and simplification of complex system structure. These methods permit to summarize a large amount of data into a small number of groups or classes [9,15,19,41].

7. Configuration of the Algorithms in Real World Finances

Let us make an illustrative development of the previous concepts in the financial sphere. But before, it is necessary to say that this paper does not include a case that describes a real situation. This work tries to expose a methodology mainly, that is able to solve a series of the problems that affect the financial sphere of the companies. We describe a finite number of financial objects using the fuzzy subsets of the referential of their more significant attributes which form another referential. The following products could be mentioned as the financial objects: the short time credits, the mortgage credits, etc. and, as their attributes, we could consider their more important characteristics, such as: the interest rate, the period of repayment, the possibilities of the cancellation in advance, etc. We start out from the set of the financial products and the set of their attributes:

$$E_1 = \{P, Q, S, T\} \quad \text{and} \quad E_2 = \{a, b, c, d, e, f\}. \tag{19}$$

The description of four financial products is made by means of fuzzy subsets, obtaining thus a fuzzy relation between two sets mentioned above, see figure 1. Initial financial data basis can be represented using either the fuzzy numbers or the fuzzy intervals [15,29].

The level of homogeneity α could be different for each attribute, but to make our exposition simpler we determine this level the same one for all attributes $(\alpha \geq 0,7)$. So, the fuzzy relation $[\underset{\sim}{R}]$ is turned to a Boolean matrix $[\underset{\sim}{R}_{0,7}] = [B]$, see figure 2.

$[\underset{\sim}{R}] =$

	a	b	c	d	e	f
P	0,3	0,7	0,9	0,4	0,8	1
Q	0,8	0,9	0,6	0,9	0,3	0,7
S	0,9	0,4	0,8	0,8	0,7	0,2
T	0,6	0,8	0,9	0,5	1	0,9

Figure 1. Financial products described by means of fuzzy subsets.

$[B] =$

	a	b	c	d	e	f
P		1	1		1	1
Q	1	1		1		1
S	1		1	1	1	
T		1	1		1	1

Figure 2. Relation between two subsets obtained using Boolean sets.

We proceed to the treatment of Boolean matrix $[B]$ using the algorithm of the maximum inverse correspondence. E_1 is the referential with the lowest number of elements and its "power-set" is as follows:

$$P(E_1) = \{\varnothing, P, Q, S, T, PQ, PS, PT, QS, QT, ST, PQS, PQT, PST, QST, E_1\} . (20)$$

We establish the right connection $R^{+}_{0,7}$ as shown in figure 3, and for each non-empty set $R^{+}_{0,7}$ we select the set that corresponds to $P(E_1)$ that has a highest number of elements. The results obtained are shown in figure 4:

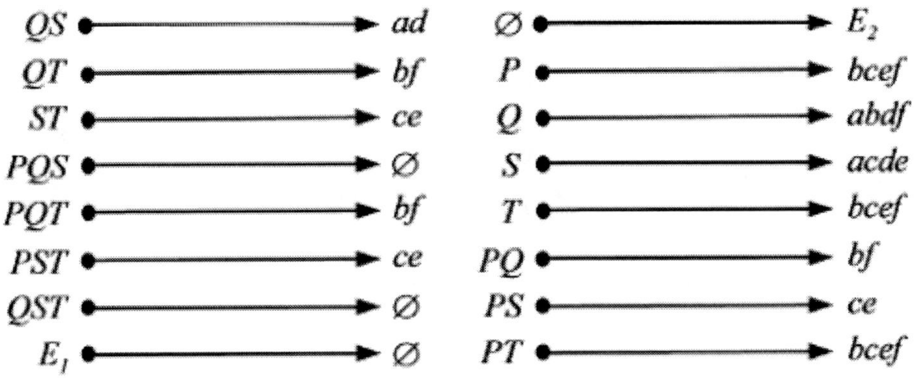

Figure 3. The results of the connection to the right R^{+}.

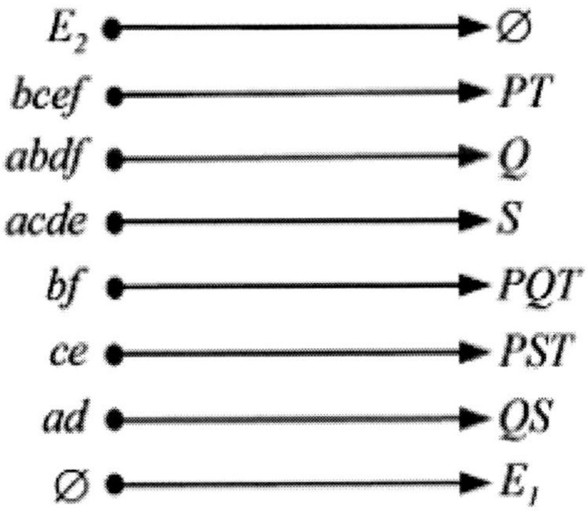

Figure 4. The set with the highest number of elements.

The elements of the "power set" of E_1 and E_2 form the lattices that are isomorphic and dual for each other. They are also antitone. See figure 5.

When superposition these lattices adequately we obtain a Galois lattice, taking into consideration that there are $(E_2, \varnothing)$ and $(\varnothing, E_1)$ as the upper and lower ends, see figure 6:

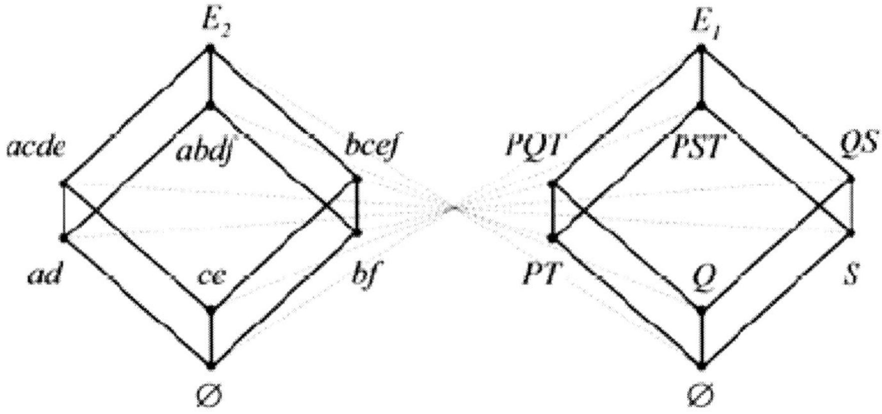

Figure 5. Two lattices that are isomorphic and dual for each other.

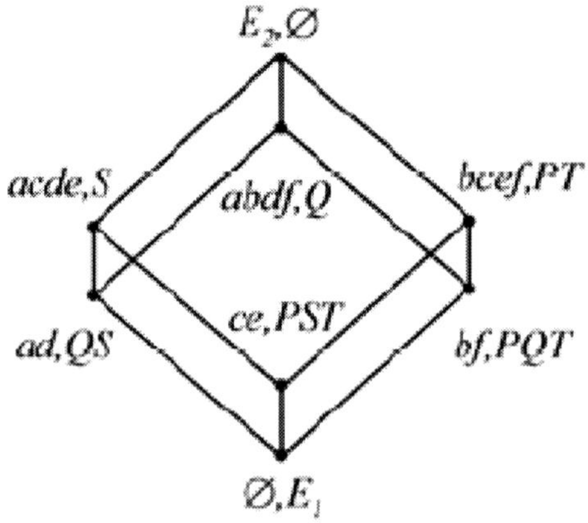

Figure 6. Galois lattice.

We obtained the affinities or maximum homogeneous groups limited to the established level α .

Let us verify that the result obtained by using the algorithm mentioned above will coincide with the one which is obtained by means of the algorithm of the complete maximum matrices. To develop this algorithm the right connection R_α^+ is obtained and its non-empty image is shown as follows:

$$C(E_1,\, M_\alpha^{(2)}) = \{ad,\ bf,\ ce,\ abdf,\ acde,\ bcef,\ E_2\}. \tag{21}$$

Let us find the left connection R_α^-, see figure 7:

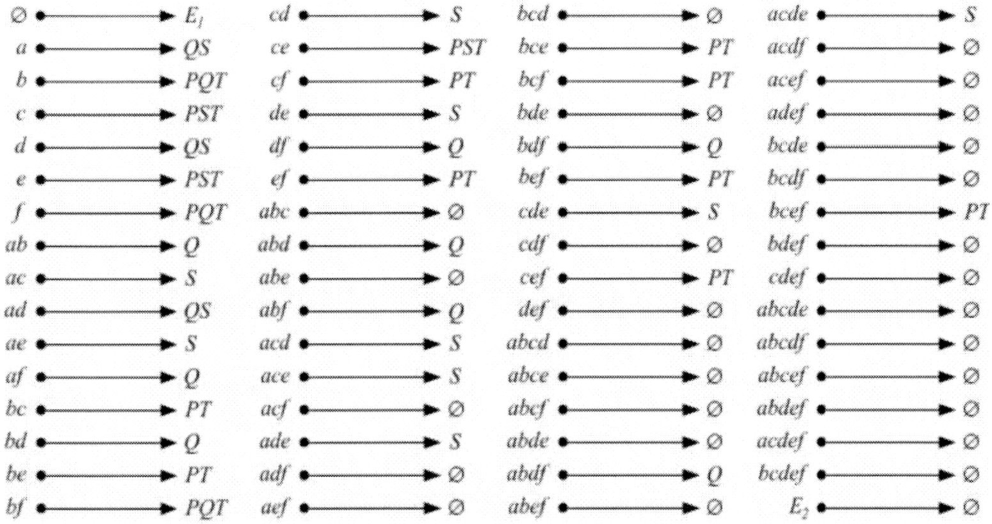

Figure 7. The results of the connection to the left *R*.

A non-empty image of R_α^- is as follows:

$$C(E_2,\ M_\alpha^{(1)}) = \{Q,\ S,\ PT,\ QS,\ PQT,\ PST,\ E_1\}. \tag{22}$$

We obtain a Cartesian product:

$$C(E_1,\ M_\alpha^{(2)}) \times C(E_2,\ M_\alpha^{(1)}). \tag{23}$$

The results are the following:

$ad \times Q$, $ad \times S$, $ad \times PT$, $ad \times QS$, $ad \times PQT$, $ad \times PST$, $ad \times E_1$
$bf \times Q$, $bf \times S$, $bf \times PT$, $bf \times QS$, $bf \times PQT$, $bf \times PST$, $bf \times E_1$
$ce \times Q$, $ce \times S$, $ce \times PT$, $ce \times QS$, $ce \times PQT$, $ce \times PST$, $ce \times E_1$
$abdf \times Q$, $abdf \times S$, $abdf \times PT$, $abdf \times QS$, $abdf \times PQT$, $abdf \times PST$, $abdf \times E_1$
$acde \times Q$, $acde \times S$, $acde \times PT$, $acde \times QS$, $acde \times PQT$, $acde \times PST$, $acde \times E_1$
$bcef \times Q$, $bcef \times S$, $bcef \times PT$, $bcef \times QS$, $bcef \times PQT$, $bcef \times PST$, $bcef \times E_1$
$E_2 \times Q$, $E_2 \times S$, $E_2 \times PT$, $E_2 \times QS$, $E_2 \times PQT$, $E_2 \times PST$, $E_2 \times E_1$

There are 49 complete and incomplete matrices. Some of them are represented below (figure 8):

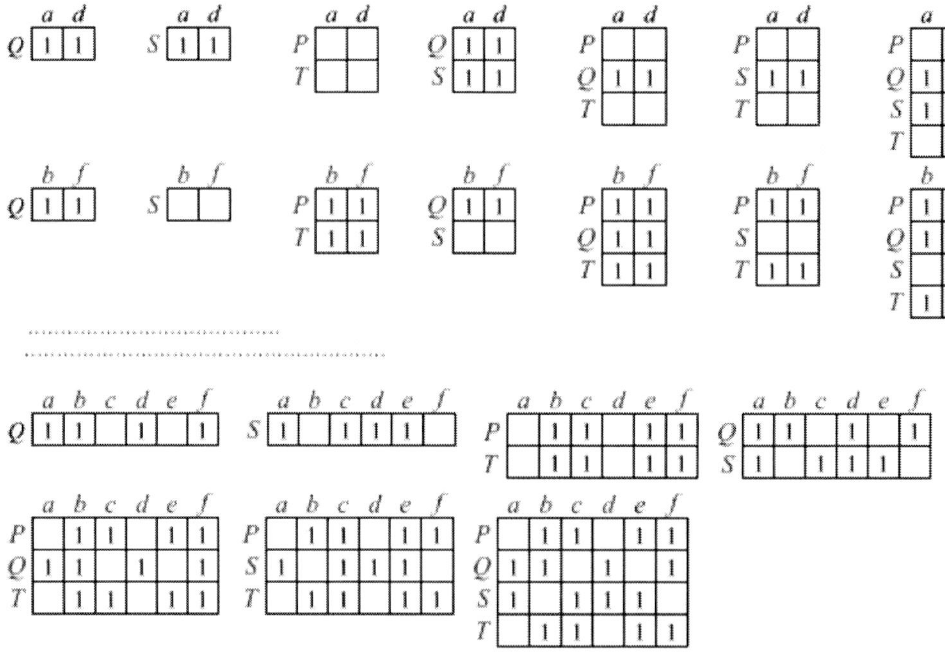

Figure 8. Complete and incomplete matrices.

After eliminating the incomplete matrices and the sub-matrices contained in the other matrices we obtain, as a result, the affinities expressed through the following sub-matrices, figure 9:

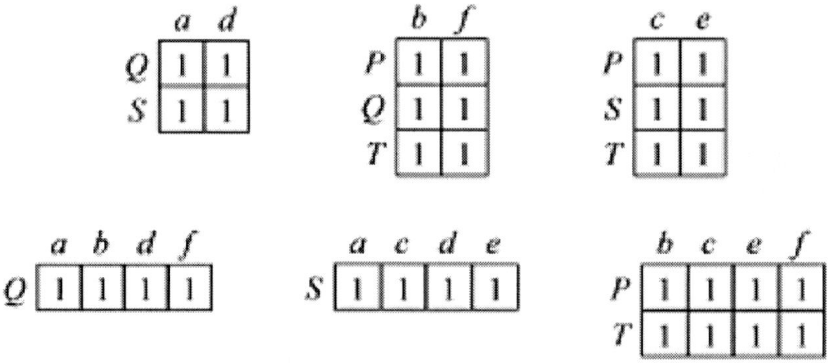

Figure 9. Affinities between the financial products and their attributes.

We obtained the result identical to the one which we got by using the inverse maximum correspondence algorithm. The reason of this is that the basis of both algorithms is the same.

To make the calculations it is reasonably to use some packages developed for these purposes in such software, as SAS, S-PLUS, MATLAB and with the use of the C/C++

programming language too. They are integrated environments that provide mathematical computing, visualization, and a powerful technical language [20,33,37,45].

Conclusion

We proceed to synthesize the contributions made in the area of generalization of different axiomatics well-known in traditional studies that give them validity in the context of uncertainty:

1. Ways to form a referential set. Two concepts can represent the elements of the "power set" originated from the referential. In accordance with the first concept, a referential is formed of the referentials of fuzzy subsets, and the second one considers their own fuzzy subsets as a referential.
2. Transition from one axiomatic to the other in pretopologies. A process was developed to pass from one pretopology to another by adding and eliminating the axioms.
3. Obtaining the strictest uncertain pretopology. A possibility to include new axioms into isotone pretopology makes it possible to obtain a very strict pretopology determined as uncertain pretopology of Moore.
4. Process for obtaining maximum groupings by using a Moore closure. The processes of getting Moore closures and closeds in the cases of fuzzy rectangular relations are found. Existence of two Moore closeds makes it possible to verify isomorphism and duality of these lattices. The vertexes form maximum groupings.
5. Generalization of existing algorithms. The theory of affinities is based on two principle elements: Moore closeds and a Galois lattice. We inscribed the developments of this theory into isotone pretopology which satisfies a complementary condition: idempotency.
6. Practical verification of the algorithms. A supposition was developed to visualize the algorithm's mechanism and verify the identity of a result obtained by different ways. A description was made of some products which had to be grouped homogeneously by using the fuzzy subsets of the referential of their attributes. A presentation made with the help of Galois lattices showed the advantage of these algorithms. We have possibilities to adopt optimum decisions of segmentation.

Throughout this work we demonstrated the usefulness of pretopological spaces in the process of making economic decisions and the possibilities they have, developed in [1,2,4,6,22,23,31,40]. The technical elements that form algorithms capable to deal with a wide range of actual and future economic situations immersed in uncertain environment are developed, step by step.

References

[1] Adnadjevic, D. and Sostak, A.P. (2002), "On inductive dimensions for fuzzy topological spaces", *Fuzzy Sets and Systems*. 31, 5-12.

[2] Bourbaki, N. (1940), Eléments de Mathématique. III. Topologie Générale, Hermann & Cie., Paris.

[3] Daowen Qiu (2004), "Characterizations of Fuzzy Finite Automata", *Fuzzy Sets and Systems.* 141, 391-414

[4] Daowen Qiu (2004), "Fuzzifying topological linear spaces", *Fuzzy Sets and Systems.* 147, 249-272.

[5] Daowen Qiu (2006), "Pumping lemma in automata theory based on complete resituated lattice-valued logic: A note", *Fuzzy Sets and Systems.* 157, 2128-2138.

[6] Das, P. (1999), "A fuzzy topology associated with a fuzzy finite state machine", *Fuzzy Sets and Systems.* 105, 469-479.

[7] Edwards, A. and Cavalli-Sforza, L. (1965), "A method for cluster analysis", *Biometrics.* 21(2), 362-375.

[8] Erceg, M.A. (1976), "Metric spaces and fuzzy set theory", *Journal of Mathematical Analysis & Applications.* 69, 205-230.

[9] Fielding, A. (2007), Cluster and Classification Techniques for the Biosciences, Cambridge University Press, UK.

[10] Florek, K., Lukaszewicz, J., Steinhaus, H., and Zubrzycki, S. (1951), "Sur la liaison et la division des points d'un ensemble fini", *Colloquium Mathematicum.* 2, 282-285.

[11] George, A. and Veeramani, P. (1995), "Some theorems in fuzzy metric spaces", *Journal of Fuzzy Mathematics.* 3, 933-940.

[12] Gil Aluja, J. (1999), Elements for a Theory of Decision in Uncertainty, Kluwer Academic Publishers, London, Boston, Dordrecht.

[13] Gil Aluja, J. (2001), "La pretopología en la gestión de la incertidumbre", in: Discurso de investidura como Doctor "Honoris Causa" por la Universidad de León, Universidad de León.

[14] Gil Aluja, J. (1998), Interactive management of human resources in uncertainty, Kluwer Academic Publishers, London, Boston, Dordrecht.

[15] Gil Lafuente, A.M. (2001), Nuevas estrategias para el análisis financiero en la empresa, Ariel, Barcelona.

[16] Gil Lafuente, J. (September, 2001), "Model for the homogeneous grouping of the sales force", in: Proceedings of Congress M.S. 2001, Changsha (Hunan) R.P. China, 332-335.

[17] Gil Lafuente, J. (2002), Algoritmos para la excelencia. Claves para el éxito en la gestión deportiva. Milladoiro, Vigo.

[18] Gordon, A. (1996), "Hierarchical classification", in: P. Arabie, L. Hubert, and G. Soete (ed.), Clustering and Classification, 65-121. River Edge, World Scientific, NJ.

[19] Guojun, G., Chaoqun, M., and Jianhong, W. (2007), Data clustering: theory, algorithms, and applications, ASA-SIAM Series on Statistics and Applied Probability, Pennsylvania, Virginia, USA.

[20] Herniter, M. (2001), Programming in MATLAB, Pacific Grove, CA, Brooks/Cole.

[21] Höhle, U. (2001), Many Valued Topology and its applications, Kluwer Academic Publisher, Dordrecht.

[22] Höhle, U., Rodabaugh, S.E. and Sostak, A. (1995), "Special Issue on Fuzzy Topology", in: *Fuzzy and Sets Systems.* 73.

[23] Höhle, U. and Sostak, A. (1999), "Axiomatic foundations of fixed-basis fuzzy topology", in: U. Höhle and S.E. Rodabaugh (ed.), Mathematics of Fuzzy Sets: *Logic,*

Topology and Measure Theory, Handbook of Fuzzy Sets Series, vol.3, Kluwer Academic Publishers, Dordrecht.

[24] Jain, A. and Dubes, R. (1988), Algorithms for Clustering Data, Engelwood Cliffs, Prentice-Hall, NJ.

[25] Johnson, S. (1967), "Hierarchical clustering schemes", Psychometrika, 32(3), 241-254.

[26] Kaufmann, A. (1977), Introduction à la thèorie des sous-ensambles flous à l'usage des ingénieurs,4. Compléments et nouvelles aplications. Masson, Paris.

[27] Kaufmann, A. (1983), Prétopologie ordinaire et prétopologie floue. *Note de Travail.* 115, La Tronche.

[28] Kaufmann, A. and Gil Aluja, J. (Julio, 1991), "Selection of affinities by means of fuzzy relations and Galois lattices", in: Proceedings of XI Euro O.R. Congress, Aachen Germany.

[29] Kaufmann, A. and Gil Aluja, J. (1992), Técnicas de gestión de empresas. *Previsiones, decisiones y estrategias.* Pirámide, Madrid.

[30] Kaufman, L. and Rousseeuw, P.J. (2005), Finding Groups in Data. *An Introduction to Cluster Analysis.* Wiley-Interscience, NJ.

[31] Khedr, E.H., Zeyada, F.M. and Sayed, O.R. (2001), "On separation axioms in fuzzifying topology", *Fuzzy Sets and Systems.* 119, 439-458.

[32] Kruskal, J.B. (1956), On the shortest spanning sub-tree of a graph and the travelling salesman problem, in Proceedings of the American Mathematical Society, 7(1), 48-50.

[33] Kuncicky, D. (2004), MATLAB Programming, Upper Saddle River, Pearson Education, NJ.

[34] Lance, G.N. and Williams, W.T. (1967), "A general theory of classificatory sorting strategies", *The Computer Journal.* 9, 373-80.

[35] Milligan, G. (1979), "Ultrametric hierarchical clustering algorithms", *Psychometrika.* 44, 343-346.

[36] Murtagh, F. (1983), "A survey of recent advances in hierarchical clustering algorithms", *The Computer Journal.* 26(4), 354-359.

[37] Nabney, I. (2002), NETLAB: Algorithms for Pattern Recognition. Advances in Pattern Recognition, Springer, London, New York.

[38] Pichat, E. (1969), "Algorithm for finding the maximal elements of a finite universal algebra", in: Inform. Processing 68, North Holland.

[39] Ponsard, C. (1969), Un modèle topologique d'equilibre économique, Dunod, Paris.

[40] Rodabaugh, S.E. (1980), "The Hausdorff separation axiom for fuzzy topological spaces", *Topology Applications.* 11, 319-334.

[41] Sadaaki Miyamoto (1990), Fuzzy sets in information retrieval and cluster analysis, Kluwer Academic Publishers, Dordrecht, Boston, London.

[42] Sapena, A. (2001), "A contribution to the study of fuzzy metric spaces", *Applications of General Topology.* 2, 63-76.

[43] Sugeno, M. (1977), "Fuzzy measures and fuzzy integrals, a survey", in: M.M. Gupta, G.N. Saridis and B.R. Gaines (ed.), *Fuzzy automata and processes.* North-Holland, Amsterdam.

[44] Veeramani, P. (2001), "Best approximation in fuzzy metric spaces", *Journal of Fuzzy Mathematics.* 9, 75-80.

[45] Vesanto, J., Alhoniemi, E., Himberg, J., Kiviluoto, K., and Parviainen, J. (1999), "Self-organizing map for data mining in MATLAB. *The SOM toolbox", Simulation News Europe.* 54.

[46] Willett, P. (1988), "Recent trends in hierarchical document clustering: A critical review", *Information Processing and Management.* 24(5), 577-597.

[47] Zadeh, L. (1965), "Fuzzy Sets", *Information and Control.* 8, 338-353.

[48] Zadeh, L. (1968), "Fuzzy Algorithms", *Information and Control.* 12, 94-102.

[49] Zadeh, L. (1971), "Similarity Relations and Fuzzy Orderings", *Information Sciences.* 3, 177-200.

[50] Zimmermann, H.J. (1978), "Results of empirical studies in fuzzy set theory", in: G.J. Klir (ed.), *Applied General Systems Research.* Plenum Press., New York.

In: Computational Techniques in Economics and Finance ISBN: 978-1-61324-558-3
Editor: Constantine Zopounidis

Chapter 4

SPATIAL MODELING BASED ON ECONOMIC, DEMOGRAPHIC AND GEOGRAPHICAL CRITERIA: AN APPLICATION ON THE REGIONALIZATION OF GREECE

***Kostas Rontos*[*a], *Christos Tzimos*[†b] *and Christos Mavroudis*[‡c]**

[a]Aegean University, Sociology Department, Alkaiou 1, Theofrastio Building, Mytilene, 81.100, Greece

[b] National Statistical Service of Greece, Delfon 218, 3455102, Greece

[c]National Statistical Service of Greece, Piraeus 46 & Eponiton, Piraeus 18510, Greece

ABSTRACT

The systematic classification of a united space and its distribution according to specific criteria, such as the homogeny, the polarity, the level of development or the degree of problems forms a basic subject of the regional science. Specifically, the regions' formation with united characteristics that are, usually, identified with the definition "homogenic regions" are essential for the implementation of effective regional programs and rational policy for each region, meaning the regional policy. In this framework, and in the current application, the homogeneity of the Greek space is surveyed according to the specific demographic, geographical and economic characteristics of the departments of the country, in order to create a basic supportive tool of a rational regional policy. For the needs of the current study, the method of the Hierarchical Cluster Classification is used, with the GDP, the level of rurality and insularity of the departments as criteria. The homogenic groups of the departments, derived from the application, present, in a large extent, a geographic continuity and a distinguishable geographic character, a fact that proves the dynamic of the "economic area" and, in every occasion, compose geographic units with common geographic, demographic and economic characteristics, the knowledge of which could contribute to

* Email: k.rontos@soc.aegean.gr (Corresponding author)

† Email: ctzimos@the.forthnet.gr

‡ Email: cmav@statistics.gr

the definition of the kind and intensity of measures of the regional policy that has to be applied. The results of the method are expected to contribute to the effort of the examination of the rationality of the regional structuring system and the formation of a modification proposal, based on combined criteria-variables, in order to compose a further discussion on a new regionalization currently developed in Greece.

Keywords: Space classification, homogenic regions, Hierarchical Cluster Classification, demographic, economic and geographic criteria-variables.

INTRODUCTION

The splitting of a united space, usually of the national one, into several parts, composes the basic subject of the Regional Economics. Furthermore, in the case that each of these consists of spaces in continuity and geographically oriented, the definition of the Economic Region is used (Boudeville, 1972).

The structure of the regions with united characteristics, that are usually referred as "homogenic regions" are essential for the application of the effective regional programs and the rational policy for each region, in other words, of the regional policy. In the case that the principals of homogeneity and the polarity are associated with the administrative division of the country, so that there is practically the feasibility of policy enforcement, the regional procedure is intended to form programming regions.

The above mentioned criteria of the homogeneity and administrative correspondence, combined with the polarity, compose substantial regional classifications based on the basic pattern of Boudeville (1968) and other subsequent researchers occupied with the regional science, while the level of development constitutes a classic criterion of regional classification (Konsolas, 1983).

The classical methods of regionalization differentiate according to the type of the region that is asked to be formed (homogenic, polaric, programming). In general, the regionalization methods use statistical data and fall into the quantitative analysis with the weighted index number as the basic method for the orientation of the homogenic regions.

The shift-share analysis (Edwards, 1976) which, combined with the Boudevilles criteria (1966) for the definition of 8 types of areas are used to specify mainly polaric regions, while, the classification methods for the programming regions, approach either those of the homogeneity or those of the polarity, depending on the nature of the intervention in macro or micro level (Papadaskalopoulos, 1990). In the bibliography there are, also, advanced techniques of spatial classification, such as the Principal Component Analysis and Synthetic Small Area Estimation Techniques (Amarasingh et al, 2005) or the Cluster and Discriminant Analysis (Csanyi,1993).

The division system of Greece into 13 regions, since 1987 (see the map in appendix), is considered, by some, to not correspond with the current needs of a regional policy enforcement and forming of regional programs. It is proposed that they should be reduced considering the populative and spatial characteristics of the country (Makridimitris & Papadimitriou, 2006, Papadaki & Kostopoulos, 2006).

Furthermore, the use of the regional accounts system is recently proposed for the administrative division of the country in spatial units NUTS2–Region and NUTS3–Department (Vlachos & Lagos, 2006).

The scientific approach for the regionalization of the Greek space based on the economic, demographic, geographical and other objective characteristics has not concentrate the interest of the researchers and the policy. The relevant applications have mainly turned to methodologies proposed by international organizations, such as OECD or Eurostat, for the grouping of the municipalities and communes by level of urbanity (urban, rural) or even mountainous and inferiority. Moreover, relative methodologies of national entities as of the Ministry of Economy and Finance and the National Statistical Service of Greece (NSSG), as well as, a proposal of alternative approaches towards the same direction, are developed in a study by the NSSG and the Agricultural University (2004), where not only population and geographic, but also, social and economic criteria were used.

These techniques as an attempt to classify the numerous municipalities and communes, refer rather to the meaning of the economic space, as the grouping is not, at least, characterized by, even a basic continuity of the space, so that to form regions. The continuity can be obtained, in the case that the municipality grouping is confined in smaller areas of the country, for example, in a region, as the Hierarchical Cluster Analysis application of the Epirus Region's method, based on combined criteria – indices of the agricultural economy (Tzimos et al, 2006).

An also recent attempt of creating homogenic groups among the departments of the country with the same method and the use of variables from the agriculture and livestock survey and the employment in the agricultural sector, combined with the applied typology from the European union, presented a compatibility in the results among the several applications for each variable. A geographic continuity in an adequate extent was also presented, so that it can be further studied and practically to be a base for a support of the regional policy in the agricultural sector (Rontos et al, 2007).

The present study consists of an application to the same direction, that, with the use of economic, geographic and population criteria – indices, it aims at the formation of the Greek space typology and the creation of the infrastructure of a rational policy application. It also aims at the trial and establishment of the objective and reliable methodological tools of the Greek space orientation, so that the relative results will compose an attempt to a large discussion on a new regionalization currently developing in Greece.

METHODOLOGY AND DATA

As already mentioned in the introduction, the Hierarchical Cluster Analysis (CAH) is used as a statistical method, with the 51 Departments of the country (objects) as dimensions and certain indices as variables that present basic characteristics – problems of the Greek economy.

For the implementation of the relevant methods, it is important that the typology should not, particularly, be complex as a result of the combination of many criteria-variables. This would have as a result a fragmentary and specialized application of policies per area and therefore, to miss the target of the cluster analysis to define common characteristics and opportunities. For this reason, only three variables were chosen: the level of rurality, the GDP and the insularity. Of course, the choice was made upon specific justification, as they reflect either basic developed parameters of the departments of the country or geographic and demographic characteristics that define the developing procedure in the Greek reality at a large extent.

Despite the fact that the Gross Domestic Product (GDP) takes criticism as a measure of the development level and of the regional inequalities (Petraki-Kotti, 1980, Nordhavs and Tobin, 1973, Heilbroner and Thurow, 1984, Chletsos et al, 2007), it continues to constitute a basic economic index on national and international level for the measurement of the material prosperity of the societies and its comparison among them and the evaluation of the regional development (Konsolas, 1983, Papadaskalopoulos, 1990).

It is widely used, especially for the regional analysis, as the problems of its calculation concern, more or less, all the spatial units and therefore, they do not cause serious problems to relative comparisons. The basic advantage to the use of the GDP is its simplicity and the coherent and continuous dissemination of statistical data, as a result of the national and regional accounts system. The relative to the GDP subjects are examined at the large sector of the economic science, the Economics of Development (Stonier & Hague, 1972).

The rural areas internationally, lack in level and in growth rate of development compared to the urban areas. The last, though, in the framework of the capitalistic development, systematically concentrate population from the rural areas, resulting in the creation of enormous inequalities among them concerning the productive and reproductive population and finally, the development itself. Neoclassical (Isaac, 1947), as well as, neokensianic theories (Chatzimichali & Chatzimichalis, 19798) and the theories of development for the labor morbidity and the urban accumulations (Perrou, 1950, Myrdal, 1957, Boudeville 1972 and Friedman, 1975), that it should be noted that were not confirmed (Andrikopoulou-Kafkala, 1983), composed the foundation for these evolutions.

In the frameworks of these main theoretical approaches and the international evolutions, there was an enormous "agricultural exodus" towards the big urban centers of Greece, after the 50's (Rontos K. & Papanis S, 2006). This resulted in the creation of the worse living conditions in the countryside, in relation to the urban pattern, while the primary sector followed a continuous diminishing course with low labor productivity, small potentials for productive investments. Another result was the weakness on the application of new methods in the production, organization and administration of the agricultural units, as well as, the promotion and the trading of the products (Pepelasis, 1976, Harissis & Rontos, 1996).

The use of the level of rurality in the model, as an alternative of the widely used concept of urbanity is imposed, due to the lagging behind of the rural areas compared to the urban ones. The rurality is, precisely, defined by the particularities of the rural areas and it is a fact that its definition has not yet been established scientifically and practically worldwide. A usual policy not being able to give the above mentioned particularities is the definition of the rural, just like the rest that don't belong to the urban definition. The lack of a unified methodology, impose that the basic contributions of the definition and the typology of the rural areas are presented, before the selection of the method to be used in this study.

In the framework of the numerous and various theories for the definition of a rural area, the main theme is that, if this composes a geographic object, a location with identified borders on the map or a social object, a society of interest, a cultural picture and a life style. According to Whitaker (1982), the concept "Rural" was used for the first time by the "U.S. Bureau of the Census" in 1874 to define the population outside the cities with population of

8000 inhabitants and over. Finally, in 1980, the definition was modified by rejecting the definition of what is rural. The urban population is defined as all inhabitants of the urban areas and of those with more than 2500 inhabitants outside urban areas. The population not listed as urban is defined as rural. After the industrial revolution and the economic progress that followed, the city lost its unity and started to enter into the rural areas. Consequently, the distinction between "urban" and "rural" became more and more difficult. However the word "rural" stopped being a synonymous of the agricultural economy and became an area with a differentiated economy consisting of activities of the secondary and tertiary sector. As a result, the contemporary techniques try to create clusters in relation with a continuous urban-rural, contrary to the beginning of the rural at the end of the city's boundaries. According to the contribution of the Politechnico di Milano (1999), the environment balance and regional effectiveness are not only based on the success of the urban production but also to the capability of the agricultural communes to produce a satisfying income for the social and demographic stabilization of the local communes.

Despite the intense differentiations on the concept of rurality, there is a general acceptance that the agricultural typology is a basic tool for the development policy, as it can also help in the tracking down of the various needs and opportunities of the agricultural areas that, consequently, have similar needs for policy implementation.

During the last 3 decades, there were a large number of multivariate studies on the classification of the rural areas with Leavy et al (1999) as a current example. He used the cluster analysis to classify the 155 rural areas of Ireland. Several approaches of the subject differentiate the rural areas based on the population, the contribution of the employment in the primary sector, the contribution of the agricultural land, the distances from the urban centers and the infrastructures, as well as, the population density. There are strong and weak points in every occasion. Deavers and Brown (1985) classified 7 categories of the agricultural areas based on the socioeconomic and demographic characteristics. The agriculture, the industry, the mines and the governing were used for the economic criteria. The social dimensions included the eminent poverty and the increase of the pensioners. The last category of indices is the proportion of the land under the possession of the state. Horn (1985) chooses the values, the socioeconomic factors, the political administrative structures, and the priorities in education. Whitaker (1982) is, also, in favor of complex and multi-dimensional definitions. He suggests 10 categories of urban-rural typology based on 15 indices that consist of number of permanent population in households, level of concentration of the occupations in a few activities, percentages of permanent workers in agriculture or fishing, monthly variation of employment, percentage of the housing increase before 1940, etc.

One of the most popular and widely used patterns, intended to be also used in the current study, is the definition of OECD. Despite the weaknesses of the specific classification, for the reason that it is only based on the population density, it composes an internationally accepted typology, offering also comparability on international level. This is, also, widely used for the total of the member states of the European Union. According to the OECD, two hierarchical levels of geographic breakdown are used. The level of Local Administrative Units (LAU2) and the regional level of Departments (NUTS3). The local Communes and Municipalities are only classified as rural or urban according to the population density. Communes and Municipalities with less than 150 inhabitants per square km are considered to be rural.

The secondary classification separates the departments in three categories (Polytechnico Di Milano, 1999).

- Predominantly Rural: Departments that more than 50% of the population lives in agricultural communes.
- Significantly Rural: Departments that the 15 up to 50% of the population live in agricultural communes.
- Predominantly Urban: Departments that less of the 15% of the population lives in agricultural communes.

In Greece, there are more than 3000 island, from which some hundreds are inhabited and developing in the Aegean and Ionian Seas, covering about half of the coastline of Greece and the 12% of the EU25 (Ministry of Environment, Physical Planning and Public Works, 2006). The 4 out of the 13 regions (NUTS2) consist of islands that include 13 departments (NUTS3) in total out of the 51 of the country. The characterization of a department as an insular or not, composed the third variable, based on the fact that the insular areas have different characteristics, development problems and potentials. Those of the insular areas in Greece that were not touristic developed are characterized by a bad sectoral structure, excessively concentrated on the primary sector, with isolation and regionality, small capability of development of the products' market and a specific identity (Rontos, 2004, Spilanis, 1997). Given that the tourist development was not rationally developed (Spilanis and Vayanni, 2003), the tourist islands in Greece faced significant developing problems that made them a special category of areas. Consequently, the insularity, combined with the level of the economic development and the demographic factor included in the pattern, is expected to be an important component of the definition of the homogenic areas in Greece.
After the description of the variables and their significance for Greece, we return to the selected method of analysis, emphasizing the fact that with the description of the variables, the breakdown of the departments in homogenic groups, as for the variables, is succeeded. In this way, they significantly differ among them, in order to define the qualities that contribute to the characterization and the fragmentation of the groups that are created, without any a priori hypothesis to the initial data (Behrakis et al, 1999, Papadimitriou, 2005, Drosos, 2005, Rontos et al, 2006, Tzimos, 2006, Florou, 1997).

The main characteristic of the method is that a successful analysis should lead to groups, where the observations in each group are as much homogenic as possible and, at the same time, comparing observations of differed groups, to significantly differ among them. Consequently, the method comes closer to the logic of the structure of the homogenic areas, as presented in the introduction and therefore, it composes an appropriate tool of regionalization.

The data for the GDP and the population density derive from the National Accounts and the Population Census 2001 results, correspondingly, by the (NSSG) National Statistical Service of Greece.

IMPLEMENTATION AND RESULTS

The values of the level of rurality are calculated with the OECD method and are the following: RURAL3 = Urban, RURAL2 = significantly rural, RURAL1 = predominantly rural. The breakdown of the departments of Greece according to the OECD's criteria, based on the population data of 2001, is presented in Figure 1. The insularity is a dummy variable with values LAND 1= Not insular and LAND 2= Insular. GDP takes the values GDP1 = low, GDP2 = medium, GDP3 = high, according to criteria explained in the following.

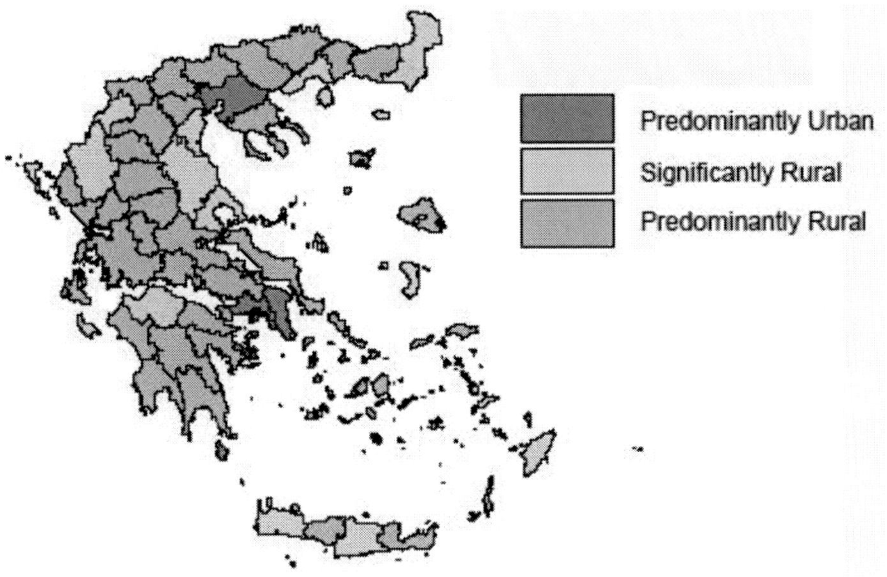

Figure 1. Breakdown of the departments of Greece by level of rurality, based on the OECD's criteria.

The algorithm chosen for the Hierarchical Cluster Analysis application is VACOR (Benzeri 1973, Karapistolis 1999, Papadimitriou 2007) and it functions agglomerative. In other words, it starts uniting one by one the objects (departments) creating groups with common characteristics. The thing that is of interest is mainly the relative position of the departments as for the variables-indices studied. For this reason, we categorize our data creating a new table where on the rows there are the departments that are characterized from the low, medium or high values of the variables that are on the columns.

In this particular application, the categorization concerns only the GDP, as all the other variables are already qualitative. If we observe the GDP breakdown in the departments, we find out that there are 20 departments that their GDP is lower than 1000 million €, another 20 departments with their GDP between 1000 to 2000 million €, 9 departments from 2000 to 3660 million € and 2 departments with much higher GDP (Attikis 66,225 million € and Thessalonikis 13,433 million €). What interests us mostly is the relevant position of the departments as for the variables-indices studied. If we exclude the two departments with the very high values, the distribution presents a light positive (right) asymmetry. Based on the information we have for the normality of the GDP distribution, we categorize our data in low, medium and high GDP, with the sense that the 17 departments (33.3 %) with the lowest values (under 950 million €) compose the first class (low). The 17 departments (33.3 %) with the higher values (GDP more than 1600 million €), compose the 3rd class (high) and the rest 17 departments (33.4 %) compose the 2nd class (medium) with GDP between 950 and 1600 million €. This is how the initial data was transformed to categorical data (Table 1), where in the rows there are the departments that are characterized by the low, medium or high index of GDP, as well as, the rest of the variables that are on the columns.

Table 1. Transformation of initial data to categorical

AREA	RURAL	LAND	GDP
100	PREDOM. URBAN	Not Island	66.225
101	PREDOM. RURAL	Not Island	1.822
103	PREDOM. RURAL	Not Island	3.664
⋮	⋮	⋮	⋮
321	SIGN. RURAL	Island	600
322	SIGN. RURAL	Island	1.318
323	PREDOM. RURAL	Island	462

→

AREA	RURAL	LAND	GDP
100	3	1	3
101	1	1	3
103	1	1	3
⋮	⋮	⋮	⋮
321	2	2	1
322	2	2	2
323	1	2	1

Then, the categorized initial table of data transforms into a logical table with values 0 and 1 (Table 2). On column RURAL_1, with value 1, there are the departments that are intensively rural, on column RURAL_2 with value 1, there are the departments with relevant rurality, etc. In the logic table, qualities are revealed (high, relevant, or low rurality, etc.) that characterize the departments, in contrast with the initial table, where the departments are characterized by the variables. The size of the logical table 0-1 is as follows: 51 (departments) x 8 (qualities). Furthermore, in the logic table, all the departments participate in the algebraic operations with the same weight, as the sum of their elements is stable and equal with three (3), the same as the number of the variables studied.

In the logical table, we apply the Hierarchical Cluster Analysis, where the results are represented in the dendrogram (Fig. 2) that can be read divisive. The results are also presented on Figure 3, where the findings are more obvious.

Table 2. Transformation of variables as 0,1 logical

AREA	RURAL_1	RURAL_2	RURAL_3	LAND_1	LAND_2	GDP_1	GDP_2	GDP_3
100	0	0	1	1	0	0	0	1
101	1	0	0	1	0	0	0	1
103	1	0	0	1	0	0	0	1
⋮	⋮	⋮	⋮	⋮	⋮	⋮	⋮	⋮
321	0	1	0	0	1	1	0	0
322	0	1	0	0	1	0	1	0
323	1	0	0	0	1	1	0	0

As observed on the top of the dendrogram, all the departments are united in a group. Following, we observe the first breakdown of the group (101) consisting of the two biggest urban departments of the country, the Attiki (ATT) and Thessaloniki departments (THE). The algorithm gives us the possibility to know the reasons for the breakdowns. So, as it is also shown in the diagramme, these departments are characterized by high urbanity and high GDP.

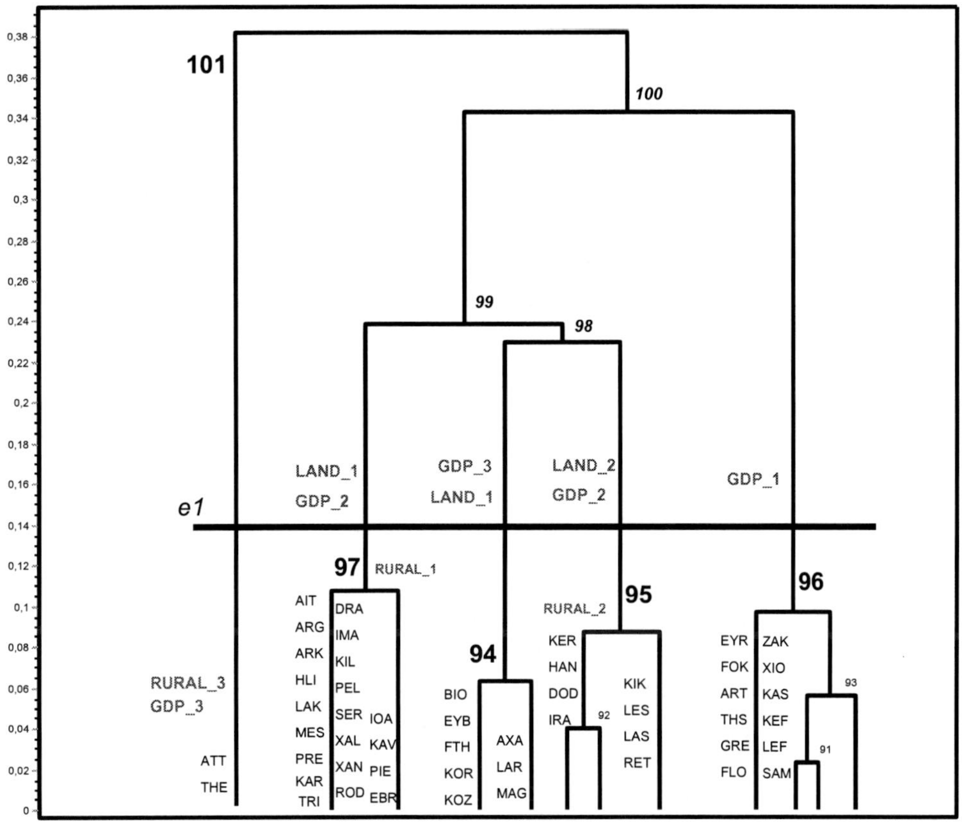

Figure 2. Dendrogram of the Hierarchical Cluster Analysis.

The departments (NUTS 3) and the Regions (NUTS 2) of Greece are presented in the map in appendix.

The second group (97) consists of 21 departments (Etoloakarnanias, Argolidas, Arkadias, Ilias, Lakonias, Messinias, Prevezis, Karditsas, Trikalon, Dramas, Hmathias, Kilkis, Pellas, Serron, Chalkidiki, Rodopis, Ioanninon, Kavalas, Pierrias, Evrou and Xanthis). These departments are not insular, they are intensely agricultural and are characterized by average GDP.

The departments of Viotias, Evias, Fthiotidas, Korinthias, Achaias, Larissas, Magnisias and Kozanis, that compose the 3rd group (94), are characterized by high GDP.

The insular departments of Kerkyras, Dodekannissou, Kykladon, Lesvou and the 4 departments of Kriti compose a 4th group (95) with the average GDP as a common characteristic.

In the 5th group (96), there are the departments with the low GDP. These are the departments of Evritanias, Fokidas, Artas, Thesprotias, Grevenon, Kastorias, Florinas, Zakinthou, Samou, Chiou, Kefallinias and Lefkadas.

Conclusion

The method's application gives an interesting grouping of the departments of the country, that helps to the successful selection of the general developmental and geographic demographic criteria used. Initially, combined with the high GDP, it groups (group 101) the two unique urban areas of the analysis. In other words, the two large metropolitan centers of the country, the Attiki and Thessaloniki department, that concentrate the 37% of the country's population 2001 and were the basic immigrant's destinations from all the remaining areas during the postwar period. At the same time, there are the places where the largest part of the industrial and tertiary activities is concentrated, creating enormous regional inequalities on the rest non-metropolitan areas of the country (Rontos, 2004). Particularly, the Attiki department, based on the appliance of the Dacen-Nystween algorithm (Rokos, 1984) had the biggest influence concerning the immigration pressures, in all the areas of the country, except from the Thraki Region, which, situated at the Northeastern part of the country, was mainly dominated by the Thessaloniki (Rontos, 1987).

Today, even though the populative and economic development of the Metropolitan centers of the country has not stopped and they have remained powerful administrative and economic centers of the country (see capital and co-capital), it is considered that they compose satiated areas with intense problems of negative economies of accumulation and magnitude (Konsolas et al, 1991). They form, indeed, a unified economic space where the policy exercised should deal with the problems of the saturation and that of the negative external economies.

Secondly, a large group of the continental departments is formed (97) with an intense agricultural character and medium GDP, that is extended to the Southern Greece and, more precisely, to the Southern Peloponnissos, to areas of the Western and the Northeastern Greece (Thraki).

It consists of the administrative region of Peloponnissos, with the exception of one department (Korinthias), the whole region of Eastern Makedonia and Thraki, as well as, the region of the Central Makedonia, with the exception of the department of Thessaloniki (Figure 4).

This is a fact that shows and points out possible adjustments, in the framework of a new official regionalization of the country. The keystone of a political development of the group would be the policy of holding down of the agricultural population, the policy of the support of the dynamic activities of the primary sector, the strengthening of the administrative-economic independence of the local urban centers and the support of the branches that the areas have a comparative advantage, in the framework of the endogenous development.

Another group of departments (94) consists of the continental departments that differentiate themselves from the previous ones, as they are intensely characterized by the high GDP.

Basically, they are the departments that compose the developmental arch, showing the industrial development of the country and it includes (together with the metropolitan centers of Attiki and Thessaloniki), the Northwestern Peloponnissos (Corinthian, Achaia), departments of the Eastern Sterea Ellada, the Thessalia and the department of Kozanis.

The development of the road transport infrastructure, the strengthening of the important ports of these areas and the formation of the metropolitan areas among the important neighboring urban centers will strengthen the industrial foundation of the areas of this group and will lead them to the preservation and extension of their developmental potentials

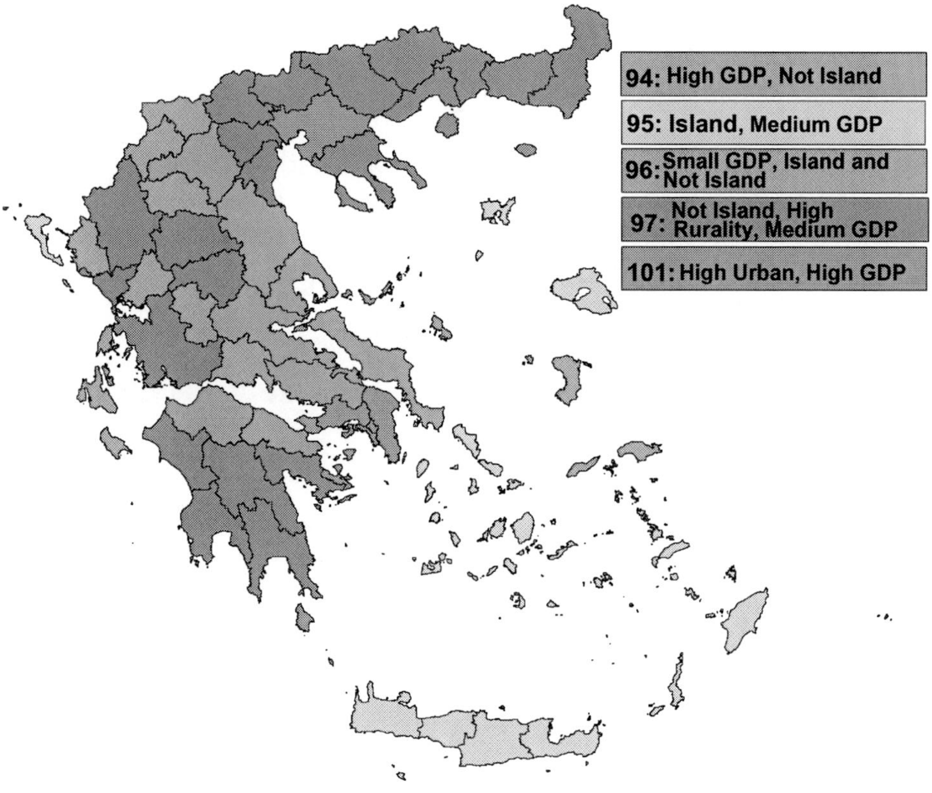

Figure 3. Homogeneous areas in Greece according to the Hierarchical Cluster Analysis/

The next group (95) is characterized by the insularity combined with the average GDP. Substantially, it is about the most touristic island' destination of Greece, whereas, for the departments of Kriti, the main characteristic composed is a more balanced development based on more activities. The regionalization that, also, occurred includes two whole administrative regions of the country, the region of Kriti and of the Southern Aegean, as well as, the largest department of the region of the Northern Aegean, Lesvos Department. The tourism development based on the sustainable tourism development on a new base, (Spilanis & Vayanni, 2003, Tsartas, 2004), the development and decrease of the cost of the sea transportation will contribute to the further development of the mentioned group of islands.

The underdevelopment, as this is determined by the GDP, composes the only powerful criterion of grouping of the 5th group (96) , where the insularity or the rurality do not seem to compose important factors, as they include insular or non-insular departments, as well as, intense or medium rural ones. It consists of 3 from the 4 departments of the Ionian Islands and the 2 from the 3 departments of the Northern Aegean Islands. The development of the infrastructure, the provision of aids for the quantitative and the qualitative development of the local labor and product markets, as well as, the support of a procedure concerning the endogenous development, are prior, as policy measures for the foundation of a developmental progress of these areas.

In general, the insularity proves to be a quite important factor for the grouping of the departments, as it defines and distinguishes the 4 of the 5 clusters that are formed, especially in departments with medium or high GDP, showing the different needs that the insular departments present. The level of development distinguishes a series of developed continental departments from some others, also continental and at the same time, intensely rural, showing the particularities and the special needs of the rural areas. Furthermore, the economic factor, wherever there is underdevelopment, limits the importance of the geographic and demographic factors and characterizes some insular or non-insular, relative or intense rural areas. Finally, the categorization of the two large urban areas of Greece in one group, combined with the high GDP, show the pattern of regional development of the country that is distinguished, in general, from the pattern Developed Metropolitan Centers – Other Less Developed or Underdeveloped Areas.

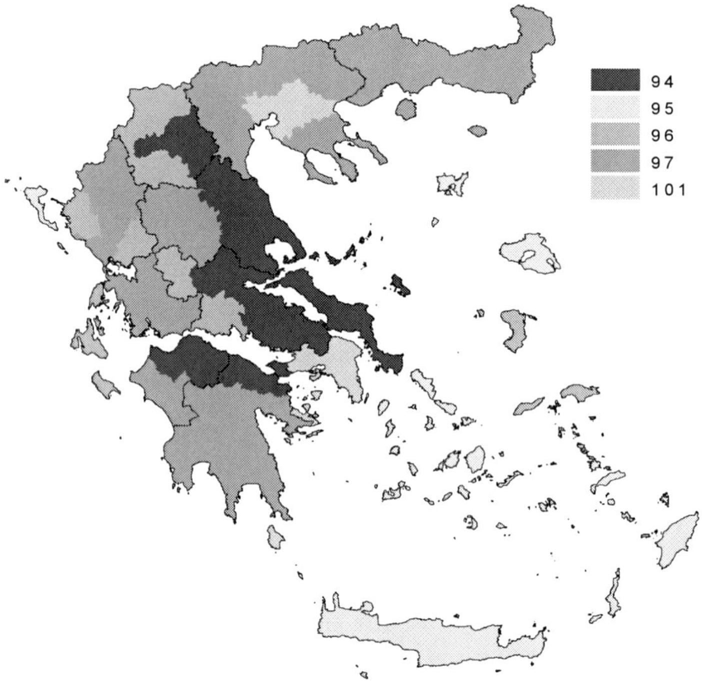

Figure 4. A comparable presentation of the administrative regions of the country and the clusters of the Hierarchical Cluster Analysis.

The relevant continuity of the area that occurred to the groups of the present application and the existence of the whole or part of the existed regions in the same group are an indication of the utility of the method. The continuity of its usage in the present and in other applications, shows that it can be a useful tool for the formation of homogenic areas and regions or for the supervision of the rationality of other criteria and techniques.

APPENDIX

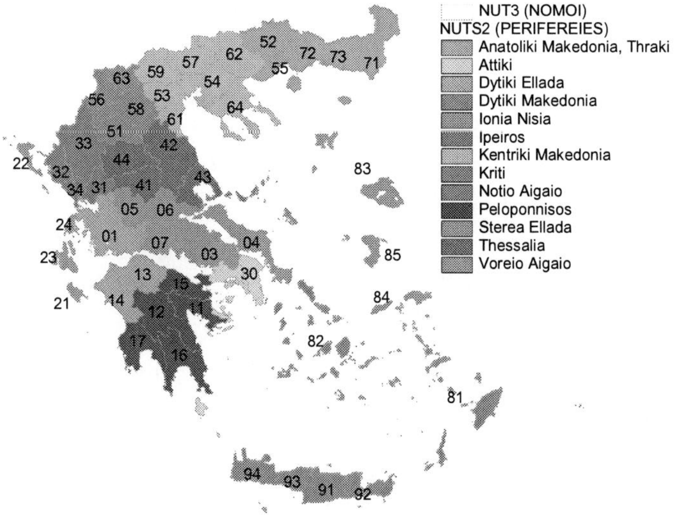

Code	Nomos	Code	Nomos
01	Aitoloakarnania	51	Grevena
03	Voiotia	52	Drama
04	Evvoia	53	Imathia
05	Evrytania	54	Thessaloniki
06	Fthiotida	55	Kavala
07	Fokida	56	Kastoria
11	Argolida	57	Kilkis
12	Arkadia	58	Kozani
13	Achaia	59	Pella
14	Ileia	61	Pieria
15	Korinthia	62	Serres
6	Lakonia	63	Florina
17	Messinia	64	Chalkidiki
21	Zakynthos	71	Evros
22	Kerkyra	72	Xanthi
23	Kefallinia	73	Rodopi
24	Lefkada	81	Dodekanisos
30	Attiki	82	Kyklades
31	Arta	83	Lesvos
32	Thesprotia	84	Samos
33	Ioannina	85	Chios
34	Preveza	91	Irakleio
41	Karditsa	92	Lasithi
42	Larisa	93	Rethymni
43	Magnisia	94	Chania
44	Trikala		

REFERENCES

Amarasinghe, U., Samad, M. & Anputhas, M. (2005). "Spatial clustering of rural poverty and food insecurity in Sri Lanka", *Food Policy, vol. 30*, no. 5-6, 493-509.

Andrikopoulou, H. (1981). "Marxistic approaches in the analysis of regional themes: A critical presentation", *City and Region, vol. 1*, 29-45.

Ballas, D., Kalogeresis, T. & Labrianidis, L. (2003). "A comparative study of typologies for rural areas in Europe" *Paper submitted to the 43rd European Congress of the Regional Science Association*, Jyväskylä, Finland,

Bechrakis, T. (1999). *"Multi-dimensional Data Analysis and Applications"* Athens : Nea Sinora Editions.

Benaki, V., Rontos, K., Apostolopoulos, C., Kazazis, E. & Mavroudis C. (2005). "Rural Areas in Greece: Definition, Typology and Data Needs for the Monitoring and Evaluation of Rural Development", Rome: *Contributed Paper for the joint UNECE/EUROSTAT/OECD/FAO Conference.*

Benzecri, J.P. (1973). "L' *analyse des donnes. Tome 1: La Taxinomie*" , Paris : Dunond.

Benzecri, J.P. (1973). "*L'analyse des donnes. Tome 2: L' analyse des correspodances"*, Paris : Dunond.

Boudeville, J. (1966). *"Problems of regional economic planning"*, Edinburgh :UP

Boudeville, J. (1968). *"L' espace et les poles de croissance"*, Paris : PUF

Boudeville, J. (1972) *"Aménagement du territoire et polarisation"*, Paris :Editions M.-Th. Genin, Librairies Techniques.

Chatzimichali, N. & Chatzimichalis, K. (1979). "Regional inequalities: Ideology and theory in the framework of the market economy", *Economy and Society*, vol. 3, 32-46.

Chletsos, M., Rontos, K. & Tragaki, A. (2007). *"Greek Economic Statistics: Evaluation and Proposals of Improvement"*, Athens, Greece: Athens Academy.

Csanyi, S., (1993), "A basis for sustainable wise use of game in Hungary: defining management regions", *Landscape and Urban Planning*, vol. 27, No 2-4, 199-205.

Deavers, K. L. & Brown, D. L. (1985) *"Natural resources dependence, rural development, and rural poverty"*. Washington, DC: U.S. Department of Agriculture, ED 258 775.

Drosos, G. (2005) *"Statistical Analysis of the data on linguistic information"*, PHD Thesis, Thessaloniki: Aristotelio University of Thessaloniki.

Edwards, J. A. (1976). "Industrial Structure and Regional Change: a shift-share analysis of the British Columbia economy 1961-70" *Regional Studies vol. 10* no3, 307-317.

Florou, G. (1997). *"Definition of the more ideal metric distance and better way of grouping at the various methods of automatic classification by ascending hierarchy"* PhD Thesis, Thessaloniki:University of Makedonia.

Friedman, J. (1975). A generalized theory of polarized development. In Niles, M. Hansen (Ed.), *"Growth Centers in Regional Economies Development"* New York: The Free Press.

Harissis, K. and Rontos, K. (1996) "Development of the State and Municipal Areas – a proposal for the Greek Agriculture", *Scientific Yearbook of Applied Study*, Technical and Professional Institution (TEI) of Pireas, vol. 3, no 1, 185 – 207.

Heilbroner, R. & Thurow, L.C. (1984). *Economic Problem*. N.J: Prentice Hall, 7th Edition.

Horn, Jerry G. (1985) *"Recruitment and preparation of quality teachers for rural schools. Manhattan"* KS: Kansas State University, ED 258 785.

Isaac, I. (1947). *Economics of migration*. N.Y: Oxford University Press.

Karapistolis, D., (1999), "*Data Analysis and Market Research*", Thessaloniki:Anikoulas Publishing.

Konsolas, N., (1983), *"Regional Economic Policy"*, Athens: Papazisi Editions.

Konsolas, N., Papadaskalopoulos, A., Ranos, K. & Rontos, K. (1991). "Development Prospects of the Community Lagging Regions and the Socio-economic Consequences of the Completion of the Internal Market", *a CREMI-E.E.C Research Project: National Report for Greece*, Athens: Regional Development Institute.

Leavy, A., McDonagh, P. & Commins, P. (1999). "Public Policy Trends and Some Regional Impacts", Dublin: Rural Economy, Research Series, no 6.

Makridimitris, A. &Papadimitriou, K. (2006). "Challenges and Perspectives of Regional Restructuring. Region as a B' level of Self-governance",*at the proceedings of the conference "Metropolitan Municipalities and Elected Regional Authority"*, Athens: Association of Greek Regionalists, December 3rd, 2005.

Ministry of Environment, Physical Planning and Public Housing (2006). Athens: *Report of Greece on Coastal Management.*

Myrdal, G. (1957). *"Economic Theory and Underdeveloped Regions"*, London:Duckworth.

Nordhaus, W. & Tobin J. (1973). *"Is Growth Obselete?", in M. Moss (E.), The Measurement of Economic and Social Performance"(pp 509-532)*, Studies in Income and Welth, Vol. 38, N.Y: National Bureau of Economic Research,

Papadaki, O. & Kostopoulos, T. (2006). "The Regional Policy in the Framework of the European Integration" *at the proceedings of the conference "Metropolitan Municipalities and Elected Regional Authority"*, Athens: Association of Greek Regionalists, December 3rd, 2005.

Papadaskalopoulos, A., (1990), *"Basic Methods of Regional Analysis*", Athens: Papazisis Editions.

Papadimitriou, G. (2004) "*Multivariable Statistical Analysis, methods of Data Analysis"*, Thessaloniki:University Notes, University of Makedonia,

Papadimitriou, G., (2005), *"Introduction on the Principles of the Factoral Analysis of the Correspondence (AFC)"*, Thessaloniki: University Lectures, University of Makedonia.

Papadimitriou, I. (2007)7. "*Data Analysis*", Athens: Gutenberg Editions.

Papadimitriou, G. (1997). *"Methods of Data Analysis"*. Thessaloniki: University of Makedonia.

Pepelassis, A. (1976) "*Agricultural policy and development*", Athens: Papazisis Editions.

Perrou, F. (1950). Economic Space: Theory and application. *Quarterly Journal of Economics, vol. 64*, 89-104.

Petraki-Kotti Athina, (1980), *"Macroeconomic Theory and Policy"*, vol A', Athens: Papazisis Editions.

Politechnico Di Milano, Dipartimento Economia e Produzione (1999) *"Indicators on strength and weakness of rural territories and selection of areas (Nuts III)"* Study programme on European Spatial planning of the European Commission, Brussels: E.C.

Rokos, K. (1984). *"Notes on Regional Analysis"*, Athens: Institute of Regional Development.

Rontos,K (1987) *"A Study on Regional Demography of Greece"*, Ph.D. thesis, Panteion University 1987, Greece.

Rontos, K. and Papanis, E. (2006) *"The progress of the internal immigration in Greece and its impact on the creation of a regional development standard"*, at the proceedings of the 1st Conference of Social Studies of the Social Science School of the Aegean University, Mytilini:29th March – 2nd April.

Rontos, K., Benaki, V., Tzimos, C. and Mavroudis, C., (2007), "Techno-economic orientation of the agricultural and livestock holdings and clustering the boundaries of the homogeneous agricultural areas in Greece", *Data Analysis Bulletin, vol 8*, 165-183.

Rontos, K. (2004). "Demographic Evolution, Regional Particularities and Developmental Patterns of North Aegean Region" in I. Spilanis & T. Iosifidis (Eds) "Development strategies for Less Favored Areas"(pp. 107-142), Athens: Gutenberg Publishers.

Spilanis, I. (1997). "Strategic Plane of Local and Insular Development of Northern Aegean Region", Mytilini: *Laboratory of Local and Insular Development, University of Aegean.*

Spilanis, I. and Vayanni, H. (2004). "Sustainable Tourism. Utopia or Necessity? The Role of New forms of Tourism in the Aegean Islands". In B. Bramweel (Ed.), "Coastal Mass Tourism:Diversification and Sustainable Development in Southern Europe (pp. 269-291), Great Britain: Channel View Publications

Stonier, A. and Hague, D., (1972), "A text book in Economic Theory", 4th ed., London: Logman Group Company.

Terluin, I.J. (2001) *"Rural Regions in the EU: Exploring Differences in Economic development"*, Utrecht/ Groningen: Netherlands Geographical Studies.

Tsartas, P., Stogiannou, M. and Stavrinoudis, T. (2004)"Less Favored Areas as tourism destinations" in I. Spilanis & T. Iosifidis (Eds) "Development strategies for Less Favored Areas"(pp. 295-306), Athens: Gutenberg Publishers.

Tzimos, C., (2006), *"Data Analysis in Ramified Relations and Structures of the Greek Economy. A Ramified Research of Production, Employment and Imports, in the framework of the Input-Output Model"* PhD Thesis, University of Makedonia, Thessaloniki.

Tzimos, C., Rontos, K., & Mavroudis C. (2006). "Structural Characteristics of the Agricultural-Livestock branch of the Epirus Region", *at the proceedings of the 9th Panhellenic Conference of the Agricultural Economy with subject "The Economy and the Society towards the new Challenges of the Universal Agro food System*, Athens: GPA, Aristotelio University of Thessaloniki, Charokopio University, Technological, Educational Foundation of Thessaloniki, University of Agricultural Development and Food & GEOTEE.

Vlachos, P. & Lagos, D. (2006). *"The Regional Accounts as an instrument for the administrative breakdown of the Country in NUTS territorial areas"* at the proceedings of the Conference"Metropolitan Municipalities and Elected Regional Authority", Athens: Association of Greek Regionalist, December 3rd, 2005.

Whitaker, W. H. (1982) The many faces of Ephraim: in search of a functional typology of rural areas. ED 242 459.

In: Computational Techniques in Economics and Finance ISBN: 978-1-61324-558-3
Editor: Constantine Zopounidis

Chapter 5

TRADING KNOWLEDGE

Thomas Bassetti[*]

ABSTRACT

This paper proposes a sophisticated empirical analysis on the presence and the nature of interaction effects between human capital and trade openness in the processes of productivity growth. According to our results, this interaction is not always linear. In particular, we will see how trade openness has a positive impact on productivity growth only above a minimum level of human capital. That is, less developed countries may take advantage of trade liberalization only after having reached a certain level of human capital. Obviously this will imply that it is not indifferent for a less developed country to decide first for a trade liberalization policy or for an education development policy.

JEL: C13, C14, O47

Keywords: Semiparametric estimates, Threshold variables, Human capital, trade openness, productivity growth.

1. INTRODUCTION

Theoretical literature has identified many channels through which trade openness could play an important role in economic growth. According to Bayoumi, Coe, and Helpman (1996), importing foreign goods may raise the flow of new ideas in the domestic R&D sector, that is, openness may facilitate knowledge externalities. In the same article, Bayoumi et al. suggest that imports can boost economic growth by increasing the variety of intermediate goods available for the production. Moreover, following Frankel and Romer (1999), we can say that trade liberalization implies a larger market, which, given the presence of a larger number of firms, can lead to positive knowledge externalities. At the same time, trade increases international competition forcing firms to invest in productivity growth and

[*] Dipartimento di Scienze Economiche "Marco Fanno", Università di Padova, Via del Santo 33, 35123 Padova, Italy, e-mail: thomas.bassetti@unipd.it.

innovation. Finally, since knowledge is at least partially contained in goods and services, trade liberalization can facilitate the process of technology diffusion [see e.g. among others Krugman (1979), Grossman and Helpman (1991), Eaton and Kortum (1999)]. That is, less advanced countries could imitate and adopt foreign technologies by importing goods.

Despite these arguments, a consistent number of empirical works shows that the hypothesis of a positive impact of trade on growth is not supported by data [see e.g. Levine and Renelt (1992), Harrison and Hanson (1999) and Rodriguez and Rodrik (2000)].

There are different explanations for the lack of evidence in favor of a positive trade-growth link. Grossman and Helpman (1991) argue that international competition may cause a migration of workers from the R&D sector to the final good sector. In terms of endogenous growth this will imply a lower economic growth rate. According to Baldwin and Sbergami (2000), the reason of a weak relationship between trade and growth depends on the unjustified, aprioristic imposition by empirical researchers of a linear relationship between openness proxies and growth. Girma et al. (2003) explore whether there is evidence for heterogeneity in the openness-productivity growth relationship. Allowing for geographical and institutional differences among countries, they find that the relationship between trade and productivity growth changes above and below a certain threshold level of natural barriers, while institutions are not so crucial to explain the trade-growth link. In like manner, Isaksson (2002) investigates if the impact of trade liberalization on GDP growth depends on a country's endowment of human capital. Isaksson finds that trade openness interacts with human capital in order to enhance economic growth.

This paper starts from Isaksson's contribution in order to better characterize the relationship between trade and Total Factor Productivity (TFP) growth. In particular, by using a panel of 78 countries for the period 1960-1995, we investigate the existence and the nature of interaction effects between trade openness and human capital on TFP growth. Following Miller and Upadhyay (2000), we use as dependent variable the rate of TFP growth instead of GDP growth. This is due to the fact that many of the independent variables do not enter directly into the production function of income as real inputs but affect the productivity of inputs such as physical capital and labor.

First of all, by using a linear regression analysis, we test the hypothesis of a linear interaction between human capital and trade openness on TFP growth. Subsequently, through a partial linear regression (PLR) model, we investigate the presence of possible nonlinear interactions between human capital and trade openness. Finally, by using an endogenous sample splitting technique, provided by Hansen (2000), we analyze the presence of threshold effects of human capital and trade openness on TFP growth rate.

According to our results, a less developed country may take advantage of a trade liberalization policy only after having reached a certain level of human capital, that is, productivity growth is conditioned by the presence of a minimum level of human capital. In contrast with Miller and Upadhyay (2000), we find that trade openness does not seem to be a threshold variable in the process of TFP growth. Specifically, the degree of trade openness influences the impact of human capital on TFP growth but not its nature of positive factor for productivity growth. Here, we also study the existence of threshold effects of human capital on TFP growth, an issue that has not been sufficiently studied before. Our results suggest that the level of human capital influences the shape and the nature of the relationship between trade openness and TFP growth. In other words, human capital acts as threshold variable in a very significant way.

Therefore, this paper helps to explain two important facts of economic growth: the persistence of poor countries in a free international market and the contemporary presence of poor and rich countries when the education gaps across countries are small. A direct consequence of our results is that the effectiveness of some policies, devoted to acquiring foreign technology through international trade, will depend on the stock of human capital present in a country.

The rest of the paper is organized as follows: Section 2 presents the econometric specifications used in the analysis; Section 3 contains the data description; Section 4 illustrates our results; Section 5 summarizes the main conclusions of this work.

2. Econometric Specifications

2.1 A Linear Regression Model

In this section, we present the econometric specifications on which our analysis is based. The first specification is a standard specification based on a simple linear regression model.

In order to test if human capital interacts or not with trade openness to determine TFP growth, we estimate the following linear regression model without interaction term between human capital and trade openness:

$$TFPG_{it} = \alpha_0 + \alpha_1 H_{it} + \alpha_2 \sigma_{it} + \delta X_{it} + \varepsilon_{it} \tag{1}$$

where i and t are indexes of country and time respectively, TFPG is the growth rate of TFP, H is the stock of human capital proxied by average years of schooling, σ represents a measure of openness, X is a vector of control variables, and ε is the disturbance term. In equation (1), the intercept captures the possibility for a country to observe a certain technological progress even when the explanatory variables of the model are zero.

Equation (1) implies the absence of interaction effects between human capital and trade openness on TFP growth. In order to explore the possibility of a significant interaction between human capital and trade, we also estimate a linear model in which human capital interacts with trade openness:

$$TFPG_{it} = \beta_0 + \beta_1 H_{it} + \beta_2 \sigma_{it} + \beta_3 (H_{it} \cdot \sigma_{it}) + \delta X_{it} + \varepsilon_{it} \tag{2}$$

In this equation, the interaction term is represented by $(H_{it} \cdot \sigma_{it})$. A positive and significant value of β_3 will imply the existence of complementarities between human capital and trade openness in the process of productivity growth.

Following Girma et al. (2003), we consider these models as constant coefficients models (sometimes also called pooled regression models) and estimate them by a Feasible GLS (FGLS) method in order to avoid the problem of heteroscedasticity.[6]

[6] This literature based on pooled regressions implicitly considers panel data on TFP growth as a stationary time series, where cross-country differences are captured by control variables. Nonetheless, heteroscedasticity remains a problem even under these strong assumptions. FGLS and PLR estimates are obtained by using R

2.2. A Partial Linear Regression Model

Even if the presence of a linear interaction term in Equation (2) can capture mutual influences between human capital and trade openness, we must say that it does not capture any nonlinear interaction between human capital and trade openness in the determination of TFP growth rate. To test this hypothesis, we will use a semiparametric technique already used by Liu and Stengos (1999). In particular, we estimate a semiparametric model of TFP growth, in which human capital and trade openness enter the nonparametric part of a PLR model:

$$TFPG_{it} = \gamma_0 + f(H_{it}, \sigma_{it}) + \delta X_{it} + \varepsilon_{it} \tag{3}$$

where *f(.,.)* is an unknown function estimated by a spline regression with two smoothing parameters obtained by cross-validation; the parametric part of Equation (3) will be estimated by iteratively re-weighted least squares (IWLS). With respect to previous studies, such as Isaksson (2002) and Miller and Upadhyay (2000), the advantage of specification (3) is that, now, human capital may interact with trade openness in an unconstrained way. In other words, we do not impose any aprioristic model, allowing data to reveal the shape of this relationship.

2.3. A Threshold Analysis

In this section, as a further step of the analysis, we test if human capital and trade openness act as threshold variables in the process of technology diffusion. In particular, by using an endogenous threshold selection technique, we aim to verify the presence of threshold effects of human capital and trade openness in the process of TFP growth. In empirical literature there are essentially two typologies of methods to determine the existence of threshold effects in regression analyses:

1. Exogenous methods. These methods involve the splitting of a sample into groups based on exogenous values of the threshold levels. In these methods, the critical switching value is not determined by the data but it is determined exogenously. Miller and Upadhyay (2000) use a sample splitting method that belongs to this class of techniques.
2. Endogenous methods. These methods involve the splitting of a sample into groups based on a self-selection of the threshold values. In these methods, the critical switching value comes from the data itself rather than from an exogenous assumption.

Exogenous selection methods are strongly conditioned by the initial assumptions made by a researcher; moreover, as suggested by Hansen (2000), they generate serious inference problems. For these reasons, we prefer to study the presence of threshold effects by an endogenous selection method. To determine any threshold values of human capital and trade

programs provided by Abbey (1988) and Wood (2006), respectively; while threshold analysis is obtained by using Gauss programs provided by Hansen (2000).

openness in the process of TFP growth and their relative confidence intervals, we use the endogenous search technique provided by Hansen (2000) and briefly illustrated in the Appendix.

By following Girma et al. (2003), if this analysis reveals the existence of threshold values in the levels of trade openness and/or human capital, we will employ these values to re-estimate Equation (1) by using both the linear and the partially linear approach.

In particular, by considering the threshold value of trade $(\overline{\sigma})$, Equation (1) will become

$$TFPG_{it} = \alpha_0 + \alpha_1[H_{it} \cdot I(\sigma_{it} < \overline{\sigma})] + \alpha_1'[H_{it} \cdot I(\sigma_{it} \geq \overline{\sigma})] + \alpha_2\sigma_{it} + \delta X_{it} + \varepsilon_{it} \quad (4)$$

where I(.) is the indicator function, $H_{it} \cdot I(\sigma_{it} < \overline{\sigma})$ represents the stock of human capital of a country with a trade openness ratio below the found threshold value, and $H_{it} \cdot I(\sigma_{it} \geq \overline{\sigma})$ represents the stock of human capital of a country with a trade openness ratio at least equal to the threshold value.

Similarly, the PLR method illustrated in the previous section will imply the following specification:

$$TFPG_{it} = \alpha_0 + \alpha_1 H_{it} + \alpha_2\sigma_{it} + \delta X_{it} + \varepsilon_{it} \quad (1)$$

where ϕ_1 and ϕ_2 are unknown functions estimated in the same way of Equation (3).

Likewise, for the threshold level of human capital $(\overline{H})$, we will have

$$TFPG_{it} = \beta_0 + \beta_1 H_{it} + \beta_2[\sigma_{it} \cdot I(H_{it} < \overline{H})] + \beta_2'[\sigma_{it} \cdot I(H_{it} \geq \overline{H})] + \delta X_{it} + \varepsilon_{it} \quad (6)$$

where $\sigma_{it} \cdot I(H_{it} < \overline{H})$ represents the trade openness level of countries with a stock of human capital below the found threshold value, and $\sigma_{it} \cdot I(H_{it} \geq \overline{H})$ represents the trade openness levels of countries with a stock of human capital at least equal to the threshold value.

Whereas, given the threshold level $(\overline{H})$, the PLR specification can be written as follows

$$TFPG_{it} = \alpha H_{it} + \psi_1[\sigma_{it} \cdot I(H_{it} < \overline{H})] + \psi_2[\sigma_{it} \cdot I(H_{it} \geq \overline{H})] + \delta X_{it} + \varepsilon_{it} \quad (7)$$

where ψ_1 and ψ_2 are still unknown functions.

The results of this analysis are discussed in the next sections.

3. DATA AND VARIABLES

Data come from Beck et al. (1999, 2000). The sample consists of 78 countries observed for the period 1960 to 1995.[7] Yearly data have been transformed into five-year averages in order to eliminate the influence of business cycle effects, that is, we have seven data points for each country. Therefore, in this dataset the effects of short run variations are reduced.

The dependent variable is the rate of TFP growth, which was estimated from a Cobb-Douglas production function with constant returns to scale by setting the capital share at 1/3 and the labor share at 2/3.[8] Among the explanatory variables, particular attention is paid to the effect of human capital on TFP growth. The most recent approach to measuring human capital in economic growth is the so-called educational stock-approach. This approach consists in the use of several proxies for human capital, where these proxies concern measures of formal education. As human capital proxy we use the average years of schooling of the population aged 15 years and older.[9]

There are important reasons to use average years of schooling instead of adult literacy rates or enrollment rates. Literacy is not univocally defined across countries and thus creates biases in cross-country analyses. Furthermore, adult literacy rates omit important components of human capital such as logical and analytical reasoning and scientific and technological knowledge. That is, adult literacy rates ignore the contribution of advanced skills and knowledge to production of output. Enrollment rates are poor proxies for the present stock of human capital. In fact, enrollment rates measure the education of students, who do not constitute the current labor force. On the contrary, average years of schooling takes into account the total amount of formal education acquired by the workforce, that is, average years of schooling proxy more accurately the existing stock of human capital in a country. For this reason, in line with recent literature, we consider average years of schooling as one of the most reliable human capital proxies available at the moment.

Following Isaksson (2002), we use as measure for trade openness the ratio of exports plus imports to GDP. Miller and Upadhyay (2000) use as measure of openness only the export share, but, as argued by Grossman and Helpman (1991), both sectors, export and import, could lead to productivity gains through the imitation and adoption of foreign technologies.

Finally, we also estimate the effects of some control variables on TFP growth: the population growth rate (pop); the investment share (inv), measured as fixed investment share of GDP; the inflation rate (p) in order to consider macro policy outcome; the financial depth (lly), measured as the ratio of liquid liabilities to GDP, in order to control for the effect of financial development on growth; two dummy variables (D70, D80), to control for time

---

[7] In the appendix we provide the list of countries contained in the sample.

[8] These values are rather standard in the growth accounting literature [see e.g. Keller (2002)].

[9] In our dataset, average years of schooling come from Barro and Lee (1996). De la Fuente and Doménech (2006), Krueger and Lindahl (2001), Temple (2001) and Cohen and Soto (2007) stress the importance of data quality in order to find a robust relationship between education and growth. For instance, according to De la Fuente and Doménech (2006), Barro and Lee's dataset performs poorly if the data is used in first differences. It is also true that Barro and Lee's dataset probably remains the most widely used reference for educational attainment in the economic literature. Moreover, De la Fuente and Doménech (2006) provide data only for 21 OECD countries, while Cohen and Soto (2007) take a single observation for each decade, and this notably reduces the number of observations. For all these reasons we have decided to use this dataset.

period effects with reference to decades '70 and '80.[10] As usual explanatory variables are expressed in terms of logarithms.

4. Estimation Results

Table 1 reports our estimates for all equations specified in Section 2. In all regressions, the coefficients of the constant term, the financial depth and the dummy variable for 1970s are not statistically significant at the 5% level of confidence, hence we cannot conclude that they are significantly different from zero. At the same time, as in Miller and Upadhyay (2000) and Isaksson (2002), population and inflation have a negative impact on TFP growth, while investments have a positive impact on TFP growth. In line with the productivity slowdown literature, the coefficients for the dummy variable D80 are all negative and statistically significant at 1% level of confidence. Let us examine the results obtained for human capital, H_i, and trade openness, σ_i.

4.1. Linear Interaction between Human Capital and Trade Openness

Columns (1) and (2) of Table 1 present the estimated coefficients for Equations (1) and (2), respectively. In Column (1), where we have estimated the linear specification without interaction term, human capital has a positive and significant impact on TFP growth, while impact of trade seems to be insignificant or even negative, confirming Isaksson's results.

As we can see in Column (2), the introduction of a linear interaction term does not improve the fitting of the data with respect to a linear model without interaction term. As in Miller and Upadhyay (2000), the marginal effect captured by the linear interaction term is positive but not so significant. That is, trade openness could slightly increase the positive effect of human capital on TFP growth and vice-versa. The coefficient of human capital remains positive, but now it is not statistically significant at the 5% of confidence. Miller and Upadhyay find a negative and significant impact of human capital on TFP growth when they insert the interaction term.

At this level of the analysis, given our results, two conclusions are possible: human capital and trade openness do not significantly interact, or this interaction is more complex than a linear interaction. In order to answer this question, we will study the presence of a nonlinear relationship between human capital and trade openness more in depth.

4.2. Nonlinear Interaction between Human Capital and Trade Openness

Column (3) of Table 1 presents the estimated coefficients for the PLR model given by Equation (3). As we can see, this specification fits the data much better.

---

[10] There are several reasons to control for specific time effects. In fact, the 70s and the 80s are decades dominated by oil shocks and high inflation in many countries. In particular, oil shocks, which raised the real price of energy between 1973 and 1974, may have caused the so called "productivity slowdown" during the 80s. Moreover, there are significant differences in GDP volatility between the 1970s and the 1980s [see, e.g., Easterly (2001)]. All these effects seem to be exogenous and this is why the inclusion of two dummy variables for periods 70s and 80s is quite common in growth regressions.

Figure 1 provides a graphical representation of these nonlinearities. Since the nonparametric part of Equation (3), that is function *f(.,.)*, contains two independent variables, in Figure 1 the relationship between pairs (H_i, σ_i) and TFP growth has been represented in a level curve plot. By looking at Figure 1, a fact emerges immediately: level curves do not always have the same shape. In particular, for some values of H and σ, level curves are concave with respect to the origin of axes, while for other values of H and σ, level curves are convex with respect to the origin of axes. Moreover, level curves converge to a vertical asymptote close to a unitary value of the log of education. On the other hand, if we compare the effect of an additional investment in education for high and low levels of trade, we can see that the impact of education (captured by the distance between two contiguous level curves) changes considerably. This suggests that human capital and trade openness may have some threshold effects on the process of productivity growth.

Table 1. Cross-Country Regressions on TFP growth rate (1960-95)

	FGLS Eq. (1)	FGLS Eq. (2)	PLR Eq. (3)	FGLS Eq. (4)	PLR Eq. (5)	FGLS Eq. (6)	PLR Eq. (7)
Control Variables							
Intercept	-0.0037 (0.692)	0.0005 (0.084)	0.0045 (0.889)	-0.0005 (0.823)	-0.0002 (0.030)	-0.0035 (0.660)	-0.0066 (1.258)
pop	-0.0731 (5.438)**	-0.0718 (5.347)**	-0.0737 (5.186)**	-0.0730 (5.454)**	-0.0822 (5.969)**	-0.0644 (4.764)**	-0.0799 (5.798)**
inv	0.0442 (3.263)**	0.0462 (3.405)**	0.0524 (3.593)**	0.0393 (2.878)**	0.0744 (4.687)**	0.0608 (4.277)**	0.0679 (4.732)**
p	-0.0244 (3.509)**	-0.0244 (3.520)**	-0.0291 (4.077)**	-0.0264 (3.779)**	-0.0239 (3.441)**	-0.0246 (3.590)**	-0.0248 (3.655)**
lly	0.0015 (0.309)	0.0005 (0.099)	-0.0014 (0.278)	0.0002 (0.280)	-0.0049 (0.937)	-0.0037 (0.725)	-0.0068 (1.352)
D70	-0.0020 (0.764)	-0.0019 (0.702)	-0.0018 (0.695)	-0.0022 (0.819)	-0.0025 (0.965)	-0.0023 (0.880)	-0.0017 (0.647)
D80	-0.0087 (3.307)**	-0.0087 (1.311)	-0.0077 (2.942)**	-0.0082 (3.109)**	-0.0084 (3.264)**	-0.0085 (3.248)**	-0.0070 (2.728)**
Main Variables							
H_i	0.0076 (4.234)**	0.0041 (1.512)				0.0050 (2.606)**	0.0078 (3.878)**
σ_i	-0.0022 (0.679)	-0.0114 (1.854)		-0.0057 (1.593)	0.0040 (0.955)		
$\ln H_i \cdot \sigma_i$		0.0070 (1.755)	NP[a] edf 17.30				
$H_i \cdot I(\sigma_i < \overline{\sigma})$				0.0077 (4.226)**	NP[a] edf 3.68		
$H_i \cdot I(\sigma_i \geq \overline{\sigma})$				0.0234 (3.140)**	NP[a] edf 6.83		
$\sigma_i \cdot I(H_i < \overline{H})$						-0.0085 (2.328)*	NP[a] edf 7.53
$\sigma_i \cdot I(H_i \geq \overline{H})$						0.0064 (1.611)	NP[b] edf 1.93
Obs	468	468	468	468	468	468	468
Log-Lik	1062.307	1059.244	1124.256	1060.663	1122.829	1063.719	1127.125
GCV			$5.337 \cdot 10^{-4}$		$5.232 \cdot 10^{-4}$		$5.113 \cdot 10^{-4}$
DF	9	10	25.30	11	19.51	10	18.46

Parentheses contain the values of t-statistics: **(1%), *(5%).

NP means that the variable enters in the nonparametric part of the regression, while edf means estimated degrees of freedom.

(a) F-test: we cannot reject the nonlinear hypothesis with a significant level of 5%.

(b) F-test: we reject the nonlinear hypothesis with a significant level of 5%.

According to this hypothesis, the impact of human capital and trade openness on productivity growth should crucially depend on the levels assumed by our main variables. Therefore, we must test the possibility of threshold effects of human capital and trade openness on TFP growth.

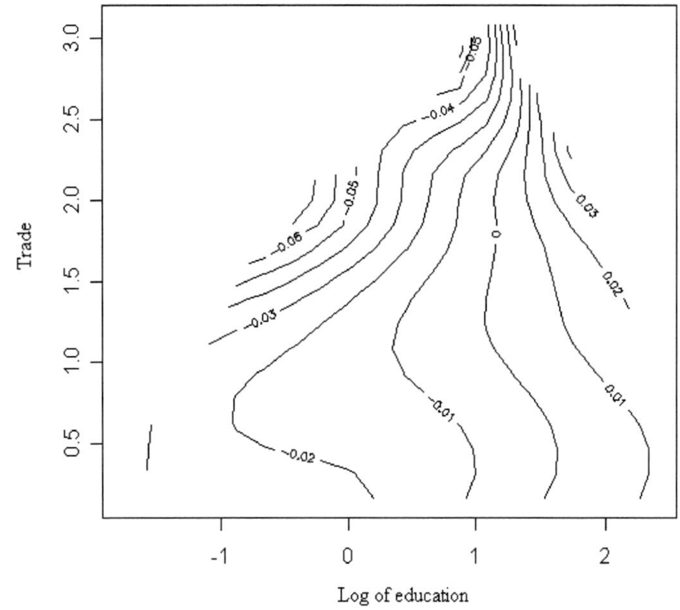

Figure 1. The estimated interaction between human capital and trade for TFP growth.

4.3. Threshold Effects for Human Capital and Trade Openness

Table 2 shows the estimated threshold values for human capital and trade openness obtained by the Hansen's method.[11]

Table 2. Threshold Analysis

TRADE	
Threshold estimate	1.8523
95% confidence interval	[0.5214, 2.1112]
Numbers of bootstrap replications	1000
Bootstrap (p-value)	0.0800
Heteroscedasticity test (p-value)	0.0120
HUMAN CAPITAL	
Threshold estimate	1.6233
95% confidence interval	[1.5369 , 1.6714]
Numbers of bootstrap replications	1000
Bootstrap (p-value)	0.0020
Heteroscedasticity test (p-value)	0.0063

[11] In the appendix, we provide a brief description of this method.

4.3.1. Trade as a Threshold Identifying Variable

Following Miller and Upadhyay (2000) and Papageorgiou (2002), we have tested if trade openness is a threshold variable for TFP growth. If our results are not comparable with Miller and Upadhyay's findings because they use the export share, we also cannot compare them with Papageorgiou's findings because he considers a cross-section of countries and the GDP growth rate as dependent variable.

Here, we have found a threshold value for trade openness of 1.85 with a bootstrapped p-value of 0.08. Figure 2 shows the normalized likelihood ratio test as a function of trade openness LRn(σ). The estimated critical level is the value that minimizes the function LRn(σ). The asymptotic ninety-five percent critical value of LRn(σ) is represented by the dashed line. The likelihood ratio function crosses the dashed line in the extreme values of the confidence interval [0.5214, 2.1112]; this means that at the 5% significance level there is a threshold effect of trade openness in this interval. Since the confidence interval is rather wide, we cannot be so confident on the threshold value we found. Nonetheless, we use this value to divide our sample into two groups: a low-trade group and a high-trade group.

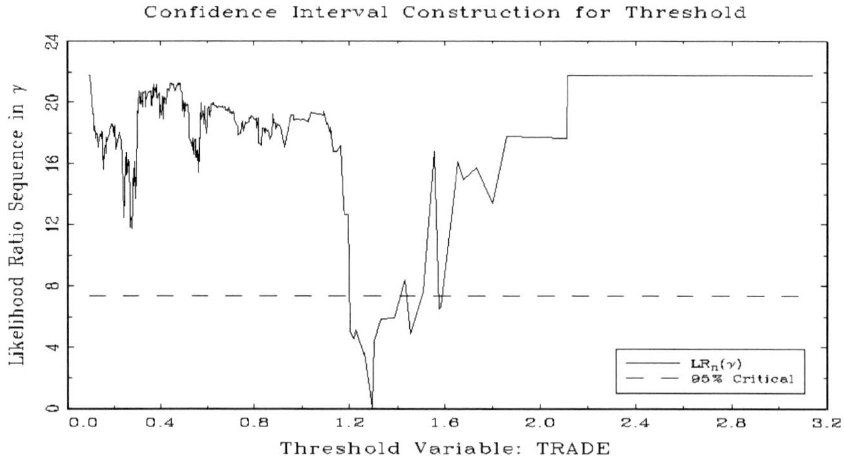

Figure 2. Likelihood Ratio for trade as threshold variable.

Columns (4) and (5) of Table 1 provide the estimated coefficients for Equations (4) and (5). There, both regressions are based on the critical value for trade of 1.85. Column (4) shows that the linear contribution of human capital to TFP growth is always positive and significant at 1% level of confidence. However, human capital plays an important role in TFP growth especially in the high trade group, where the coefficient is three times the coefficient observed for the low trade group.

In Column (5) we have estimated the PLR model as specified by Equation (5). That is, we have taken into account possible nonlinear effects of human capital on TFP growth either for low levels of trade openness or for high levels of trade openness. Through an F-test, we can say that the hypothesis of a nonlinear contribution of human capital to TFP growth cannot be rejected with a significance level of 5% in both groups. Figures 3.a and 3.b show the nonparametric contributions of human capital, as presented in Column (5), for low and high levels of trade openness, respectively. In these figures, we have also reported the 95% confidence interval band.

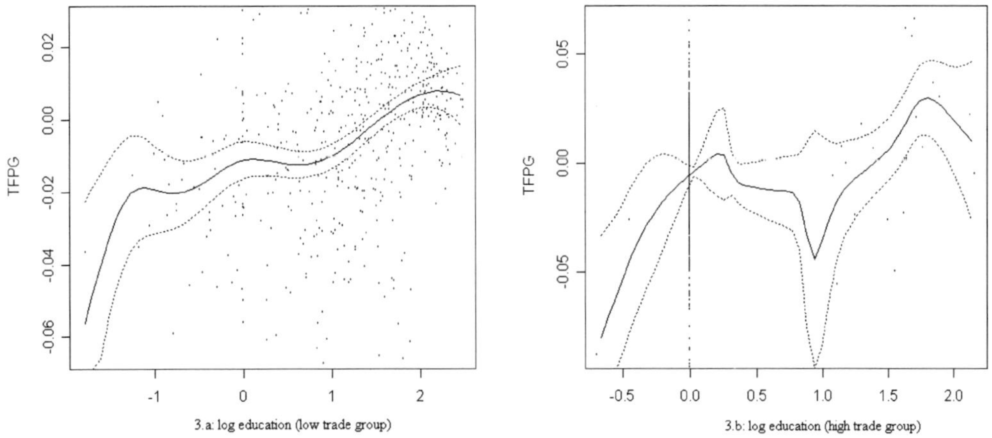

Figure 3. Nonlinear parts of Equation (5).

Figure 3.a suggests that, for low levels of trade openness, investments in human capital slightly increase productivity growth. That is, in countries with low levels of trade openness investments in human capital play a marginal role in productivity growth. A possible explanation is that in these countries the only source of technological progress is the domestic research activity, while in a open economy countries may also benefit from foreign technology diffusion.

Although Figure 3.b suggests that, for high levels of trade openness, the effect of human capital on TFP growth is nonlinear. The main reason of these strong nonlinearities can be the small number of observations contained in the high-trade group.[12]

4.3.2. Human Capital as a Threshold Identifying Variable

According to Figure 1, human capital may be a threshold variable for TFP growth, thus we must also test this hypothesis. The estimated threshold level for human capital is 1.62 (5.07 average years of schooling) and its confidence interval is [1.5369 , 1.6714]. A bootstrap test shows that this threshold level of human capital is statistically significant at the 5%, that is, we reject the null hypothesis of no threshold in the interval already mentioned. In fact, the estimated confidence interval is rather narrow. Figure 4 shows the normalized likelihood ratio test as a function of the stock of human capital LRn(H).

Columns (6) and (7) of Table 1 provide the estimated coefficients for Equations (6) and (7), respectively. There the TFP growth regressions are based on the critical value for human capital of 1.62. This threshold value divides our sample into a low-education group and a high-education group. Column (6) shows that the coefficients of trade for low levels of human capital is negative and statistically significant at the 5% of confidence, whereas the same coefficient for high levels of human capital is positive but not so significant. This confirms the fact that trade openness facilitates the TFP growth of a country only if its stock of human capital is sufficiently high.

[12] The number of observations is 458 for countries with low levels of trade openness and only 10 for countries with high levels of trade openness.

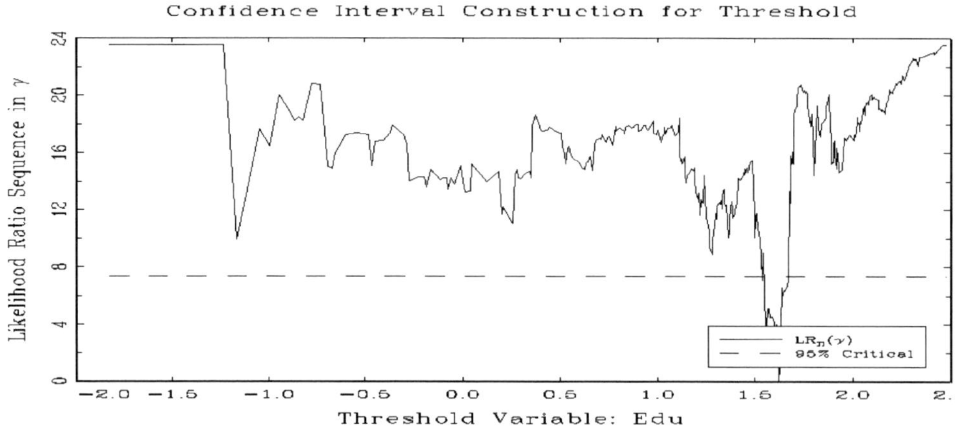

Figure 4. Likelihood Ratio for human capital as threshold variable.

In Column (7) we have estimated Equation (7). That is, we have taken into account possible nonlinear effects of trade openness on TFP growth either for low levels of human capital or for high levels of human capital. Here the Generalized Cross Validation (GCV) score is the lowest and the log-likelihood ratio is the highest, that is, specification (7) provides the best fitting of the data.[13]

By using an F-test, we cannot reject, at the 5% significance level, the hypothesis of a nonlinear relationship between trade and TFP growth for low levels of human capital. The same test shows that the hypothesis of a nonlinear relationship between trade and TFP growth must be rejected, at the 5% significance level, for countries with high levels of human capital.

Figures 5.a and 5.b show the nonparametric contributions of trade openness, as presented in Column (7), for low and high levels of human capital, respectively. The dotted line represents the 95% confidence interval band.

Figure 5.a suggests that, for low levels of human capital, trade openness has a nonlinear effect on TFPG. In Figure 5.a, the estimated relationship between trade openness and TFP growth seems to be decreasing except for relatively high levels of openness, but it is due to the presence of an outlier: Malta during the periods 1960-64, 1965-69, 1970-74. We can say that trade liberalization has negative effects, on TFP growth in countries with low levels of human capital. At the same time, Figure 5.b shows that, for high levels of human capital, the effect of trade openness on TFPG is positive, confirming the results obtained in Column (6). Moreover, we must reject the hypothesis of a nonlinear relationship between trade openness and TFP growth for high levels of human capital. Before opening up to international competition a country must have a sufficient stock of human capital.

[13] GCV criterion is a technique used to guide the selection of optimal parameters in smoothing splines and related regularization problems. The optimal combination of parameters is, typically, the one that produces a minimum GCV score. The GCV score function is defined as: $GCV(\alpha,\rho)=\sum_{i=1}^{n}(\frac{e_i^2}{n-m})^2$ where e is the vector of error terms, m is the number of parameters, n is the number of data points, α=(K/n) (K is the number of sub-samples) and ρ is the order of polynomial used to fit the data into the sub-samples.

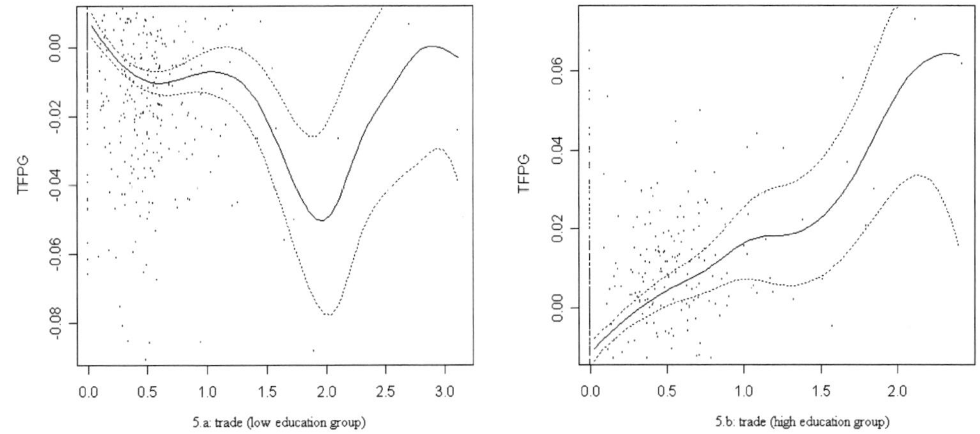

Figure 5. Nonlinear parts of Equation (7).

In Figure 7, we re-propose Figure 1 with the critical values found by Hansen's technique. The first threshold refers to trade openness (the critical value is 1.85), while the second threshold refers to human capital (the critical value is 1.62). These two values divide the space (Hi, σi) into four quadrants.

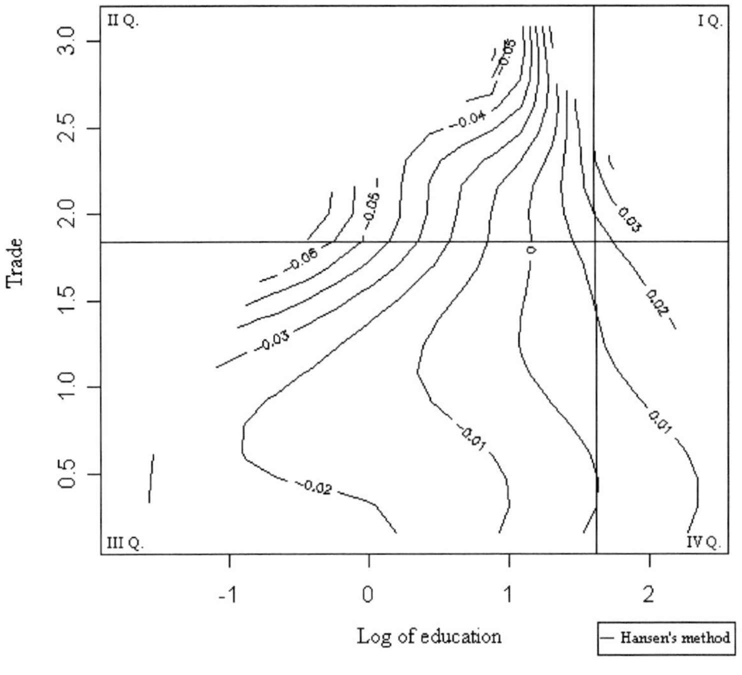

Figure 7. Threshold and interaction effects on TFP growth.

Quadrant I contains observations with high levels of human capital and trade openness. Quadrant II contains observations with low levels of human capital and high levels of trade openness. Quadrant III contains observations with low levels of human capital and trade openness. Quadrant IV contains observations with high levels of human capital and low levels of trade openness.

In Quadrant I, level curves are convex with respect to the origin of axes. This means that, for high levels of human capital and trade openness, both of these variables are positively correlated with TFP growth rate. Countries with high levels of human capital and trade openness can use their stock of human capital to produce new technologies as well as adopt foreign technologies that come from international trade. In this situation, further investments in education and policies in favor of trade liberalization have positive effects on productivity growth.

In Quadrant II, the level curves are concave with respect to the origin of axes. If the trade openness ratio of countries with low levels of human capital increases, they might experience a severe reduction in their TFP. This can be due to the fact that international competition may be too strong for countries with an insufficient endowment of human capital; these countries do not have the minimum level of human capital necessary to absorb foreign technologies and consequently they do not import knowledge. For countries in this situation the way out from a continuous loss of productivity is investing in human capital but not in trade liberalization.

Quadrant III contains countries with low levels of human capital and trade openness. With respect to countries in Quadrant II, countries in Quadrant III are in a better situation. In fact, they are not so exposed to international competition; in general, their TFP growth rates are less negative than those shown by countries in Quadrant II. By investing in education and trade openness, these countries can increase their TFP growth rates.

Finally, since countries in Quadrant IV have a sufficient stock of human capital, they can open up to international trade in order to take advantage of trade liberalization.

CONCLUSIONS

This paper has investigated how human capital and international trade influence TFP growth. Here, we have carried out an econometric analysis in order to characterize the shape of the interaction between human capital and trade openness for TFP growth.

According to our results, a model in which human capital may interact with trade openness in a nonlinear way fits the data much better than a model in which human capital may interact with trade openness only in a linear way. In particular, we have seen that the role played by trade openness in TFP growth depends on the stock of human capital of a country.

By using an endogenous sample splitting technique, the last part of the analysis has been devoted to the search for possible threshold effects of human capital and trade on TFP growth. While trade openness does not show any threshold behavior, it is important to distinguish between countries with high and low levels of human capital. For high levels of human capital a country might take advantage (in terms of TFP growth) of a policy of trade liberalization, whereas, for low levels of human capital the same policy could be negative. This evidence supports the idea that international competition could be too strong for economies with an insufficient stock of human capital. Therefore, to take advantage of trade liberalization, countries with low levels of human capital must invest in education in order to improve their absorptive capacity and then catch up with the most advanced countries.

The existence of nonlinearities and threshold effects between human capital and trade openness could explain why the impacts of human capital and trade openness on TFP growth are found to be statistically insignificant, or even negative, in many growth regressions. Moreover, our results help to explain two important facts of economic growth: the persistence of poor countries in a free international market and the contemporary presence of poor and rich countries when the education gaps across countries are small.

A. The Country-List

Algeria	Guatemala	Pakistan
Argentina	Guyana	Panama
Australia	Haiti	Papua New Guinea
Austria	Honduras	Paraguay
Belgium	India	Peru
Bolivia	Indonesia	Philippines
Brazil	Iran, Islamic Republic of	Portugal
Cameroon	Ireland	Rwanda
Canada	Israel	Senegal
Central African Republic	Italy	Sierra Leone
Chile	Jamaica	South Africa
Colombia	Japan	Spain
Congo	Kenya	Sri Lanka
Costa Rica	Korea, Republic of	Sudan
Cyprus	Lesotho	Sweden
Denmark	Malawi	Switzerland
Dominican Republic	Malaysia	Syria
Ecuador	Malta	Thailand
Egypt, Arab Rep.	Mauritius	Togo
El Salvador	Mexico	Trinidad and Tobago
Finland	Nepal	United Kingdom
France	Netherlands	United States
Gambia, The	New Zealand	Uruguay
Germany	Nicaragua	Venezuela
Ghana	Niger	Zaire
Greece	Norway	Zimbawe

B. A Brief Illustration of Hansen's Method

Hansen (2000) provides an econometric technique of endogenous sample splitting based on a threshold regression model in which observations can be divided into classes that depend on an unknown value of an explanatory variable. Hansen's method satisfies two important statistical requisites: the threshold values come from data, thus nonlinearities are not exogenously imposed; the method offers asymptotic properties useful to test the statistical significance of the results.

Consider a general regression model in which Yt is the dependent variable at time t, Xt is the explanatory variable of interest, Zt is a vector of other regressors, and εt is a with noise term:

$$Y_t = \beta_0 + \beta_{X,1} X(t) \cdot I(X(t) \leq \mu) + \beta_{X,2} X(t) \cdot I(X(t) > \mu) + \beta_z Z(t) + \varepsilon_t \quad \text{(B.1)}$$

given different critical values (μ), the indicator function I(.) creates various sub-samples of data.

Hansen's selection technique can be divided into three steps:

1. Estimate the Threshold Value μ

By the least squares estimation method, Hansen (2000) obtains μ as the value that minimizes the concentrated sum of squared errors (SSE), $S(\mu)$. The SSE function depends on μ only through the indicator function. The minimization problem is solved by a sequential procedure. There each step is characterized by a distinct value of the potential threshold variable (X). For each of these values, the threshold regression model is estimated and the SSE is obtained. The critical value μ is the one that minimizes the SSE function.

In general, Equation (B.1) is nonlinear. Nevertheless, at each step we take only a given value of μ, thus, (B.1) becomes linear and correct estimates can be obtained by OLS method. Therefore, once $\overline{\mu}$ is obtained, the slope coefficients can be obtained as $\overline{\beta} = \beta(\overline{\mu})$.

2. Test the Hypothesis that a Threshold Exists

After having identified the threshold value μ, we must test whether it is statistically significant. In other words, we test the null hypothesis, $H_o : \beta_{X,1} = \beta_{X,2}$, against the alternative hypothesis $H_o : \beta_{X,1} \neq \beta_{X,2}$. The null hypothesis states that a linear regression model is a proper specification, while the alternative hypothesis assumes the existence of a threshold. Unfortunately, the threshold $\overline{\mu}$ is not identified under the null hypothesis, then classical tests do not have standard distributions and critical values cannot be find into distribution tables. Hansen proposes to bootstrap the p-value of the hypothesis test.

3. Define a Confidence Interval for $\overline{\mu}$

If the previous analysis suggests to reject the null hypothesis, we need to define a confidence interval in which $\overline{\mu}$ lies (that is, an interval that contains the correct threshold value). In this endogenous sample splitting proposal, the parameter μ fails to be identified when $\beta_{X,1} = \beta_{X,2}$ and the asymptotic distribution of $\overline{\mu}$ is non standard. To obtain the appropriate distribution function and the relative critical values, cα, Hansen (2000) uses the following likelihood ratio statistic:

$$LR_n(\mu) = \frac{S_n(\mu) - S_n(\overline{\mu})}{S_n(\overline{\mu})} n \tag{B.2}$$

The confidence interval of $\overline{\mu}$ contains all those values of X for which the likelihood ratio statistic is less than cα. This is equivalent to a no rejection area of the likelihood ratio test.

Hansen (2000) also presents a normalized likelihood ratio statistic, $LR_n^*(\mu)$, useful to make robust inference tests even in presence of heteroscedasticity. Moreover, Hansen (2000) shows that even if the estimator β depends on the threshold estimate μ, the asymptotic normal distribution theory can be used to make inference analyses on the estimated coefficients.

REFERENCES

Abbey, S. (1988), "Robust measures and the estimator limit", *Geostandards Newsletter*, 12, 241-248.

Barro, R. J. and Lee, J. W. (1996), "International Measures of Schooling Years and Schooling Quality", *American Economic Review*, 86(2), 218-223.

Baldwin, R. and Sbergami, F. (2000), "Non-Linearity in Openness and Growth Links", *Working Paper of the Graduate Institute of International Studies, Geneva.*

Bayoumi, T., Coe, D.T. and Helpman E. (1996), "R&D Spillovers and Global Growth", *Journal of International Economics*, 48, 399-428.

Beck, T., Levine, R. and Loayza (1999), "Finance and the Sources of Growth", *Journal of Financial Economics,* 58(1-2), 261-300.

Beck, T. Levine, R. and Loayza (2000), "Financial Intermediation and Growth: Causality and Causes", Journal of Monetary Economics, 46(1), 31-77.

Cohen, D. and Soto, M. (2007), "Growth and Human Capital: Good Data, Good Results", *Journal of Economic Growth*, 12(1), 51-76.

De la Fuente, A. and Doménech, R. (2006), "Human Capital in Growth Regressions: How Much Difference Does Data Quality Make?", *Journal of European Economic Association,* 4(1), 1-36.

Easterly, W. (2001), "The Lost Decades: Developing Countries' Stagnation in Spite of Policy Reform 1980-1998!, *Journal of Economic Growth*, 2(6), 135-157.

Eaton, J. and Kortum, S. (1999), "International Technology Diffusion: Theory and Measurement*", International Economic Review*, 40, 537-570.

Frankel, J. and Romer, D. (1998). "Does Trade Cause Growth?", *American Economic Review*, 89, 379-399.

Gerschenkron, A. (1962), Economic Backwardness in Historical Perspective, Cambridge, Mass.: *Belknap Press of Harvard University Press*.

Girma, S., Henry, M., Kneller, R. and Milner, C. (2003), "Threshold and Interaction Effects in the Openness - Productivity Growth Relationship: The Role of Institutions and Natural Barriers, *GEP Research Paper*, 2003/32, University of Nottingham.

Grossman, G. M. and Helpman, E. (1991), "Trade, Knowledge Spillovers, and Growth", *European Economic Review*, 35, 517-526.

Hansen, B.E. (2000), "Sample Splitting and Threshold Estimation", *Econometrica*,68,575-603.

Harrison, A. and Hanson, G.H. (1999), "Trade Liberalization and Wage Inequality in Mexico", *Industrial and Labor Relations Review*, 52(2), 271-288.

Isaksson, A. (2002), "The Importance of Human Capital for the Trade-Growth Link", *Working Paper* 2, UNIDO.

Keller, W. (2002), "Trade and the Transmission of Technology", *Journal of Economic Growth,* 7, 5-24.

Krueger, A. and Lindhal, M. (2001), "Education for Growth: Why and For Whom?", *Journal of Economic Literature,* 39, 1101–1136.

Krugman, P. (1979), "A Model of Innovation, Technology Transfer, and the World Distribution of Income", *Journal of Political Economy*, 87(2), 253-266.

Levine, R. and Renelt, D. (1992), "A Sensitivity Analysis of Cross-Country Growth Regressions", *American Economic Review*, 82, 942-963.

Liu, Z. and Stengos, T. (1999), "Nonlinearities in Cross-Country Growth Regressions: A Semiparametric Approach", *Journal of Applied Econometrics*, 14, 527-538.

Miller, S. M. and Upadhyay, M. P. (2000), "The effects of openness, trade orientation, and human capital on total factor productivity", *Journal of Development Economics*, 63(2), 399-423.

Papageorgiou, C. (2002), "Trade as a Threshold Variable for Multiple Regimes", *Economics Letters,* 77(1), 85-91.

Rodriguez, F. and Rodrik, D. (1999), "Trade Policy and Economic Growth: A Skeptic's Guide to the Cross-National Evidence", in: B. S. Bernanke and K. Rogoff (eds), *NBER Macroeconomics Annual,* Cambridge: MIT Press.

Temple, J. R. W. (2001), "Generalizations that aren't? Evidence on education and growth", *European Economic Review*, 45(4-6), 905-918.

Wood, S. (2006), Generalized Additive Models: An Introduction with R, *CRC/Chapman & Hall.*

In: Computational Techniques in Economics and Finance ISBN: 978-1-61324-558-3
Editor: Constantine Zopounidis

Chapter 6

IMPACT OF OUTLIER RETURNS ON THE CAPM MODEL: AN INVESTIGATION USING THE HUBER'S M ROBUST ESTIMATION METHOD

***Alexandra Theodossiou*[*1] *and Panayiotis Theodossiou*[*2]**

[1] Drexel University, US

[2] Cyprus University of Technology, Cyprus and Rutgers University, US

ABSTRACT

This paper investigates the impact of outliers on the estimated parameters of the CAPM model. A mixed return process, consisting of a regular and an outlier component, is used to model returns for individual stocks. The regular component of stock returns is estimated using Huber's Robust M estimation (HRM) method. The results show that when positive (negative) outlier returns are matched with high (low) market returns a stock's OLS beta is larger than its respective HRM beta, and when matched with low (high) market returns, a stock's OLS beta is smaller than its respective HRM beta. The impact of outlier returns on a stock's estimated alpha is not as straightforward. (JEL: G11, G12).

Keywords: CAPM, M Robust Estimator, OLS and Outlier Returns.

1. INTRODUCTION

Stock outlier returns are extremely large returns triggered by major company specific events such as acquisitions, class action lawsuits, financial distress and the development of a major product line. These events appear randomly and infrequently over a company's life and have a more profound impact on the prices of smaller rather than larger capitalization stocks.

* atheodoss@gmail.com

* theodoss@gmail.com or theodoss@camden.rutgers.edu

Because of their size, outliers have a significant effect on the estimated alphas and betas of the Capital Asset Pricing Model (CAPM).

The impact of outliers on the CAPM model has been discussed in several published articles.[14] Many authors advocate that outlier returns should be removed from the data so that the estimated CAPM regression slope (beta) would reflect the "true" stochastic relationship between the returns of the stock and the market portfolio. Although this solution is not the best, an estimated beta in the absence of influential outliers yields a better measure of a company's systematic risk, at least on intuitive grounds.

It is well known that the OLS method is particularly sensitive to outliers and that its efficiency declines dramatically as the data divert away from normality; e.g., Sharpe (1971), Chan and Lakonishok (1992), Martin and Simin (2003) and McDonald et al. (2008). In all cases, these authors show that robust estimation methods produce more reliable estimators of stock return models than OLS.

A natural question to ask is which estimators are more appropriate to use in the estimation of the CAPM model? Should CAPM estimators be resistant to outliers? These are extremely important questions for financial researchers and practitioners involved in the estimation of cost of capital and portfolio inputs or the investigation of how different events impact company stock prices. Theodossiou and Theodossiou (2009) find that outliers have insignificant impact on the overall company risk and conclude that outlier resistant estimation methods of stock return models are more appropriate than OLS.

This paper demonstrates how outlier returns impact the CAPM alphas and betas estimated via the OLS method. Outlier resistant estimates for the alphas and betas are obtained using Huber's Robust M (HRM) method. These alphas and betas are estimates of the regular component of the CAPM regression model, therefore, they can be used as benchmarks to examine the impact of outliers on the CAPM alphas and betas.

The paper is organized as follows. Section 2 presents the mixed return model in the presence of outliers and Huber's Robust M (HRM) method. Section 3 presents a description and descriptive statistics of the sample companies. Section 4 discusses the empirical findings when the OLS estimated parameters are compared to those obtained through the HRM method. The last section presents the summary and concluding remarks.

2. MIXED RETURN MODEL AND HUBER'S ROBUST M (HRM) ESTIMATORS

Mixed return processes are often used to model the stochastic behaviour of stock returns in the presence of outlier events. The general format of the mixed return process employed in this paper is written as:

$$R_{i,t} = \alpha_{k,i} + \beta_{k,i} R_{M,t} + e_{i,t} + d_{i,t} H_{i,t} \tag{1}$$

where $R_{i,t}$ is the return for stock i during period t, $\alpha_{k,i} + \beta_{k,i} R_{M,t} + e_{i,t}$ and $d_{i,t}$ $H_{i,t}$ are the regular and outlier components of company's i stock return, $R_{M,,t}$ is the historical market return at

[14] Martin and Simin (2003), Gray et al. (2005) and Genton and Ronchetti (2008).

time t, $\alpha_{k,i}$ is the intercept and $\beta_{k,i}$ is the beta coefficient of the company's regular component of return and $e_{i,t}$ is a white noise error term $d_{i,t}$ is a dichotomous (Bernouli) random variable that takes the value of one with probability q when an outlier is present and the value of zero with probability $(1-q)$ otherwise, and $t = 1, 2, \ldots, T$, N is the number of stocks and T is the number of historical returns.

For the estimation of the parameters of the regular return component, equation 1 is written as

$$R_{i,t} = \alpha_{k,i} + \beta_{k,i} R_{M,t} + u_{i,t} \tag{2}$$

where the error $u_{i,t} \equiv e_{i,t} + d_{i,t} H_{i,t}$ is decomposed between its regular and outlier components using the rule

$$e^{*}_{i,t} = \begin{cases} sign(u_{i,t}) c\sigma_{e,i} \text{ for} |u_{i,t}| > c\sigma_{e,i} \\ u_{i,t} \text{ for} |u_{i,t}| \leq c\sigma_{e,i} \end{cases} \tag{3a}$$

and

$$H^{*}_{i,t} = u_{i,t} - e^{*}_{i,t} \tag{3b}$$

where $\sigma_{e,i}$ is the standard deviation of $e_{i,t}$, c is a predetermined constant, and *sign* is the sign function assigned the value of one for positive values of $u_{i,t}$ and the value of minus one for negative values. According to these equations, values of $u_{i,t}$ falling outside the interval $[-c\sigma_{e,i}, c\sigma_{e,i}]$ are truncated to $-c\sigma_{e,i}$ or $c\sigma_{e,i}$ (depending on whether $u_{i,t}$ is negative or positive) and are assigned to $e^{*}_{i,t}$. The excesses or trimmed values of $u_{i,t}$ are assigned to $H^{*}_{i,t}$. Note that $e^{*}_{i,t}$ and $H^{*}_{i,t}$ are proxy variables for $e_{i,t}$ and $d_{i,t}H_{i,t}$, respectively.

The estimation of the regular return regression is accomplished using Huber's Robust M (HRM) estimator. Huber (1964, 1973) shows that when data follow a mixed probability distribution process, robust M estimators for the regression model can be obtained from the minimization of the following maximum-likelihood type function:

$$\min_{\alpha_{k,i}, \beta_{k,i}} S_i = \sum_{t=1}^{T} \rho(u_{i,t} \mid F_t) \tag{4a}$$

where

$$\rho(u_{i,t} \mid F_t) = \begin{cases} 0.5u^2_{i,t} \text{ for } |u_{i,t}| \leq c\sigma_{e,i} \\ |u_{i,t}| c\sigma_{e,i} - 0.5c^2\sigma^2_{e,i} \text{ for } |u_{i,t}| > c\sigma_{e,i} \end{cases} \tag{4b}$$

and

$$u_{i,t} = R_{i,t} - \left(\hat{\alpha}_{k,i} + \hat{\beta}_{k,i} F_t\right) \tag{4c}$$

and the other notation is as defined previously.[15] Note that the derivative of $\rho(u_{i,t}|F_t)$ with respect to $u_{i,t}$ is

$$\partial\rho\left(u_{i,t}\middle| F_t\right)/\partial u_{i,t} = e^{*}_{i,t} \tag{5}$$

where $e^{*}_{i,t}$ is as defined previously. The HRM estimators for the regression intercept and slope satisfy the following normal equations (first order conditions for minimization),

$$\frac{\partial S_i}{\partial \alpha_{k,i}} = \sum_{t=1}^{T} \hat{e}_{i,t} = 0 \tag{6a}$$

and

$$\frac{\partial S_i}{\partial \beta_{k,i}} = \sum_{t=1}^{T} F_t' \hat{e}_{i,t} = \underset{\sim}{0} \tag{6b}$$

These equations are solved iteratively using the algorithm

$$\hat{\theta}_i^{s+1} = \hat{\theta}_i^{s} + \left(\sum_{t=1}^{T} Z_t' Z_t\right)^{-1} \sum_{t=1}^{T} Z_t' \hat{e}_{i,t} \tag{8a}$$

where

$$\hat{e}_{i,t} = \begin{cases} \hat{u}_{i,t} = Y_t - Z_t\hat{\theta}_i \text{ for } |\hat{u}_{i,t}| < c\hat{\sigma}_{e,i} \\ sign\left(\hat{u}_{i,t}\right) c\hat{\sigma}_{e,i} \text{ for } |\hat{u}_{i,t}| \geq c\hat{\sigma}_{e,i} \end{cases} \tag{8b}$$

$\theta_i' = \left[\alpha_{k,i}, \beta_{k,i}'\right], Z_t = \left[1, F_t\right]$, $\hat{\sigma}_{e,i}$ is the HRM estimator for $\sigma^2_{e,i}$ and s is for the sth iteration. OLS estimates for θ can be used as starting values for the algorithm. The regression variance is estimated using

$$\hat{\sigma}^2_{e,i} = \left(\frac{g_i^2}{T-2}\right) \sum_{t=1}^{T} \hat{e}^2_{i,t} \tag{8c}$$

[15] A review of the estimation and statistical properties of Huber's method can be found in Judge et al. (1985), Ch. 20. pp. 828-834; see also Huber (1981). For a thorough analysis of robust estimation methods, see Hampel et al. (1986). An extensive review on outliers in statistics can be found in Beckman and Cook (1983).

where

$$g_i = \left[1 + \frac{2}{T}\left(\frac{1-m_i}{m_i}\right)\right]\frac{1}{m_i} \tag{8d}$$

m_i is the proportion of non-trimmed (non-winsorized) returns for company i. Standard errors for the estimator are computed from

$$\operatorname{var}\left(\hat{\theta}_i\right) = \hat{\sigma}_{e,i}^2\left(\sum_{t=1}^{T} Z_t' Z_t\right)^{-1} \tag{9}$$

Excess or abnormal returns for individual stocks are computed from the data using the equation

$$\hat{u}_{i,t} = R_{i,t} - \left(\hat{\alpha}_{k,i} + \hat{\beta}_{k,i} F_t\right) \tag{10}$$

and outlier excess returns using the equation

$$\hat{H}_{i,t} = \hat{u}_{i,t} - \hat{e}_{i,t} \tag{11}$$

Most $\hat{H}_{i,t}$ values are zero. Large positive or negative values are indicative of outlier returns. Unlike $\hat{e}_{i,t}$, the residual $\hat{u}_{i,t}$ captures the full impact of outlier returns.

3. Sample Description

The impact of outlier returns on the OLS-estimated CAPM alphas and betas is demonstrated using a selected group of four US publicly traded companies. These companies are (1) the AES Corporation, (2) Questcor Pharmaceuticals Inc, (3) the Gentyle Group Inc and (4) the Marathon Oil Corporation. The first three companies present cases in which the OLS estimates of the CAPM model are affected by outlier returns in different ways. The last company presents a case in which the OLS estimates of the CAPM model are not affected by outlier returns. The relevant data and information for the four companies were obtained from the CRSP, Lexis Nexis and Factiva databases. The data cover the months of January 2003 to December 2007.

The proxy for the market return is the Fama and French market factor. This is the value weighted return of all stocks listed on the NYSE, NASDAQ and AMEX stock exchanges obtained from the CRSP database. During the examination period, the market monthly return fluctuated between –4.9 percent (November 2007) and 8.3 percent (April 2003). Its average and median monthly returns for the period were 1.21 percent 1.48 percent, respectively.

The AES Corporation was established in Texas during 1981. The company is a global power company operating and providing energy in 29 countries. The company maintains an extensive portfolio of "thermal and renewable fuel sources such as coal, diesel, gas, hydro power, solar and wind.[16] In the early 1990's, when regulatory restrictions were lifted and the global markets opened up, the company started operations in the United Kingdom, Argentina, Pakistan, Hungary, China and Brazil. During the examination period, the company was listed on NYSE and was categorized as operating in the generation, transmission and/or distribution of electric energy (SIC code 4911[17]). During the examination period, the company's market capitalization fluctuated between 1.8 and 15.8 billion dollars. Its mean and median market capitalization of the company was 9.5 and 10.4 billion dollars. The company's return during the examination period fluctuated between –19.8 percent (June 2003) and 8.3 percent (April 2003).

Questcor Pharmaceuticals Inc. was incorporated in California during 1990. The company develops and commercializes pharmaceutical products mainly in the US (SIC code 2834). The company's two main products are the Achtar Gel and Doral. The Achtar Gel is used for the treatments of multiple sclerosis exacerbations and infantile spasms. Doral is used for the treatment of insomnia. Currently, the company is researching a tablet for the treatment of patients with difficulty in swallowing. The company is listed on AMEX. The company's stock is characterized by great volatility. During the examination period, its market value ranges between 20.44 million (August 2004) and 401.92 million (November 2007). The company's average and median market value was 40.4 and 61.8 million dollars. Its stock return fluctuated between the minimum of –41 percent (August 2004) and 326 percent (November 2007).

Genlyte Group Inc was founded in Louisville, Kentucky during 1985. The company engages in the design, manufacturing, and marketing and selling of lighting fixtures, controls and other related products (SIC code of 3640). It operates mainly in the US, Canada and Mexico. The company was acquired in January 2008 by Philips Holding US Inc. for 2.81 billion dollars. During the examination period, the company was listed on the NASDAQ stock exchange, and its market value ranged between 0.38 billion (February 2003) and 2.69 billion (December 2007). Its average and median value were 1.38 and 1.35 billion dollars, respectively. The company's stock return reached as low as –11.82 percent in July 2007 and as high as 44.78 percent in November 2007.

The fourth company, Marathon Oil Corporation, was established in Ohio during 1887. Today, the company is among the leaders in integrated energy worldwide (SIC code 1311). The company supplies global markets with liquid hydrocarbons and natural gas. During the examination period, the company was listed on the NYSE, and its market capitalization fluctuated between 6.48 billion dollars (January 2003) and 43.23 billion dollars (December 2007). Its average and median capitalization were 21.46 and 19.33 billion dollars, respectively. During the same period, the company's stock monthly return dipped to a low of –12.72 in October 2005 and reached a high of 26.08 percent in January 2006.

---

[16] www.aes.com

[17] www.osha.gov

4. HRM vs. OLS Return Estimators - Empirical Findings

Figures 1 to 4 show the CAPM regression lines for the OLS and HRM methods along with a scatter plot of the excess returns for each stock and the market. It is clear from the figures that the OLS regression lines for three of the four stocks are impacted by outliers in different but significant ways. Nevertheless, these outliers have little or no impact on the HRM regression lines which appear to provide a robust representation of the bulk of the data for all four stocks. The estimation of the HRM regression line was based on a value of c = 1.645.

In the case of the AES corporation (figure 1), the OLS-CAPM regression line is tilted up by a single outlier return of about 65% which occurred during a month of a well above average stock market excess return of about 8% (highest excess return of the estimation period). Other outliers do not appear to have as much impact on the OLS regression line. The aforementioned outlier occurred in April of 2003 as a result of an announcement that AES was making a tender offer to acquire some of its senior and subordinated notes through the private placement of new debt securities.

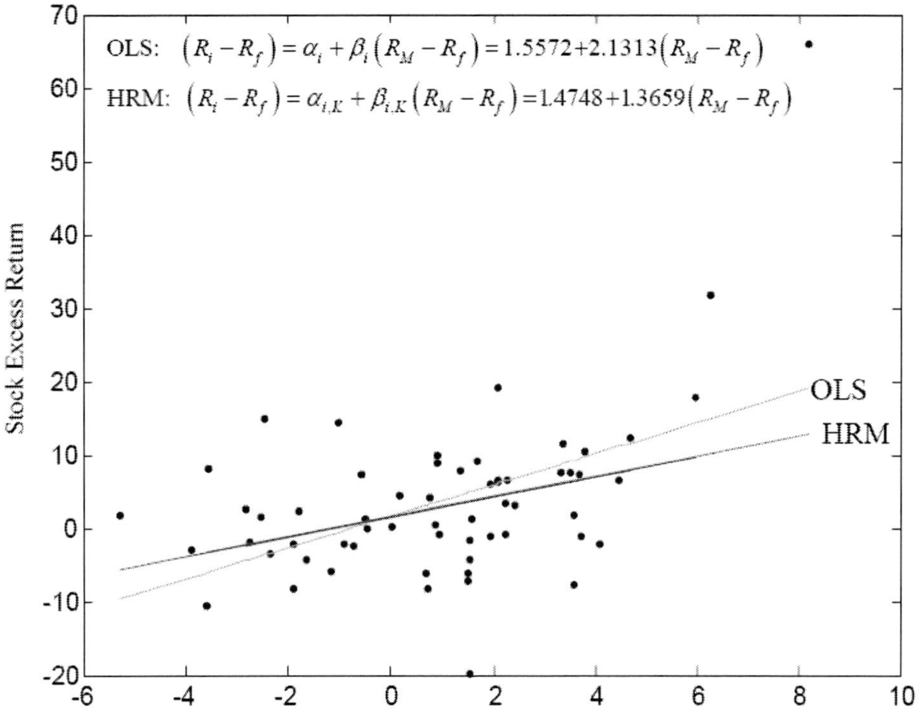

Figure 1. A E S Corporation.

In the case of Questcor (figure 2), a large positive outlier return of about 325 percent coupled with a below market excess return of about –5 percent "pulls up" the tail of the OLS regression line and reverses its slope from positive to negative. As a result, the intercept increases from 0.5432 to 11.31, and the slope decreases 0.77 to 3.33. Both changes are significant at the 5 percent level. This outlier return occurred in November of 2007 when the company announced better than expected financial results. It followed another outlier return of about 115 percent in the month of October of 2007 when Questcor increased the price of its drug Acthar, used for the treatment of infantile spasms, from \$1,600 to \$23,000 per vial. The October 2007 return, however, does not have as much leverage (impact) on the regression line because it occurred during normal market conditions (market return of 2.58 percent).

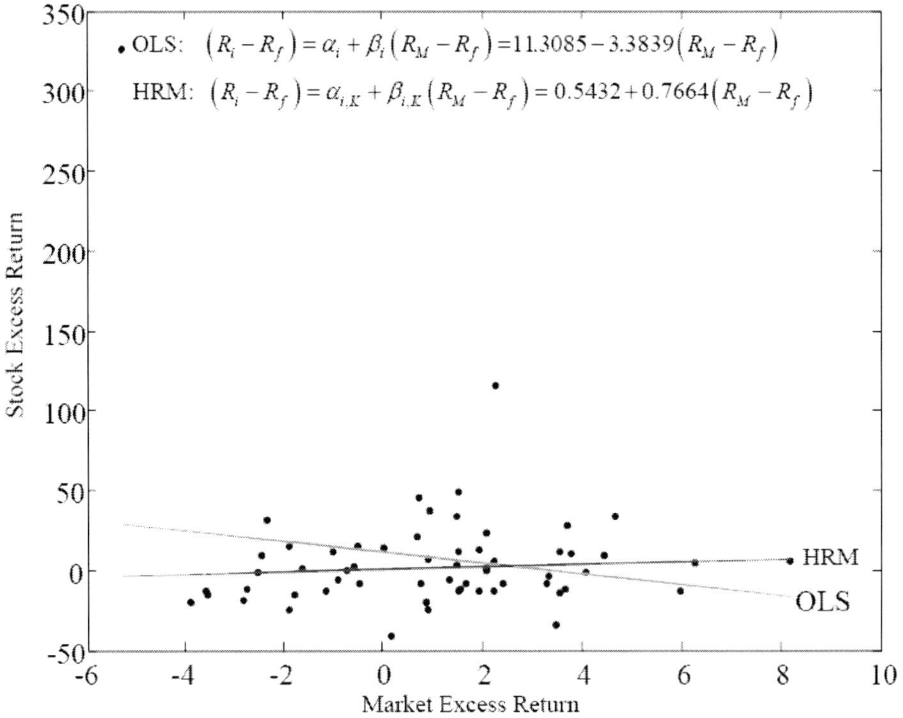

Figure 2. Questcor Pharmaceuticals, Inc.

In the case of Gentlyte (figure 3), an outlier return of about 45 percent that occurred during a month of below average stock market return (-4.93 percent) "pulls up" the tail of the OLS regression line and increases its intercept from 1.33 to 2.53 and decreases the slope from 1.32 to 0.69. Unlike Questcor, this outlier does not possess the strength to reverse the sign of the slope. The outlier occurred in November 2007 when Royal Philips Electronics announced a takeover premium of 52 percent over Genlyte's stock price. Note that there was no trimming for the minimum return of -11.81 percent that happened during a month when the market return was –2.52 percent.

Marathon Oil (figure 4) is the typical case of a company not impacted by outliers. The HRM and the OLS methods give similar estimated alphas and betas. The minimum weight given to any residual was 61.28 percent and corresponds to the monthly return of 26.08 percent (market return 4.01 percent) in January 2006. It is followed by the weight of 66.13 percent assigned to the residual of February, 2005 when the company's monthly company return was 22.95 percent (market return 2.27).

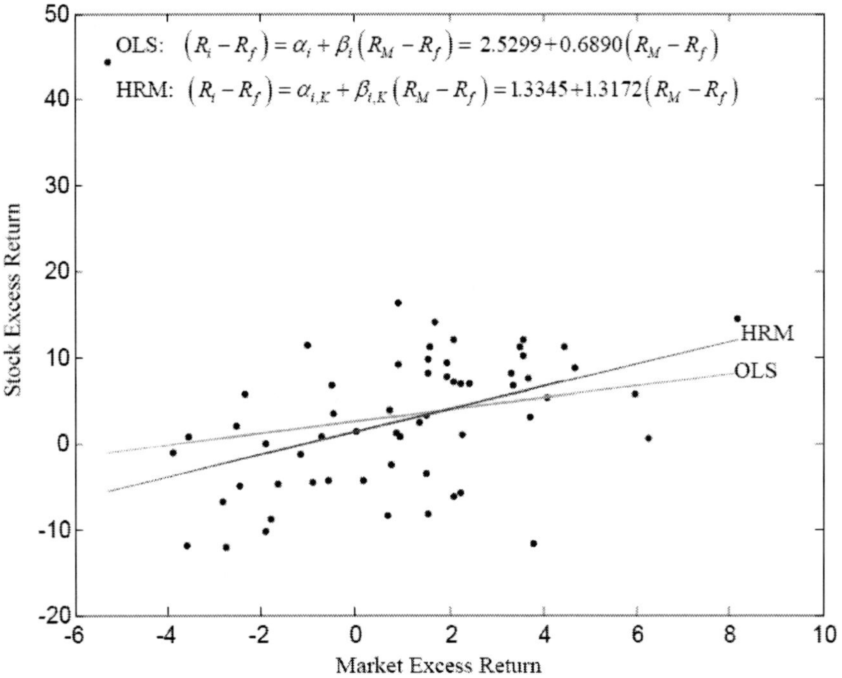

Figure 3. Genlyte Group.

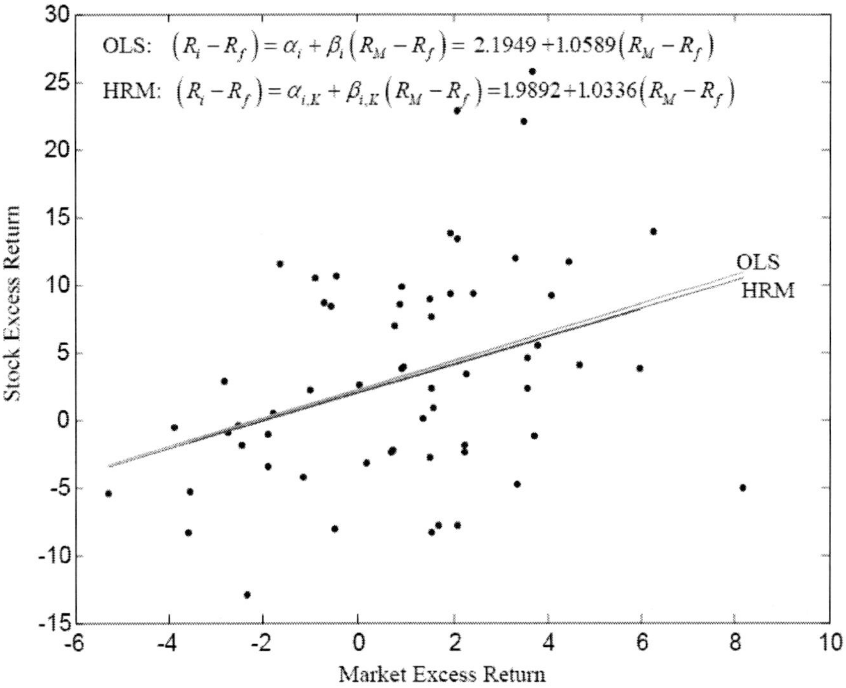

Figure 4. Marathon Oil Corporation.

Table 1 presents the regression estimated parameters for the companies according to both the OLS and the HRM methods along with test statistics. In all four cases, the OLS estimated alpha is greater than the HRM estimated alpha. This is a very important finding when measuring or testing abnormal returns since the CAPM alpha represents abnormal returns. In the case of betas the absolute value of the OLS estimated beta is greater than the absolute value of the HRM estimated beta. In the case of Questcor Pharmaceuticals where there is a beta sign reversal, the value of the OLS estimated beta is less than the HRM estimated beta.

Table 1. Estimated CAPM Model for a Selected Number of Stocks Based on the OLS and HRM Methods

	A E S Corp		Questcor Pharm. Inc		Genlyte Group Inc		Marathon Oil Corp	
	OLS	HRM	OLS	HRM	OLS	HRM	OLS	HRM
$\hat{\alpha}_i$	1.5572	1.4748 (1.41)	11.3085 (1.73)**	0.5432 (0.17)	2.5299 (2.04)*	1.3345 (1.41)	2.1949 (2.11)*	1.9892 (1.95)**
$\hat{\beta}_i$	2.1313 (4.36)*	1.3659 (3.71)*	-3.3839 (-1.47)	0.7664 (0.68)	0.6890 (1.58)	1.3172 (3.95)*	1.0589 (2.89)*	1.0336 (2.88)*
$\hat{\sigma}_i^2$	10.121	7.424	47.571	20.868	9.019	6.735	7.586	7.411
F	19.02	23.456	2.17	0.51	2.50	13.99	8.36	10.05
R^2	0.2469	0.2880	0.0361	0.0087	0.0414	0.1943	0.1259	0.1477

Notes: Data covers the period January 2003 to December 2007. Models are estimated using the OLS and the HRM methods along with 60 monthly returns. Inside parentheses t values are reported pertaining to the hypothesis testing that the estimated parameter is equal to zero. The symbols * and ** are used to denote statistical significance at the 5 and 10 percent levels of statistical significance, respectively.

SUMMARY AND CONCLUSIONS

This paper investigates the impact outlier returns have on the CAPM alphas and betas estimated via the OLS method. This is accomplished by comparing the OLS estimates to those obtained via the Huber's Robust M (HRM) estimation method. The HRM method is chosen as a benchmark because it is an outlier resistant estimation method. Moreover, it is consistent with the mixed stock return model used in the finance literature to model the stochastic behavior of stock returns in the presence of outliers.

A sample of four companies is employed for the investigation. These companies are representative examples of the effects that outliers exert on the CAPM estimated parameters. For three of the four sample companies, A E S Corp, Poniard Pharmaceuticals Inc and Genlyte Group Inc, the impact of outliers on the CAPM estimated parameters is large. In the case of Poniard Pharmaceuticals Inc., the presence of a single outlier during the 5 year examination period is strong enough not only to affect the magnitude of the estimated parameters but also to reverse the sign of the beta parameter. The fourth and largest company, Marathon Oil Corp., represents the case of large companies with no outliers or very small outliers in their historical returns. In such cases, announcements regarding the prospects of the company or its products have little impact; therefore, market reaction is not as strong as the reaction we observe for similar announcements about smaller companies. In the cases where there are no influential outliers during the examination period both the OLS and the HRM methods give similar estimated parameters.

In summary, the results show that when positive (negative) outlier returns for stocks occur during periods of high (low) market returns, the OLS beta will be higher than HRM betas. On the other hand, when positive (negative) outlier returns for stocks occur during periods of low (high) market returns, the OLS beta will be lower than HRM betas. The impact of outlicr rcturns on stock alphas tends to be positive. In all four cases we find that the OLS estimated alphas are higher than the HRM estimated alphas. Overall, we find that the impact of outliers on the CAPM estimated parameters depends not only on the size of the aforementioned outliers but also on the magnitude of the market excess returns during the month the outlier returns occur. The magnitude of excess returns acts as a lever hereby increasing or decreasing the effect of outliers on the estimated OLS parameters.

ACKNOWLEDGMENTS

We would like to thank the Editor of the Journal Kostas Zopounides and the participants at the 7th Annual Conference, Hellenic Finance and Accounting Association, Chania, Crete, December 12-13, 2009, for their comments and encouragement. This paper was based partially on the Keynote Speech of Panayiotis Theodossiou at the conference. The contribution of both authors is equal.

REFERENCES

Beckman, R. J. and R. D. Cook. 1983. "Outlier…s." *Technometrics.* 25(2):119-149.

Chan, L.K.C. and J. Lakonishok. 1992. "Robust Measurement of Beta Risk." *Journal of Financial and Quantitative Analysis.* 27: 265-282.

Genton, M. G., and E. Ronchetti. 2008. "Robust Prediction of Beta." Computational Methods in Financial Engineering, *Essays in Honour of Manfred Gilli.* Springer, 147-161.

Gray, S., J. Hall, J. Bowman, T. Brailsford, R. Faff, and B. Officer. May 2005. "The Performance of Alternative Techniques for Estimating Equity Betas of Australian Firms." Report Prepared for the Energy Networks Association, 1-41.

Hampel, F.R., E. M. Ronchetti, P. J. Rousseeuw, and W. A. Stahel. 1986. Robust Statistics: The Approach Based on Influence Functions. John Wiley & Sons, Inc.

Huber, P. J. 1981. *Robust Statistics.* John Wiley & Sons, Inc.

Huber, P.J. Mar. 1964. "Robust Estimation of a Location Parameter." *The Annals of Mathematical Statistics.* 35(5): 73-101.

Huber, P.J. Sep. 1973. "Robust Regression Asymptotics, Conjectures and Monte Carlo." *The Annals of Statistics.* 1(5): 799-821.

Judge, G.J., W. E. Griffiths, R. C. Hill, H. Lutkepohl, and T-C. Lee. 1985. *The Theory and Practice of Econometrics,* 2nd Ed. John Wiley & Sons, Inc.

Martin, R. D. and T. Simin. 2003. "Outlier Resistant Estimates of Beta." *Financial Analysts Journal.* 59, 56–69.

McDonald, J. B., R.A. Michelfelder, and P. Theodossiou. 2008. "Evaluation of Robust Regression Estimation Methods and Intercept Bias: A Capital Asset Pricing Model Application," Working Paper, Rutgers University.

Theodossiou P. and A. Theodossiou, 2009. "Impact of Outliers on Stock Return Models: Implications for Event Studies." Working Paper, Rutgers University.

In: Computational Techniques in Economics and Finance
Editor: Constantine Zopounidis
ISBN: 978-1-61324-558-3

Chapter 7

ON MODELING AN INTEGRATED MULTIPLE CRITERIA METHODOLOGY FOR SUPPORTING COMMON STOCK PORTFOLIO CONSTRUCTION DECISIONS

Panagiotis Xidonas**, *Dimitrios Askounis and John Psarras
National Technical University of Athens,
School of Electrical and Computer Engineering,
Management & Decision Support Systems Laboratory, Athens, Greece

ABSTRACT

We propose an integrated multiple-criteria methodological framework to support decisions that concern the selection of common stock portfolios. At the first stage of the methodology, two multiple-criteria methods are employed, within the context of the outranking relations theory, towards the initial appraisal of the stocks that are examined. We then utilize a non-linear optimization model, to generate portfolios that consist of the stocks that are classified as those with the optimal characteristics, during of the first stage. Finally, the portfolios designed at the previous stage are evaluated by using a wide set of well-known sophisticated evaluation criteria.

The preferences and experiences of professionals and experts in the field of portfolio management were taken into consideration, through all the stages of the process. The validity of the above methodology is tested through a large scale illustrative application on the stocks that constitute the FTSE-140 index of the Athens Stock Exchange. The advantages of the proposed model against contextual approaches are finally stressed.

* Corresponding author information: National Technical University of Athens, School of Electrical and Computer Engineering, Management & Decision Support Systems Laboratory, 9, Iroon Polytechniou Str., 15773, Athens, Greece ;Tel: +30 210 7723 514, +30 210 7723 553, Fax: +30 210 7723 550; E-mail: pxid@epu.ntua.gr

Keywords: multiple criteria decision making; outranking relations theory; portfolio construction; stock evaluation; corporate evaluation; portfolio optimization; portfolio evaluation.

1. INTRODUCTION

The portfolio management process is an integrated set of steps undertaken in a consistent manner to create and maintain an appropriate portfolio (combination of assets) to meet clients' stated goals (Maginn, 2007). The three fundamental elements in managing any business process are: planning, execution and feedback. The same steps form the basis for the portfolio management process. In the planning step, investment objectives and policies are formulated, capital market expectations are formed and strategic asset allocations are established. In the execution step, the manager constructs the portfolio and integrates investment strategies with capital market expectations to select the specific assets for the portfolio. Finally, in the feedback step, the manager monitors and evaluates the portfolio compared with the plan. Any changes suggested by the feedback must be examined carefully to ensure that they represent long-run considerations.

The emphasis in this article is on the portfolio construction phase and we focus on common stock portfolios design. The portfolio construction problem has several dimensions and the framework of multiple criteria decision making provides the solid methodological basis to resolve the inherent multicriteria nature of this problem. The main goal of the current study is to develop an integrated multiple-criteria methodology, the basic aims of which will be the:

- Standardization of the procedures of this ill-structured decision making problem
- Standardization of the decision maker's preference system and incorporation in all the methodology components
- Incorporation of combination of decision support techniques and multiple decision criteria from different dimensions
- Multi-usability offering evaluation of either the security or the corporate performance
- Flexibility without involving complex / time consuming processes
- Effectiveness for the decision maker providing reliable results

The paper proceeds as follows. In Section 2 we set the problem and within this frame we analyze the portfolio management process, we review the most popular existing portfolio selection/optimization models and we stress the necessity for modelling the problems of this kind by using multicriteria analysis. In Section 3 we review some of the coherent multicriteria studies relevant to the portfolio selection problem and we then focus on the gap that has been spotted. In Sections 4 and 5 we present the proposed methodology and the corresponding application from the Athens Stock Exchange (ASE). Finally, the concluding remarks are given in Section 6.

2. Problem Setting

2.1. The portfolio management process

According Maginn (2007), portfolio management is an ongoing process in which: (1) investment objectives and constraints are identified and specified, (2) investment strategies are developed, (3) portfolio composition is decided in detail, (4) portfolio decisions are initiated by portfolio managers and implemented by traders, (5) portfolio performance is measured and evaluated, (6) investor and market conditions are monitored, and (7) any necessary rebalancing is implemented. As stated previously, the portfolio management process is an integrated set of three steps: planning, execution and feedback (Figure 1).

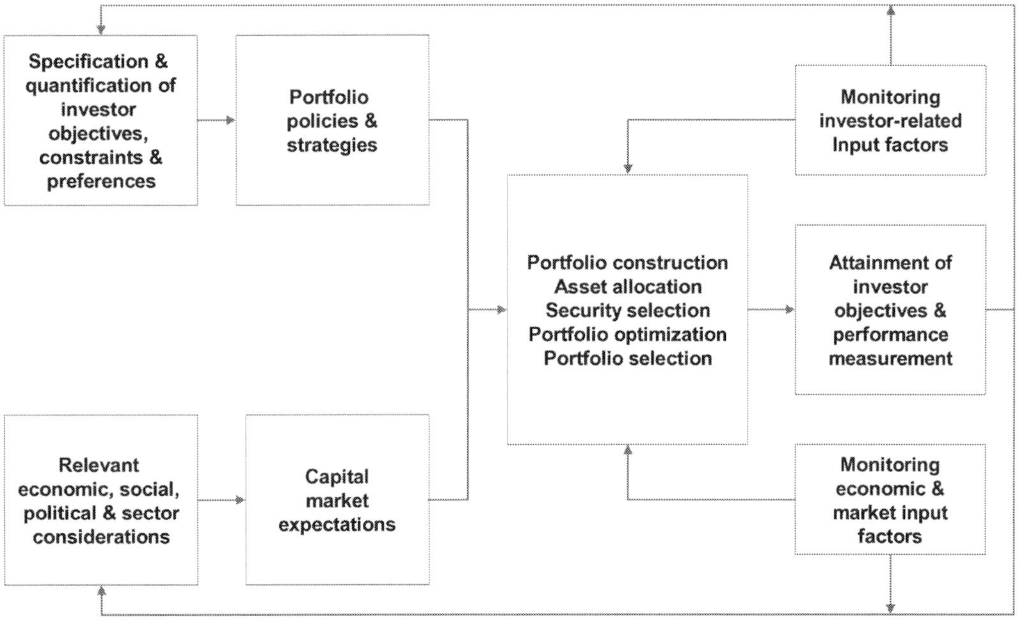

Figure 1. The portfolio management process (Maginn, 2007).

In the planning step, portfolio managers formulate investment objectives and policies, assess capital market expectations and establish strategic asset allocations. The investment policy statement (IPS) serves as the foundation for the process. The investment policy statement sets out a client's return objectives and risk tolerance over that client's relevant time horizon, along with applicable constraints such as liquidity needs, tax considerations, regulatory requirements, and unique circumstances. The IPS must clearly communicate the client's objectives and constraints. The IPS thereby becomes a plan that can be executed by any adviser or portfolio manager the client might subsequently hire. A properly developed IPS disciplines the portfolio management process and helps ensure against ad hoc revisions in strategy. When combined with capital market expectations, the IPS forms the basis for a strategic asset allocation. Capital market expectations concern the risk and return characteristics of capital market instruments such as stocks and bonds. The strategic asset allocation establishes acceptable exposures to IPS-permissible asset classes to achieve the client's long-run objectives and constraints.

In the execution step, portfolio managers initiate portfolio decisions based on analysts' inputs, and trading desks then implement these decisions (portfolio implementation decision). Subsequently, the portfolio is revised as investor circumstances or capital market expectations change; thus, the execution step interacts constantly with the feedback step. In making the portfolio selection/composition decision, portfolio managers may use the techniques of portfolio optimization. Portfolio optimization—quantitative tools for combining assets efficiently to achieve a set of return and risk objectives—plays a key role in the integration of strategies with expectations. The portfolio implementation decision is as important as the portfolio selection/composition decision. Poorly managed executions result in transaction costs that reduce performance. Transaction costs include all costs of trading, including explicit transaction costs, implicit transaction costs, and missed trade opportunity costs.

Finally, in the feedback step, managers monitor and evaluate the portfolio. Any changes suggested by the feedback must be examined carefully to ensure that they represent long-run considerations. In any business endeavor, feedback and control are essential elements in reaching a goal. In portfolio management, this step has two components: monitoring and rebalancing, and performance evaluation. Monitoring and rebalancing involve the use of feedback to manage ongoing exposures to available investment opportunities so that the client's current objectives and constraints continue to be satisfied. Two types of factors are monitored: investor-related factors such as the investor's circumstances, and economic and market input factors. Investment performance must periodically be evaluated by the investor to assess progress toward the achievement of investment objectives as well as to assess portfolio management skill. The assessment of portfolio management skill has three components. Performance measurement involves the calculation the portfolio's rate of return. Performance attribution examines why the portfolio performed as it did and involves determining the sources of a portfolio's performance. Performance appraisal is the evaluation of whether the manager is doing a good job based on how the portfolio did relative to a benchmark (a comparison portfolio).

Moreover, in order to elaborate the relationship between the decision context of the investor and the economic environment of the securities, Spronk and Hallerbach (1997) decompose the investment decision process in the following stages: (1) security analysis to determine the relevant characteristics (or attributes) of the investment opportunities, (2) portfolio analysis to delineate the set of non-dominated or efficient portfolios, (3) portfolio selection to choose the optimal portfolio from the efficient set, and (4) preference analysis.

In this article we lay emphasis on the portfolio construction phase and below we state some of the most popular portfolio selection models.

2.2. Portfolio Selection Models

Portfolio selection models are at the heart of the portfolio construction phase. Since the pioneering work of Markowitz (1952, 1959) in the theory of portfolio analysis, based on the mean-variance formulation, several portfolio selection models have been proposed. According to this formulation, an investor regards expected return as desirable and variation of return (variance) as undesirable. In the basis of the Markowitz mean-variance formulation, many researchers developed miscellaneous new methodologies. Elton et al. (2007) provide a complete overview as far as these methodologies is concerned. Apart from the mean-variance model, they cite the single index models, the multi-index models, the average correlation models, the mixed models, the utility models in which the preference function of the investor play a key role in the construction of an optimum risky portfolio, and the models which employ different criteria such as the geometric mean return, safety first, stochastic dominance and skewness. Pardalos et al. (1994), also, provide a review and some computational results of the use of optimization models for portfolio selection.

2.3. The Need for Modeling within the MCDM Frame

In recent years, the development of new techniques in operations research and management science, as well as the progress in computer and information technologies gave rise to new approaches for modeling the portfolio selection problem. Several authors have developed a new approach, using Multiple Criteria Decision Making (MCDM) for portfolio management. The multidimensional nature of the problem has been emphasized by researchers in finance, as well as by MCDM researchers.

An elaborate and completed justification for modeling portfolio management problems within the MCDM frame is provided in the milestone study of Hurson and Zopounidis (1995). According to them an analysis of the risk nature in portfolio management shows that the latter comes from various origins and then its nature is multidimensional. Also, individual goals and investor's preferences cannot be incorporated in these models. MCDM provides the methodological basis to resolve the inherent multicriteria nature of portfolio selection problem. Additionally, it builds realistic models by taking into account, apart of the two basic criteria of return and risk (mean-variance model), a number of important other criteria. Furthermore, MCDM, have the advantage of taking into account the preferences of any particular investor. To manage efficiently portfolio selection, it is necessary to take into account all the factors that influence the financial markets. Then, portfolio management is a multicriteria problem. Effectively, multifactor models point out the existence of several influence factors for the determination of the stock prices. Furthermore, fundamental analysis models, commonly used in practice, underline that stock prices are also dependant on the firm health and its capacity to pay dividends. The latter problem itself is a multicriteria problem because, in order to solve it, we must appreciate the profitability of the firm, its debt level (in the short and long terms) and quality of management. Finally, in practice, an investor has a personal attitude and particular objectives.

Moreover, it can be said that the classical approach imposes a norm to the investor's behavior that can be restrictive. Also, it cannot take into account the personal attitude and preferences of a real investor confronted with a given risk in a particular situation. However, experience has proved that the classical approach is useful, for instance concerning the diversification principle and the use of the beta as measure of risk. Thus, the use of the classical approach seems to be necessary but not sufficient, to manage portfolio selection efficiently. Some additional criteria must be added to the classical risk-return criteria. In practice, these additional criteria can be found in fundamental analysis or constructed following the personal goals of the investor. The combination of the above principles is difficult because of the complexity of multicriteria problems on the one hand and the use of criteria from different origins and of conflicting nature on the other hand. Furthermore MCDM will facilitate and favor the analysis of compromise between the criteria. It equally permits to manage the heterogeneity of criteria scale and the fuzzy and imprecise nature of the evaluation that it will contribute to clarify. Linking the multicriteria evaluation of an asset portfolio and the research of a satisfactory solution to the investor's preferences, the MCDM methods allow to take into account the investors' specific objectives. Furthermore, these methods do not impose any normative scheme to the comportment of the investors. The use of MCDM methods allows synthesizing in a single procedure the theoretical and practical aspects of portfolio management, and then it allows a non normative use of theory.

3. Review of Existing Studies

3.1. Coherent Methodologies

The portfolio construction problem can be realized as a two stage process (Hurson and Zopounidis, 1995): (1) evaluation of the available securities to select the ones that best meet the investor's preferences, (2) specification of the amount of capital to be invested in each of the securities selected in the first stage. The implementation of these two stages in the traditional portfolio theory is based on the mean-variance approach. Within this multidimensional context, the MCDM paradigm provides a plethora of appropriate methodologies to support the evaluation of the available securities as well as portfolio synthesis/optimization. The former (securities' evaluation) has been studied by MCDM researchers using discrete evaluation methods (outranking relations, multi-attribute utility theory, preference dissagregation analysis, rough sets). Studies conducted on this topic have focused on the modeling and representation of the investor's policy, goals and objectives in a mathematical model. The model aggregates all the pertinent factors describing the performance of the securities and provides their overall evaluation. The securities with the higher overall evaluation are selected for portfolio synthesis purposes in a latter stage of the analysis. This stage is realized within the MCDM framework as a multiple-objective mathematical programming/goal programming problem. The decision maker specifies the portfolio synthesis criteria, his objectives/goals and an iterative and interactive process is invoked to identify a portfolio that best meets his investment policy.

Zopounidis et al. (1998) classifies the studies concerning the use of multicriteria analysis in portfolio selection according to their special methodological background (Pardalos et al., 1995; Siskos and Zopounidis, 1993) as follows: (1) multiobjective mathematical programming, (2) multiattribute utility theory, (3) outranking relations, and (4) preference disaggregation approach. Doumpos (2000) categorizes the research studies in portfolio management in four basic classes: (1) Models focusing on the analysis and perception of the securities' behavior, (2) Forecasting models focusing on the rapid spotting of the security trends, (3) Security evaluation methodologies focusing on modeling of the investor's preferences, and (4) Portfolio synthesis and optimization methodologies. Moreover, in the papers of Zopounidis and Doumpos (2002) and Steuer and Na (2003) someone can find completed reviews of multiple criteria portfolio selection models.

In the study of Hurson and Zopounidis (1995) an excellent and detailed review is provided as well. More precisely, Saaty et al. (1980) proposed to construct a portfolio using the analytic hierarchy process methodology. Lee and Chesser (1980) present a goal programming model to construct a portfolio. Rios-Garcia and Rios-Insua (1983) construct a portfolio using multi-attribute utility theory and multiobjective linear programming. Evrard and Zisswiller (1983) use multi-attribute utility theory to perform a valuation of some stocks. Nakayama et al. (1983) propose a graphics interactive methodology to construct a portfolio using multiple criteria. Martel et al. (1988) perform a portfolio selection using the outranking methods ELECTRE I and ELECTRE II. Colson and De Bruyn (1989) propose a system that performs a stock valuation and allows the construction of a portfolio. Szala (1990) performs stock evaluation in collaboration with a French investment company. Khoury et al. (1993) use the outranking methods ELECTRE IS and ELECTRE III to select international index portfolios. The purpose of Colson and Zeleny (1979) is to construct an efficient frontier in concordance with the principles of stochastic dominance. Hurson and Zopounidis (1993) propose to manage the portfolio selection by using the MINORA system that will be presented in the following section. Zopounidis et al. (1998) propose the use of the ADELAIS system to construct a portfolio using some diversification constraints, some constraints representing the investor's personal preferences and multiple stock-market criteria. Tamiz et al. (1996) propose to use goal programming for portfolio evaluation and selection. Dominiak (1997) presents a procedure for security selection that uses a multicriteria discrete analysis method based on the idea of reference solution. Hurson and Ricci (1998) propose to combine Arbitrage Pricing Theory (APT) and MCDM to model the portfolio management process.

Steuer et al. (2007) employ six categories in order to place multiple criteria oriented portfolio analysis research into perspective: (1) overall framework, (2) portfolio ranking, (3) skewness inclusion, (4) use of alternative measures of risk, (5) decision support systems, and (6) the modeling of individual investor preferences. In the first category, he classifies articles that are overview pieces such as Hallerbach and Spronk (2002a, 2002b) and Bana e Costa and Soares (2001), in which the benefits of embracing multiple criteria concepts in financial decision making are outlined. Employing tools from multiple criteria decision analysis for portfolio ranking, there are papers represented by Yu (1997), Jog et al. (1999) and Bouri et al. (2002). In the category of skewness inclusion there are papers by Stone (1973), Konno et al. (1993), Konno and Suzuki (1995) and Chunhachinda et al. (1997). With regard to alternative measures of risk, there are the efforts by Zeleny (1977), Konno and Yamazaki (1991), Feinstein and Thapa (1993) and Doumpos et al. (1999). In the category of decision support systems employing mathematical programming techniques, there are the approaches of Ballestero and Romero (1996), Ogryczak (2000), Arenas Parra et al. (2001), Ballestero and Pla-Santamarıa (2003), Ehrgott et al. (2004) and Zopounidis and Doumpos (2000). In the sixth category, recognizing that some criteria may come from financial-economic theory and others may come from the individual investor, we have Spronk and Hallerbach (1997), Ballestero (1998), Chang et al. (2000) and Bana e Costa and Soares (2004).

3.2. The Scientific Gap

Even if the scientific activity in the field is elaborate and extended enough, there is a shortage of completed methodologies in which the below issues are integrated:

- Formulation of all the procedures of this ill-structured decision making problem
- Formulation of the decision maker's preference system and incorporation in all the methodology components

- Evaluation of both the security and the corporate performance as well, in a unified manner
- Flexibility without involving complex and time consuming processes

4. Proposed Methodology

The methodology that is proposed for constructing common stock portfolios consists of four (4) discrete components (Xidonas et al., 2007). The first two components reflect to the security selection phase (Figure 2), the third component has to do with the portfolio optimization phase, while the last component fits into the portfolio selection phase.

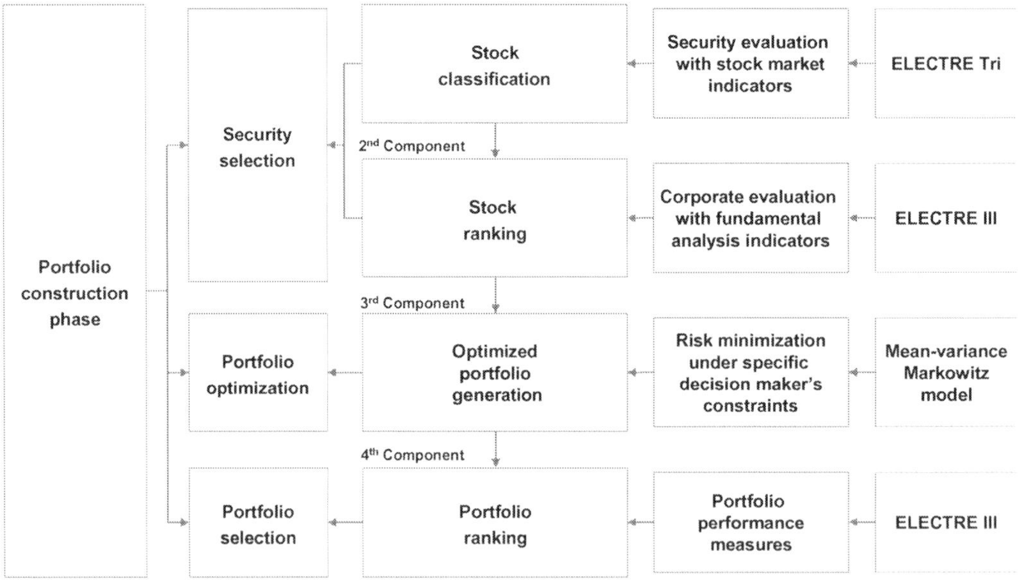

Figure 2. The proposed methodology – Matching with process logic.

The process flow diagram of the proposed methodology is presented in Figure 3.

In the first component (stock classification) the initial set of stocks is evaluated with stock market indicators and the multiple criteria method that is employed is the ELECTRE Tri (Yu, 1992) method, which belongs to the outranking relations theory frame. The stock market indicators that we use are (the sign in the parenthesis denotes the type of criterion scale: (+) for increasing scale and (-) for declining scale):

- *Stock market criteria*
  - Return dimension
    - Capital return (+)
    - Dividend yield (+)
  - Risk dimension
    - Standard deviation of capital return (-)
    - Beta coefficient (-)
  - Market acceptance dimension

- Marketability (+)
- P/E (current year) / 3-yrs Average P/E (or Relative P/E) (+)

Extended theoretical presentation of these criteria can be found in Alexander and Sharpe (1989) and Jones (1985). Besides, extended details, as far as the mathematical formulation of the above criteria is concerned, are provided in the presentation of the third component (optimization).

In the second component (stock ranking) the improved set of stocks, i.e. the stocks that are classified in the satisfactory class (which is determined according to the decision maker's preferences) during the first phase, are evaluated with fundamental analysis indicators and the multiple criteria method that is employed is the ELECTRE III method, which belongs to the outranking relations theory frame, as well [see Roy (1996) for the method's exact technical formulation]. The fundamental analysis that we use are (the sign in the parenthesis denotes the type of criterion scale: (+) for increasing scale and (-) for declining scale):

- Fundamental analysis criteria
  - Profitability dimension
    - Return on assets (+)
    - Return on equity (+)
  - Management performance dimension
    - Assets turnover (+)
    - Inventories turnover (+)
  - Capital structure dimension
    - Assets to liabilities (+)
    - Liabilities to equity (-)

Extended theoretical presentation of these criteria can be found in Niarchos (2005). It has to be noted that despite the fact that the Assets to liabilities and the Liabilities to equity criteria provide similar information, the experts' preference was for simultaneous use of these ratios in the criteria set.

In this way, except for the evaluation of the security, we apply an evaluation in the corporate level, in order to minimize the possibility spectrum to invest in an overvalued security, which represents poor and unhealthy business / corporate performance.

The criteria that are used above have to do only with commercial / industry companies, since our application in Section 5 is applied to that sector (there are four accounting plans in Greece: (1) Commerce/industry companies, (2) Banks, (3) Insurance companies, and (4) Investment companies). However, this 2nd component of the proposed methodology can easily be extended to the other three accounting plans. By using different sets of indicators for each company's accounting plan we manage to make more realistic comparisons.

Moreover, in order to model the lowest tolerance profile (LTP, is a terminology proposed by the authors) i.e. the profile under which the stocks are considered as unacceptable, a dummy stock participates in the ranking process. Samaras et al. (2007) utilize a similar formulation, named the 'lowest stock profile'. The scores of this stock in the above fundamental analysis criteria are determined by the decision maker / expert and are the minimum acceptable that he tolerates.

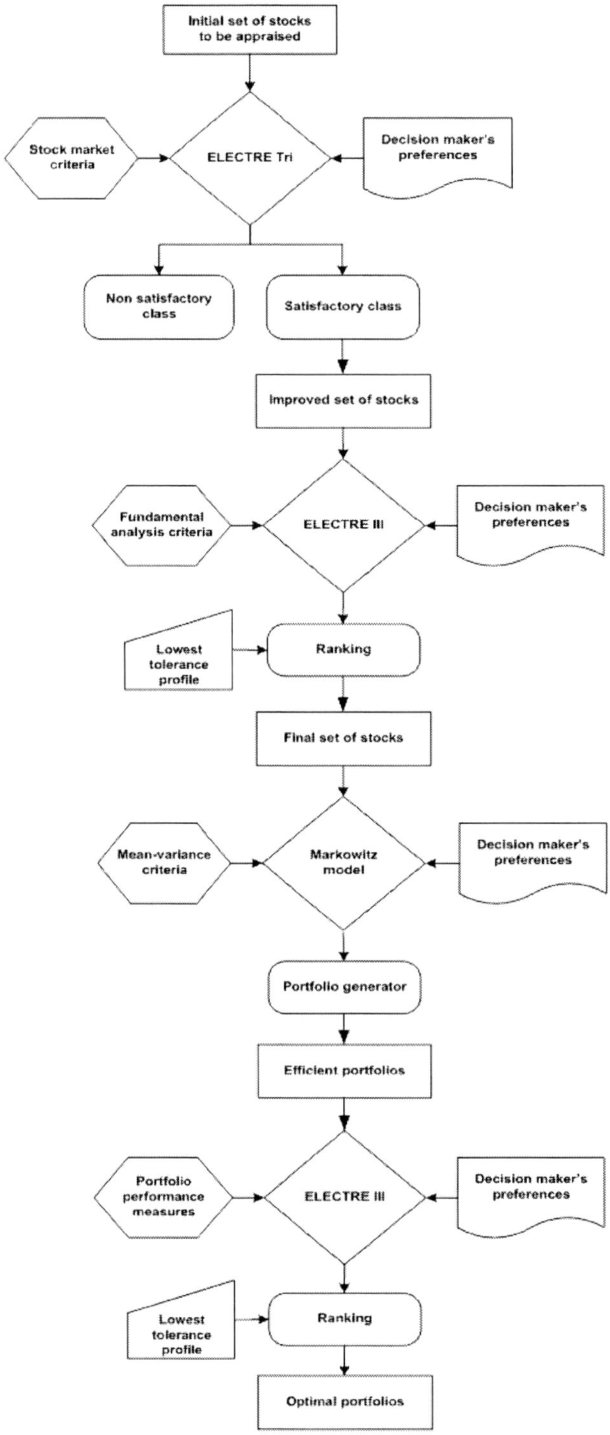

Figure 3. Process flow diagram of the proposed methodology.

In the third component (optimized portfolio generation), we utilize Markowitz mean-variance formulation in order to construct portfolios on the efficient frontier, using the final set of stocks, as resulted from the previous stage. The details of the non-linear optimization process are:

- *Modeling optimization process*
  - Objective
    - Portfolio standard deviation (see below for the detailed mathematical formulation).
  - Constraints
    - Basic constraints
      - Return: $R_t = (P_t - P_{t-1} + D_t) / P_{t-1}$, where R_t is the return on a share in period *t*t, P_t is the share price in period *t*, P_{t-1} is the share price in period *t-1* and D_t is the dividend that the share gives to the investor in period *t*.
      - Portfolio beta: $COV(R_i, R_m) / VAR(R_m)$, where R_i is the return of the share *i* and R_m is the return of the market portfolio (see Hurson and Zopounidis, 1995, 1997; Zopounidis et al. 1998).
      - Capital availability: The completeness constraint, which means that all the available capital is invested.
    - Additional constraints
      - Dividend yield: Dividend yield of a security = Dividend in period *t* / Share price closed in period *t*.
      - Marketability: Number of transactions of shares of a company during period *t* / Total number of shares of a company during period *t* (see Hurson and Zopounidis, 1995, 1997; Zopounidis et al. 1998).
      - Upper limit investment barrier for each security.

The generic mathematical formulation of the optimization model that developed follows:

Minimization of standard deviation:

$$\text{Min } \sigma_p^2 = \sum_{i=1}^{m} w_i^2 \sigma_i^2 + \sum_{i=1}^{m} \sum_{\substack{j=1 \\ j \neq i}}^{m} w_i w_j \sigma_{ij} = \sum_{i=1}^{m} \sum_{j=1}^{m} w_i w_j \sigma_{ij}$$

Subject to:

$$\sum_{i=1}^{m} w_i = 1$$

$$\sum_{i=1}^{m} w_i E(r_i) \geq R$$

$$\sum_{i=1}^{m} m_i w_i \geq M$$

$$\sum_{i=1}^{m} d_i w_i \geq D$$

$$\sum_{\forall i:\beta_i \leq 1} w_i = X$$

$$\sum_{\forall i:\beta_i > 1} w_i = Y$$

$$w_i < W, \ \forall \mathrm{i}$$

where:

w_i : the amount invested in security i
σ_i : the standard deviation of returns for security i
σ_p : the portfolios' standard deviation
$E(r_i)$: the expected return of security i
m_i : the marketability of security i
d_i : the dividend yield of security i
β_i : the beta coefficient of security i
R : the portfolios' demanded expected return
M : the portfolios' demanded marketability
D : the portfolios' demanded dividend yield
X : the amount of capital invested in defensive securities
Y : the amount of capital invested in offensive securities
W : the maximum amount of capital invested in each security

The specific decision makers' preferences under the above formulation are presented in paragraph 5 (see Figure 5).

In the fourth component (portfolio ranking) the portfolios that were constructed in the previous stage, are evaluated with portfolio performance indicators and the multiple criteria method that is employed is, again, the ELECTRE III (Roy, 1996) method. The portfolio performance indicators that we use are (the sign in the parenthesis denotes the type of criterion scale: (+) for increasing scale and (-) for declining scale):

- *Portfolio performance criteria*
    - Conventional measures
        - Portfolio return (+)
        - Portfolio volatility (-)
        - Portfolio beta (-)
    - Risk adjusted measures
        - Sharpe ratio (+)
        - Treynor ratio (+)
        - Relative Value at Risk (-)

It should be noted that the simultaneous consideration of highly correlated criteria like the Sharpe or the Treynor ratio, entails the risk of double counting, but in this case too the experts' preference was for simultaneous use of these ratios in the criteria set. As in the case of stock ranking, in order to model the lowest tolerance profile (LTP) (under which we consider the portfolios ranked as unacceptable), a dummy portfolio participates in the ranking process. The scores of this portfolio in the above portfolio performance criteria are determined by the decision maker and are the minimum acceptable that he tolerates.

The most crucial issue of the proposed methodology is the standardization and formulation of the decision maker's preferences, as well as the incorporation of them in all the methodology components. As far as the ways that the decision maker's preferences are incorporated in the decision procedure, this is achieved through his participation in the determination of:

- 1st Component / Stock classification
  - Criteria weights (risk averse / risk seeking / moderate profile)
  - Technical parameters (indifference / preference / veto thresholds & class profile)
- 2nd Component / Stock ranking
  - Criteria weights (profitability / management performance / capital structure focus)
  - Technical parameters (indifference / preference / veto thresholds)
  - Lowest tolerance profile (LTP) (dummy benchmark stock)
- 3rd Component / Portfolio optimization
  - Beta adjustment (risk averse / risk seeking profile)
  - Optimization constraints
- 4th Component / Portfolio ranking
  - Criteria weights (risk averse / risk seeking / moderate profile)
  - Technical parameters (indifference / preference / veto thresholds)
  - Lowest tolerance profile (LTP) (dummy benchmark portfolio)

The advantages of the techniques the model embodies are summarized below:

- ELECTRE family methods
  - accepts intransitivity / incomparability
  - enjoys great scientific study frequency & popularity
  - uses techniques that are easily understandable by the decision maker
- ELECTRE Tri
  - is a perfect mean for an initial dilution of a large number of alternatives since this method does not involve pair comparison
  - provides the advantage of two assignment procedures
- ELECTRE III provides sufficient satisfactory trade off analysis
- Markowitz mean-variance model
  - does not require huge amount information from the decision maker
  - is the market standard

5. APPLICATION

The above presented proposed methodology has been applied in the Athens Stock Exchange (ASE). The characteristics of the field of the application follow:

- 84 stocks of the commercial / industry sector of the FTSE-140 of the ASE
- 23 stocks of the index were excluded because of different accounting plans
    - 12 stocks from the banking sector
    - 5 stocks from the insurance sector
    - 6 stocks from financial sector
- 33 stocks from the commercial / industry sector stocks were also excluded because of lack of different types of data
- Data and data sources
    - Closing share prices (daily closes for 5 yrs ago)
    - Stock market variables (P/E, beta coefficients, marketability, dividend yields etc.) for each security (2006)
    - Balance sheet and income statement items (2006)

In Figures 4 and 5, the specified preferences of the decision maker / expert are presented. As we can see, as far as the 1st Component is concerned, three different investment profiles have been standardized (risk averse / risk seeking / moderate profile), while the same approach is followed for the 4th Component. As far as the 2nd Component is concerned, the focus is on three different dimensions (profitability / management performance / capital structure). Finally, two discrete profiles (risk averse / risk seeking profile) are modeled for the 3rd Component. The formulation of all the above profiles has been determined through different weighting in the key criteria, each time. On this basis, the key criteria in the 1st Component are capital return and volatility, the key criteria in the 2nd Component are return on assets (ROA) and return on equity (ROE), the key criterion in the 3rd Component is the beta coefficient and finally the key criteria in the 4th Component are the portfolio capital return and the portfolio volatility.

Stock classification		Capital return	Dividend yield	Volatility	Beta	Marketability	Relative P/E
	Risk averse	20%	10%	40%	10%	10%	10%
Profile weights	Moderate	30%	10%	30%	10%	10%	10%
	Risk seeking	40%	10%	20%	10%	10%	10%
Indifference thresholds		5%	0.5%	5%	0.1	5%	0.1
Preference thresholds		20%	2%	10%	0.4	20%	0.3
Veto thresholds		40%		30%			
Satisfactory class profile		55%	2%	35%	1	60%	1

Stock ranking		ROA	ROE	Assets turnover	Inventories turnover	Assets to liabilities	Liabilities to equity
	Profitability	30%	30%	10%	10%	10%	10%
Profile weights	Management	20%	20%	20%	20%	10%	10%
	Structure	20%	20%	10%	10%	20%	20%
Indifference thresholds		1%	3%	0.1	4	0.2	0.2
Preference thresholds		3%	6%	0.3	8	0.4	0.7
Satisfactory class profile		6%	17%	1	6	2	2.5

Figure 4. Decision maker's preference modeling.

Portfolio optimization		Beta > 1	Beta < 1	Capital availability	Marketability	Dividend yield	Investment limit
Amount to invest	Risk averse	40%	60%				
	Risk seeking	60%	40%				
Constraint 1				100%			
Constraint 2					65%		
Constraint 3						2.5%	
Constraint 4							40%
Portfolio ranking		**Portfolio return**	**Volatility**	**Portfolio beta**	**Sharpe**	**Treynor**	**Relative VaR**
Profile weights	Risk avert	20%	30%	12.5%	12.5%	12.5%	12.5%
	Moderate	25%	25%	12.5%	12.5%	12.5%	12.5%
	Risk seeking	30%	20%	12.5%	12.5%	12.5%	12.5%
Indifference thresholds		1.5%	0.5%	0.01	0.3	0.03	1000
Preference thresholds		3%	1.5%	0.03	0.6	0.06	3000
Lowest tolerance profile		30%	15%	1	2	0.3	36000

Figure 5. Decision maker's preference modeling.

In Figures 6 and 7 are presented the results of the 1st and 2nd component. The blue font indicates securities of high capitalization, while the green and red fonts indicate securities of medium and low capitalization correspondingly. As we can see, satisfactory diversification in the level of capitalization has been achieved. Moreover, we can see that in the satisfactory class in the 1st Component, have been classified 30 from the 84 stocks and as far as the 2nd Component, 16 of these 30 stocks ranked above the lowest tolerance profile LTP (dummy stock).

	Stock	Return	Dividend yield	Volatility	Beta	Marketability	Relative P/E
1	ΕΛΤΕΧ	57.06	1.80	34.20	0.81	94.15	1.45
2	ΙΝΛΟΤ	84.83	2.56	37.48	1.25	68.93	1.03
3	ΟΤΕ	26.59	2.48	24.13	1.00	55.42	1.05
4	ΑΒΑΞ	55.17	1.53	37.99	1.17	53.32	1.99
5	ΒΣΤΑΡ	76.39	2.33	42.00	1.61	55.69	1.25
6	ΗΡΑΚ	73.26	5.73	32.62	1.25	24.13	1.66
7	ΙΑΤΡ	83.22	1.05	37.48	1.26	91.45	0.88
8	ΛΑΜΔΑ	102.20	1.64	31.57	1.33	44.40	0.15
9	ΜΥΤΙΛ	64.40	1.49	44.92	1.91	121.68	0.75
10	ΣΙΔΕ	181.62	1.68	57.74	0.94	68.70	1.04
11	ΤΕΡΝΑ	78.38	1.56	39.94	1.66	80.75	1.78
12	ΦΟΛΙ	34.23	0.40	27.48	0.78	60.23	1.01
13	ΦΡΙΓΟ	98.38	1.43	32.86	1.09	41.85	0.89
14	ΑΒΕ	89.96	1.82	45.15	1.28	66.97	1.18
15	ΑΛΜΥ	49.67	1.58	43.27	1.19	68.90	1.13
16	ΒΕΤΑΝ	28.88	3.88	26.63	0.61	83.35	1.53
17	ΒΥΤΕ	40.01	2.30	39.99	0.79	54.41	1.03
18	ΔΙΧΘ	253.69	1.18	58.39	0.40	127.43	1.12
19	ΔΡΟΥΚ	63.47	1.74	34.50	1.50	19.51	1.29
20	ΕΒΕΡ	34.29	2.92	41.89	0.66	85.76	1.11
21	ΕΛΤΚ	75.54	2.11	42.10	0.85	45.08	1.53
22	ΕΤΕΜ	73.45	1.62	58.15	1.13	62.84	1.12
23	ΚΑΛΣΚ	62.25	0.55	37.24	0.72	30.36	1.22
24	ΜΟΤΟ	35.57	5.95	32.97	0.70	24.06	1.00
25	ΜΠΤΚ	46.49	1.17	37.21	1.15	16.56	1.61
26	ΠΕΤΡΟ	40.59	4.28	35.21	0.26	12.59	1.70
27	ΠΡΟΦ	108.73	1.32	32.50	1.08	94.74	0.92
28	ΡΕΒ	90.28	1.79	49.13	1.23	69.45	1.23
29	ΣΙΔΜΑ	96.06	2.94	44.51	0.54	47.52	0.90
30	ΣΠΥΡ	62.71	0.60	35.99	1.61	30.90	1.36

Figure 6. Results 1st Component / Stock classification (satisfactory class).

Ranking			Return on assets	Return on equity	Assets turnover	Inventories turnover	Assets to liabilities	Liabilities to equity
1	1	ΙΝΛΟΤ	17.2	51.3	1.3	41.3	3.0	2.5
2	2	ΒΣΤΑΡ	5.2	10.1	0.3	92.9	2.6	1.0
3	3	ΦΟΛΙ	11.2	39.3	0.8	4.9	3.5	3.4
	4	ΦΡΙΓΟ	11.3	27.0	1.2	4.6	1.5	1.1
	5	ΡΕΒ	4.5	12.0	8.5	154.8	1.1	2.0
4	6	ΕΒΕΡ	6.9	16.2	1.3	40.5	1.1	1.2
5	7	ΛΑΜΔΑ	11.3	25.9	0.1	1.6	2.6	1.0
	8	ΒΥΤΕ	7.4	13.6	1.2	10.7	1.6	1.1
6	9	ΗΡΑΚ	5.7	7.4	0.7	9.5	2.8	0.3
	10	ΕΛΤΚ	6.9	16.2	1.1	7.9	1.9	1.5
	11	ΜΟΤΟ	6.8	16.9	2.0	3.7	1.6	1.5
7	12	ΜΥΤΙΛ	8.3	23.4	0.7	4.4	1.3	1.3
	13	ΣΙΔΕ	8.0	22.1	0.9	4.2	1.7	1.6
	14	ΠΡΟΦ	6.8	11.2	0.7	18.2	1.6	0.7
8	15	ΟΤΕ	4.9	15.7	0.5	35.1	1.5	2.1
	16	ΔΡΟΥΚ	5.7	16.7	0.9	5.8	2.1	2.3
		LTP	6.0	17.0	1.0	6.0	2.0	2.5
9	17	ΔΙΧΘ	7.2	26.5	0.6	26.1	1.2	3.1
	18	ΠΕΤΡΟ	4.3	11.0	1.2	5.9	1.9	1.5
	19	ΣΙΔΜΑ	5.0	14.4	0.9	6.0	2.2	2.2
10	20	ΕΛΤΕΧ	3.4	6.7	0.5	24.3	1.6	0.9
	21	ΚΑΛΣΚ	3.6	7.6	0.9	3.5	2.2	1.1
11	22	ΙΑΤΡ	3.9	11.0	0.6	48.0	0.7	1.9
	23	ΑΒΕ	3.9	19.0	0.4	14.4	0.7	4.3
12	24	ΑΒΑΞ	4.0	10.3	0.7	12.6	1.1	1.8
	25	ΤΕΡΝΑ	3.4	10.5	0.6	23.0	1.4	2.3
13	26	ΕΤΕΜ	1.9	4.2	0.7	3.2	2.0	1.3
14	27	ΒΕΤΑΝ	2.7	6.8	0.4	10.8	1.7	1.7
	28	ΜΠΤΚ	3.0	10.1	0.9	4.6	1.4	2.5
15	29	ΑΛΜΥ	2.0	6.3	0.7	3.2	1.4	2.1
	30	ΣΠΥΡ	-2.1	-3.7	0.3	1.4	1.6	0.9

Figure 7. Results 2nd Component / Stock ranking.

				1	2	3	4	5	6	7	8	9	10	11	12	13	14	15	16
	Stocks	MEAN	STD	ΙΝΛΟΤ	ΒΣΤΑΡ	ΦΟΛΙ	ΦΡΙΓΟ	ΡΕΒ	ΕΒΕΡ	ΛΑΜΔΑ	ΒΥΤΕ	ΗΡΑΚ	ΕΛΤΚ	ΜΟΤΟ	ΜΥΤΙΛ	ΣΙΔΕ	ΠΡΟΦ	ΟΤΕ	ΔΡΟΥΚ
Portfolio 1	14	0.00065	0.00750	6.1%	0.0%	11.8%	1.4%	10.1%	5.7%	1.4%	6.0%	4.8%	0.0%	27.4%	0.0%	0.4%	15.0%	8.6%	1.2%
Portfolio 2	14	0.00068	0.00750	6.5%	0.0%	11.8%	2.3%	9.8%	5.2%	1.6%	5.4%	3.9%	0.4%	27.5%	0.0%	1.1%	14.9%	8.6%	1.0%
Portfolio 3	14	0.00072	0.00754	7.1%	0.0%	11.8%	3.6%	9.3%	4.4%	1.8%	4.7%	2.7%	0.9%	27.7%	0.0%	2.0%	14.7%	8.5%	0.8%
Portfolio 4	14	0.00076	0.00761	7.7%	0.0%	11.8%	4.8%	8.9%	3.7%	2.0%	3.9%	1.5%	1.5%	27.9%	0.0%	2.9%	14.5%	8.4%	0.6%
Portfolio 5	14	0.00080	0.00770	8.0%	0.0%	11.8%	5.9%	8.5%	2.8%	2.1%	3.2%	0.5%	1.9%	28.3%	0.5%	3.6%	14.1%	8.3%	0.5%
Portfolio 6	15	0.00084	0.00782	8.1%	0.0%	11.6%	6.8%	8.0%	2.0%	2.0%	2.6%	0.0%	2.4%	29.0%	1.3%	4.1%	13.7%	8.3%	0.2%
Portfolio 7	14	0.00088	0.00796	8.0%	0.0%	11.5%	7.5%	7.5%	1.2%	1.6%	1.9%	0.0%	2.8%	29.5%	2.3%	4.8%	13.2%	8.3%	0.0%
Portfolio 8	13	0.00092	0.00813	7.8%	0.0%	11.5%	8.2%	6.9%	0.4%	1.1%	1.2%	0.0%	3.2%	30.0%	3.3%	5.5%	12.7%	8.3%	0.0%
Portfolio 9	13	0.00096	0.00832	7.6%	0.0%	11.3%	9.1%	6.2%	0.0%	0.7%	0.3%	0.0%	3.7%	30.6%	4.3%	6.1%	12.1%	8.1%	0.0%
Portfolio 10	12	0.00100	0.00853	7.3%	0.0%	10.7%	10.2%	5.5%	0.0%	0.3%	0.0%	0.0%	4.0%	31.1%	5.4%	6.6%	11.2%	7.6%	0.0%
Portfolio 11	11	0.00104	0.00878	7.0%	0.0%	10.0%	11.4%	4.7%	0.0%	0.0%	0.0%	0.0%	4.4%	31.5%	6.6%	7.1%	10.3%	7.0%	0.0%
Portfolio 12	10	0.00108	0.00906	6.5%	0.0%	9.2%	12.5%	3.8%	0.0%	0.0%	0.0%	0.0%	4.8%	31.9%	7.9%	7.7%	9.4%	6.4%	0.0%
Portfolio 13	10	0.00112	0.00936	6.0%	0.0%	8.5%	13.6%	2.9%	0.0%	0.0%	0.0%	0.0%	5.1%	32.3%	9.1%	8.3%	8.5%	5.8%	0.0%
Portfolio 14	10	0.00116	0.00969	5.5%	0.0%	7.8%	14.6%	2.0%	0.0%	0.0%	0.0%	0.0%	5.5%	32.7%	10.3%	8.9%	7.6%	5.1%	0.0%
Portfolio 15	10	0.00120	0.01004	5.0%	0.0%	7.1%	15.7%	1.1%	0.0%	0.0%	0.0%	0.0%	5.9%	33.0%	11.5%	9.5%	6.6%	4.5%	0.0%
Portfolio 16	10	0.00124	0.01041	4.6%	0.0%	6.4%	16.8%	0.2%	0.0%	0.0%	0.0%	0.0%	6.2%	33.4%	12.7%	10.0%	5.7%	3.9%	0.0%
Portfolio 17	10	0.00128	0.01080	3.5%	0.0%	5.8%	17.4%	0.0%	0.0%	0.0%	0.0%	0.0%	6.6%	33.3%	14.5%	10.9%	4.6%	3.5%	0.0%
Portfolio 18	9	0.00132	0.01121	2.6%	0.0%	5.0%	18.2%	0.0%	0.0%	0.0%	0.0%	0.0%	7.1%	33.3%	16.0%	11.7%	3.3%	3.0%	0.0%
Portfolio 19	9	0.00136	0.01164	1.6%	0.0%	4.2%	19.0%	0.0%	0.0%	0.0%	0.0%	0.0%	7.5%	33.3%	17.5%	12.5%	1.9%	2.4%	0.0%
Portfolio 20	9	0.00140	0.01208	0.6%	0.0%	3.5%	19.9%	0.0%	0.0%	0.0%	0.0%	0.0%	8.0%	33.3%	19.0%	13.4%	0.5%	1.8%	0.0%
Portfolio 21	9	0.00144	0.01255	0.0%	0.0%	2.0%	19.8%	0.0%	0.0%	0.0%	0.0%	0.0%	9.1%	32.5%	20.2%	15.5%	0.0%	0.8%	0.0%
Portfolio 22	7	0.00148	0.01308	0.0%	0.0%	0.0%	19.0%	0.0%	0.0%	0.0%	0.0%	0.0%	10.8%	30.6%	21.0%	18.6%	0.0%	0.0%	0.0%
Portfolio 23	5	0.00152	0.01369	0.0%	0.0%	0.0%	17.9%	0.0%	0.0%	0.0%	0.0%	0.0%	12.3%	26.1%	22.1%	21.6%	0.0%	0.0%	0.0%
Portfolio 24	5	0.00156	0.01437	0.0%	0.0%	0.0%	16.8%	0.0%	0.0%	0.0%	0.0%	0.0%	13.7%	21.6%	23.2%	24.7%	0.0%	0.0%	0.0%
Portfolio 25	5	0.00160	0.01512	0.0%	0.0%	0.0%	15.7%	0.0%	0.0%	0.0%	0.0%	0.0%	15.1%	17.1%	24.3%	27.8%	0.0%	0.0%	0.0%
Portfolio 26	5	0.00164	0.01593	0.0%	0.0%	0.0%	14.6%	0.0%	0.0%	0.0%	0.0%	0.0%	16.6%	12.6%	25.4%	30.8%	0.0%	0.0%	0.0%
Portfolio 27	5	0.00168	0.01678	0.0%	0.0%	0.0%	13.6%	0.0%	0.0%	0.0%	0.0%	0.0%	18.0%	8.1%	26.4%	33.9%	0.0%	0.0%	0.0%
Portfolio 28	5	0.00172	0.01788	0.0%	0.0%	0.0%	3.2%	0.0%	0.0%	0.0%	0.0%	0.0%	16.2%	7.7%	36.8%	36.1%	0.0%	0.0%	0.0%

Figure 8. Results 3rd Component / Portfolio optimization.

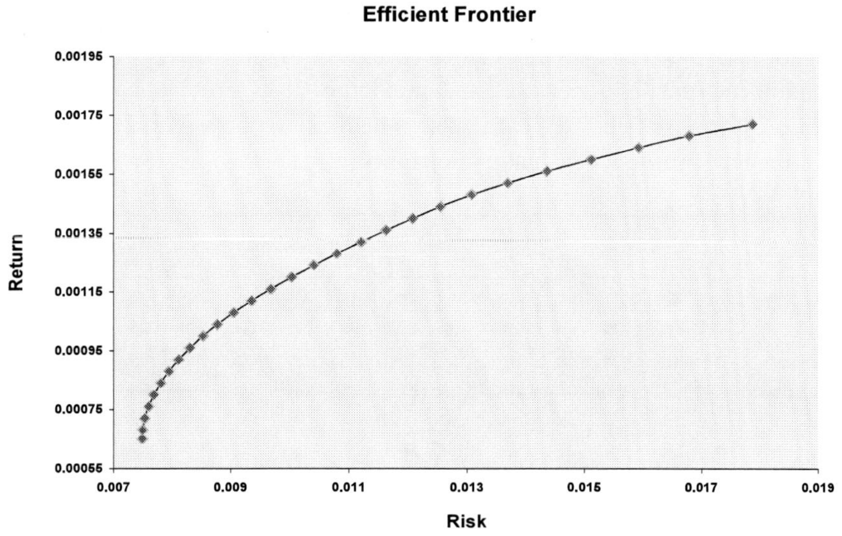

Figure 9. The efficient frontier.

		Portfolio return	Volatility	Portfolio beta	Sharpe	Treynor	Relative VaR
1	Portfolio 6	21.0%	12.4%	0.94	1.70	0.22	28765
2	Portfolio 5	20.0%	12.2%	0.94	1.64	0.21	28332
3	Portfolio 4	19.0%	12.0%	0.93	1.58	0.20	27984
	Portfolio 13	28.0%	14.8%	0.99	1.89	0.28	34442
4	Portfolio 7	22.0%	12.6%	0.95	1.75	0.23	29285
	Portfolio 14	29.0%	15.3%	1.00	1.89	0.29	35650
5	Portfolio 8	23.0%	12.9%	0.96	1.79	0.24	29896
	Portfolio 15	30.0%	15.9%	1.01	1.89	0.30	36938
	LTP	30.0%	15.0%	1	2	0.30	36000
6	Portfolio 9	24.0%	13.2%	0.97	1.82	0.25	30595
	Portfolio 10	25.0%	13.5%	0.97	1.85	0.26	31393
	Portfolio 11	26.0%	13.9%	0.98	1.87	0.27	32305
	Portfolio 16	31.0%	16.5%	1.02	1.88	0.30	38299
7	Portfolio 12	27.0%	14.3%	0.99	1.88	0.27	33324
	Portfolio 17	32.0%	17.1%	1.03	1.87	0.31	39728
	Portfolio 18	33.0%	17.7%	1.04	1.86	0.32	41234
8	Portfolio 3	18.0%	11.9%	0.93	1.51	0.19	27740
	Portfolio 19	34.0%	18.4%	1.05	1.85	0.32	42810
9	Portfolio 21	36.0%	19.8%	1.08	1.81	0.33	46169
10	Portfolio 20	35.0%	19.1%	1.07	1.83	0.33	44446
11	Portfolio 22	37.0%	20.7%	1.09	1.79	0.34	48115
12	Portfolio 23	38.0%	21.6%	1.11	1.76	0.34	50342
13	Portfolio 24	39.0%	22.7%	1.13	1.72	0.35	52854
14	Portfolio 25	40.0%	23.9%	1.14	1.67	0.35	55611
15	Portfolio 26	41.0%	25.2%	1.16	1.63	0.35	58579
16	Portfolio 27	42.0%	26.5%	1.18	1.58	0.36	61729
17	Portfolio 2	17.0%	11.9%	0.93	1.43	0.18	27605
	Portfolio 28	43.0%	28.3%	1.27	1.52	0.34	65782
18	Portfolio 1	16.3%	11.9%	0.93	1.37	0.17	27578

Figure 10. Results 4th Component / Portfolio ranking.

In Figure 8 are presented the results of the 3rd component (optimized portfolio generation) and in Figure 9 is presented the corresponding efficient frontier. In total, 28 portfolios have been constructed. Again, as we can see, satisfactory diversification in the level of capitalization has been achieved in this phase too. In Figure 10 are presented the results of the 4th component (portfolio ranking) and in Figure 11 is presented the synthesis of the acceptable portfolios. As far as this particular component, 6 of the 28 portfolios, ranked above the lowest tolerance profile LTP (dummy portfolio).

			1	2	3	4	5	6	7	8	9	10	11	12	13	14	15	16
		Stocks	ΙΝΛΟΤ	ΒΣΤΑΡ	ΦΟΛΙ	ΦΡΙΓΟ	ΡΕΒ	ΕΒΕΡ	ΛΑΜΔΑ	ΒΥΤΕ	ΗΡΑΚ	ΕΛΤΚ	ΜΟΤΟ	ΜΥΤΙΛ	ΣΙΔΕ	ΠΡΟΦ	ΟΤΕ	ΔΡΟΥΚ
1	Portfolio 6	15	8.1%	0.0%	11.6%	6.8%	8.0%	2.0%	2.0%	2.6%	0.0%	2.4%	29.0%	1.3%	4.1%	13.7%	8.3%	0.2%
2	Portfolio 5	14	8.0%	0.0%	11.8%	5.9%	8.5%	2.8%	2.1%	3.2%	0.5%	1.9%	28.3%	0.5%	3.6%	14.1%	8.3%	0.5%
3	Portfolio 4	14	7.7%	0.0%	11.8%	4.8%	8.9%	3.7%	2.0%	3.9%	1.5%	1.5%	27.9%	0.0%	2.9%	14.5%	8.4%	0.6%
	Portfolio 13	10	6.0%	0.0%	8.5%	13.6%	2.9%	0.0%	0.0%	0.0%	0.0%	5.1%	32.3%	9.1%	8.3%	8.5%	5.8%	0.0%
4	Portfolio 7	14	8.0%	0.0%	11.5%	7.5%	7.5%	1.2%	1.6%	1.9%	0.0%	2.8%	29.5%	2.3%	4.8%	13.2%	8.3%	0.0%
	Portfolio 14	10	5.5%	0.0%	7.8%	14.6%	2.0%	0.0%	0.0%	0.0%	0.0%	5.5%	32.7%	10.3%	8.9%	7.6%	5.1%	0.0%
5	Portfolio 8	13	7.8%	0.0%	11.5%	8.2%	6.9%	0.4%	1.1%	1.2%	0.0%	3.2%	30.0%	3.3%	5.5%	12.7%	8.3%	0.0%
	Portfolio 15	10	5.0%	0.0%	7.1%	15.7%	1.1%	0.0%	0.0%	0.0%	0.0%	5.9%	33.0%	11.5%	9.5%	6.6%	4.5%	0.0%

Figure 11. Portfolio synthesis of the acceptable portfolios.

Finally, in Figure 12 are presented the characteristics of the top-3 ranked portfolios.

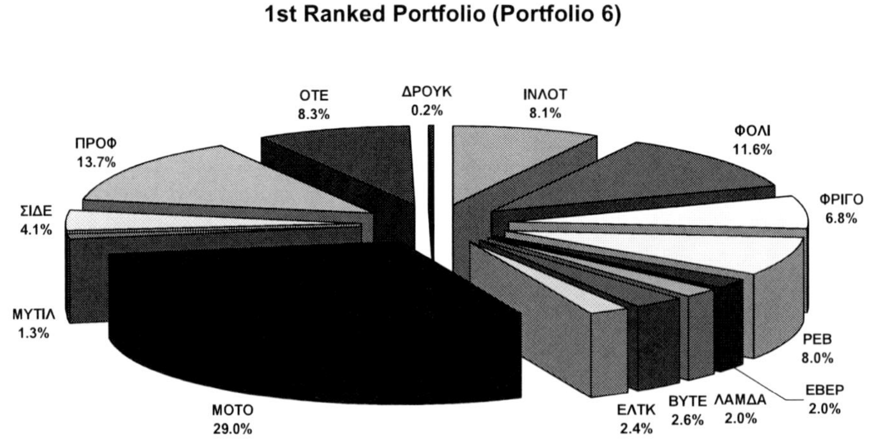

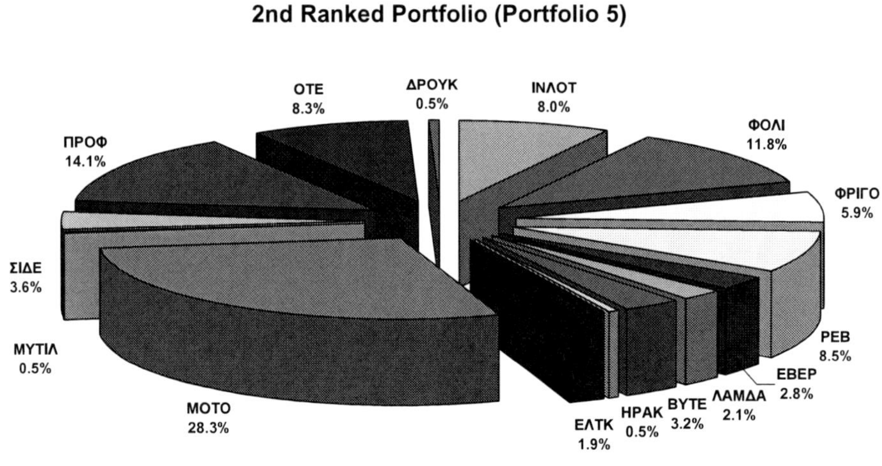

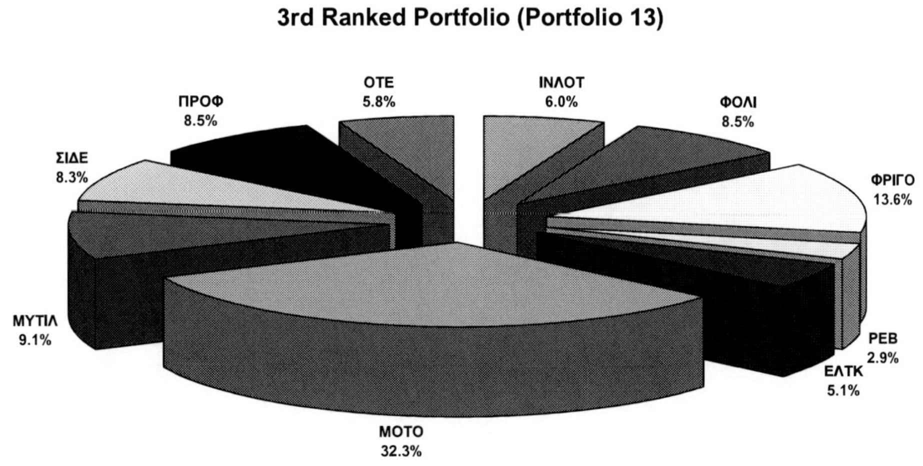

Figure 12. Portfolio synthesis of the top-3 ranked portfolios.

Concluding Remarks

The methodology that has been presented could be a useful tool for portfolio managers, financial analysts and traders in constructing and designing their portfolios. The contribution of the proposed methodology has to do with the facts that follow:

- The complex investment decision process in common stocks is scientifically structured
- Incorporation of the decision maker's preference system (choice among standard different investment profiles & LTPs)
- Incorporation of combination of decision support techniques and multiple decision criteria from different dimensions
- Multi-usability since the model can be utilized solely for corporate evaluation or single stock selection
- Flexibility for the decision maker since the model does not involve complex processes
- Reliable specialized stock evaluations based on each case specific accounting plan
- Minimization of time / costs & additional transparency in the whole process in case of incorporation in a decision support system (DSS)

Towards enhancing the proposed methodology, the issues below have to be assessed:

- Testing the model (time & benchmark)
- Expansion of the criteria sets (stock market, fundamental analysis and portfolio performance indicators)
- Widening the application to the other three accounting plans by expanding the 2nd Component / Stock ranking (four rankings & four lowest tolerance profiles LTPs)

- Embodiment of the methodology in a web-based decision information system so as real time investment decisions to be supported
- Expansion of the methodology so as to include additional asset classes

ACKNOWLEDGMENTS

We wish to express our thanks to the two anonymous referees, whose comments on an earlier version of the paper were very helpful.

REFERENCES

Alexander, G.J. and Sharpe, W.F. (1989). *Fundamentals of Investments*. Prentice Hall International, Inc., Englewood Cliffs, New Jersey.

Arenas Parra, M., Bilbao Terol, A. and Rodrıguez Urıa, M.V. (2001). A Fuzzy Goal Programming Approach to Portfolio Selection. *European Journal of Operational Research* 133(2), 287–297.

Ballestero, E. (1998). Approximating the Optimum Portfolio for an Investor with Particular Preferences. *Journal of the Operational Research Society* 49 (9), 998–1000.

Ballestero, E. and Pla-Santamarıa, D. (2003). Portfolio Selection on the Madrid Exchange: A Compromise Programming Model. *International Transactions in Operational Research* 10(1), 33–51.

Ballestero, E. and Romero, C. (1996). Portfolio Selection: A Compromise Programming Solution. *Journal of the Operational Research Society* 47(11), 1377–1386.

Bana e Costa, C.A. and Soares, J.O. (2001). Multicriteria Approaches for Portfolio Selection: An Overview. *Review of Financial Markets* 4 (1), 19–26.

Bana e Costa, C.A. and Soares, J.O. (2004). A Multicriteria Model for Portfolio Management. *European Journal of Finance* 10(3), 198–211.

Bouri, G., Martel, J.M. and Chabchoub, H. (2002). A Multi-criterion Approach for Selecting Attractive Portfolio. *Journal of Multi-Criteria Decision Analysis* 11(3), 269–277.

Chang, T.-J., Meade, N., Beasley, J.E. and Sharaiha, Y.M. (2000). Heuristics for Cardinally Constrained Portfolio Optimisation. *Computers & Operations Research* 27(13), 1271–1302.

Chunhachinda, P., K. Dandapani, S. Hamid, and Prakash, A.J. (1997). Portfolio Selection and Skewness Evidence from International Stock Markets. *Journal of Banking & Finance* 21, 143–167.

Colson, G. and Zeleny, M. (1979). Uncertain prospects ranking and portfolio analysis under the condition of partial information. *Mathematical Systems in Economics*, No. 44, Verlag Anton Hain, Maisenheim.

Colson, G. and De Bruyn, Ch. (1989).An integrated multiobjective portfolio management system. *Mathematical and Computer Modelling* 12(10/11), 1359–1381.

Dominiak, C. (1997). An Application of Interactive Multiple Objective Goal Programming on the Warsaw Stock Exchange. In R. Caballero, F. Ruiz, and R.E. Steuer (eds.), *Lecture Notes in Economics and Mathematical Systems,* Vol. 455, Berlin: Springer-Verlag, pp. 66–74.

Doumpos, M. (2000). Multicriteria classification methods and applications in financial management. Doctorate dissertation. Technical University of Crete, Chania.

Doumpos, M., Spanos, M. and Zopounidis, C. (1999). On the Use of Goal Programming Techniques in the Assessment of Financial Risks. *Journal of Euro-Asian Management* 5(1), 83–100.

Elton, E.J. and Gruber, M.J. (1987). *Modern Portfolio Theory and Investment Analysis.* 3rd edition, John Wiley and Sons Inc., New York.

Ehrgott, M., Klamroth, K. and Schwehm, C. (2004). An MCDM Approach to Portfolio Optimization. *European Journal of Operational Research* 155(3), 752–770.

Evrard, Y. and Zisswiller, R. (1983). *The Setting of Market Investors Preferences: An Exploratory Study Based on Multiattribute Models*, Centre d'Enseignement Superieur des Affaires, Paris.

Feinstein, C.D. and Thapa, M.N. (1993). Notes: A Reformulation of a Mean-Absolute Deviation Portfolio Optimization Model. *Management Science* 39(12), 1552–1553.

Hallerbach, W.G. and Spronk, J. (2002a). A Multidimensional Framework for Financial-economic Decisions. *Journal of Multi-Criteria Decision Analysis* 11(3), 111–124.

Hallerbach, W.G. and Spronk, J. (2002b). The Relevance of MCDM for Financial Decisions. *Journal of Multi-Criteria Decision Analysis* 11(4–5), 187–195.

Hurson, Ch. and Zopounidis, C. (1993). Return, risk measures and multicriteria decision support for portfolio selection, in: Papathanassiou, B. and Paparrizos, K. (eds), *Proc. 2nd Balkan Conference on Operational Research*, pp. 343–357.

Hurson, Ch. and Zopounidis, C. (1995). On the use of multicriteria decision aid methods to portfolio selection. *Journal of Euro Asian Management* 1(2), 69–94.

Hurson, Ch. and Ricci, N. (1998). Multicriteria Decision Making and Portfolio Management with Arbitrage Pricing Theory. In C. Zopounidis (ed.), *Operational Tools in the Management of Financial Risks*. Dordrecht: Kluwer Academic Publishers, pp. 31–55.

Jog, V., Kaliszewski, I. and Michalowski, W. (1999). Using Attribute Trade-off Information in Investment. *Journal of Multi-Criteria Decision Analysis* 8(4), 189–199.

Jones, Ch. P. (1985). *Investments: Analysis and Management*, John Wiley and Sons Inc., New York.

Konno, H., Shirakawa, H. and Yamazaki, H. (1993). A Mean-Absolute Deviation-Skewness Portfolio Optimization. *Annals of Operations Research* 45, 205–220.

Konno, H. and K.-I. Suzuki. (1995). A Mean-Variance-Skewness Portfolio Optimization Model. *Journal of he Operations Research Society of Japan* 38(2), 173–187.

Konno, H. and Yamazaki, H. (1991). Mean-Absolute Deviation Portfolio Optimization Model and Its Application to Tokyo Stock Market. *Management Science* 37(5), 519–531.

Niarchos, N. (2005). *Financial Statement Analysis.* 2nd Edition, Stamoulis Publications, Athens.

Maginn, J.L., Tuttle, D.L., Pinto D.E., and McLeavey, D.W. (2007). *Managing Investment Portfolios*. 3rd Edition, John Wiley and Sons Inc., New York.

Lee, S.M. and Chesser, D.L. (1980). Goal programming for portfolio selection, *The Journal of Portfolio Management*, Spring, pp. 22–26.

Khoury, N., Martel, J.M., and Veilleux, M. (1993). Méthode multicritère de sélection de portefeuilles indiciels internationaux. *L'Actualité Economique* 69/1.

Markowitz, H. (1952). Portfolio selection. *The Journal of Finance*, March, pp. 77–91.

Martel, J.M., Khoury, N.T. and Bergeron, M. (1988). An application of a multicriteria approach to portfolio comparisons. *Journal of the Operational Research Society* 39 (7), 617–628.

Nakayama, H., Takeguchi, T., and Sano, M. (1983). Interactive graphics for portfolio selection, in Hansen, P. (ed.), *Lecture Notes in Economics and Mathematical Systems* 209, Essays and Surveys on Multiple Criteria Decision Making, Springer Verlag, Berlin Heidelberg, pp. 280- 289.

Ogryczak, W. (2000). Multiple Criteria Linear Programming Model for Portfolio Selection. *Annals of Operations Research*, 97, 143–162.

Pardalos, P.M., Sandstrom, M. and Zopounidis, C. (1994). On the use of optimization models for portfolio selection: A review and some computational results. *Computational Economics* 7, 227–244.

Pardalos, P.M., Siskos, Y. and Zopounidis, C. (1995). *Advances in Multicriteria Analysis*. Kluwer Academic Publishers, Dordrecht.

RiosGarcia, S. and RiosInsua, S. (1983). The portfolio selection problem with multiattributes and multiple criteria, in Hansen, P. (ed.), *Lecture Notes in Economics and Mathematical Systems* 209, Essays and Surveys on Multiple Criteria Decision Making, Springer Verlag, Berlin Heidelberg, pp. 317–325.

Roy, B. (1996). Multicriteria Methodology for Decision Aiding. Dordrecht: Kluwer Academic Publishers.

Saaty, T.L., Rogers, P.C. and Pell, R. (1980). Portfolio selection through hierarchies. *The Journal of Portfolio Management*, Spring, pp. 16–21.

Samaras, G.D., Matsatsinis, N.F., and Zopounidis, C. A multicriteria DSS for stock evaluation using fundamental analysis. European Journal of Operational Research (2006), doi:10.1016/j.ejor.2006.09.020.

Siskos, Y. and Zopounidis, C. (1993). Multicriteria decision support systems: Editorial. *Journal of Information Science and Technology*, Special Issue 2, 2, 107–108.

Stone, B.K. (1973). A Linear Programming Formulation of the General Portfolio Selection Problem. *Journal of Financial and Quantitative Analysis* 8(4), 621–636.

Spronk, J. and Hallerbach, W.G. (1997). Financial Modelling: Where to Go? With an Illustration for Portfolio Management. *European Journal of Operational Research* 99(1), 113–127.

Steuer, R.E. and Na, P. (2003). Multiple Criteria Decision Making Combined with Finance: A Categorized Bibliography. *European Journal of Operational Research* 150(3), 496–515.

Steuer, R.E., Qi, Y. and Hirshberger, M. (2007). Suitable-portfolio investors, nondominated frontier sensitivity, and the effect of multiple objectives on standard portfolio selection. *Annals of Operations Research* 152, 297-317.

Szala, A. (1990). *L'aide a la Decision en Gestion de Portefeuille*. Diplome Superieur de Recherches Appliquees, Universite de Paris Dauphine, Paris.

Tamiz, M., Hasham, R., Jones, D.F., Hesni, B. and Fargher, E.K. (1996). A Two Staged Goal Programming Model for Portfolio Selection. In M. Tamiz (ed.), *Lecture Notes in Economics and Mathematical Systems,* Vol. 432. Berlin: Springer-Verlag, pp. 386–399.

Xidonas, P., Askounis, D., and Psarras, J. (2007). Towards modeling an integrated methodology for supporting common stock portfolio construction decisions. In: 7th Hellenic Operational Research Society Special Conference, Technical University of Crete, 27-28 September.

Yu, W. (1992). ELECTRE TRI: Aspect methodologiques et manuel d' utilization. Document du Lamsade, Universite´ Paris-Dauphine, p.74.

Yu, G.Y. (1997). A Multiple Criteria Approach to Choosing an Efficient Stock Portfolio at the Helsinki Stock Exchange. *Journal of Euro-Asian Management* 3(2), 53–85.

Zeleny, M. (1977). Multidimensional Measure of Risk: The Prospect Ranking Vector. In S. Zionts (ed.), *Lecture Notes in Economics and Mathematical Systems,* Vol. 155. Heidelberg: Springer Verlag, pp. 529– 548.

Zopounidis, C., Despotis D.K., and Kamaratou, I. (1998). Portfolio selection using the ADELAIS multiobjective linear programming system. *Computational Economics* 11/3, 189-204.

Zopounidis, C. and Doumpos, M. (2000). INVESTOR: A Decision Support System Based on Multiple Criteria for Portfolio Selection and Composition. In A. Colorni, M. Paruccini, and B. Roy (eds.), *A-MCD-A Aide Multi Critere a la Decision—Multiple Criteria Decision Aiding*. Brussels: European Commission Joint Research Centre, pp. 371–381.

Zopounidis, C., and Doumpos, M. (2002). Multicriteria Decision Aid in Financial Decision Making: Methodologies and Litrature Review. *Journal of Multicriteria Decision Analysis* 11: 167-186.

In: Computational Techniques in Economics and Finance ISBN: 978-1-61324-558-3
Editor: Constantine Zopounidis

Chapter 8

MOVING AVERAGE, NEURAL NETWORKS AND GENETIC ALGORITHMS FOR STOCK MARKET PREDICTION

G. Atsalakis[18*] and D. Nezis
Technical University of Crete, Greece

ABSTRACT

This paper presents a combination of technical analysis and neural networks based on genetic algorithms for the purposes of forecasting the stock market trend. Various time frame moving average indexes are used as inputs to a neural network. The model uses genetic algorithms as a learning method. Many tests applying various stocks and indexes were carried out. The results were evaluated by the in sample and out of sample trend accuracy rate. Further evaluation was conducted by simulating the model and the returns were measured and compared with the buy and hold strategy. The results are very significant and are subject to further investigation.

Keywords: neural networks, financial forecasting, genetic algorithms, stock market forecasting

1. INTRODUCTION

The efficient market hypothesis *(EMH)* is connected with the idea of a "random walk," which is a term loosely used in the finance literature to characterize a price series where all subsequent price changes represent random departures from previous prices. The logic of the random walk idea is that if the flow of information is unimpeded and information is immediately reflected in stock prices, then tomorrow's price change will reflect only tomorrow's news and will be independent of the price changes today. But facts are by definition unpredictable, and, thus, resulting price changes must be unpredictable and

[*] Corresponding author: George Atsalakis - Email: atsalak@otenet.gr; atsalakis@ermes.tuc.gr

random. As a result, prices fully reflect all known information, and even uninformed investors buying a diversified portfolio at the tableau of prices given by the market will obtain a rate of return as generous as that achieved by experts.

By the start of the twenty-first century, the great dominance of the efficient market hypothesis had become far less known. When the term 'efficient market' was introduced into the economics literature thirty years ago, it was defined as a market which 'adjusts rapidly to new information' Fama (1969). It soon became clear, however, that while rapid adjustment to new information is an important element of an efficient market, it is not the only one. A more modern definition is that asset prices in an efficient market 'fully reflect all available information' Fama (1991). This implies that the market processes information rationally, in the sense that relevant information is not ignored, and systematic errors are not made. As a consequence, prices are always at levels consistent with fundamentals. The words in this definition have been chosen carefully, but they nonetheless mask some of the subtleties inherent in defining an efficient asset market. Many financial economists and statisticians began to believe that stock prices are at least partially predictable. Many famous economists emphasized psychological and behavioural elements of stock-price determination, and they came to believe that future stock prices are somewhat predictable on the basis of past stock price patterns as well as certain "fundamental" valuation metrics. Moreover, many of these economists were even making the far more controversial claim that these predictable patterns enable investors to earn excess risk adjusted rates of return. There are at least three reasons for the persistence of commitment to EMH. First, the wealth of empirical evidence in support of the EMH can no longer be ignored than can the more recent counter evidence. Keane (1991) notes that "..unexplained price behaviour is not necessarily irrational, and that irrational behaviour is not necessarily exploitable, and finally that exploitable behaviour is not necessarily worth exploiting" Kean (1991). Second, tests of market efficiency necessarily involve joint tests of efficiency and the asset pricing model used in the tests. It is arguable that the anomalies are reflections of misspecification of the models used rather than of (exploitable) market inefficiency. Finally, there are some who will tend to the EMH for the sheer weight of its economic logic, at least with respect to developed markets. As a result, everybody understands from the above, that the efficient market hypothesis is almost certainly the right place to start when thinking about asset price formation. However, both academic research and asset market experience, suggest that it does not explain some important and worrying features of asset market behaviour.

Another stock market forecasting approach is *technical analysis*. Technical analysis is the practice of identifying recurring patterns in historical prices in order to forecast future price trends. The technique relies on the idea that prices 'move in trends which are determined by the changing attitudes of investors toward a variety of economic, monetary, political and psychological forces' and that these trends are therefore predictable to some extent, Pring (1985). Technical analysis has its roots in the belief that information contained in past prices is not correctly incorporated in current prices. Technical trading rules, while many and varied, aim, in general, to identify the initiation of new trends. Some of the simpler rules include filter rules, (buy when the price rises by a given proportion above a recent trough) trading range breaks (buy when the price rises by a given proportion above a recently established trading range) and moving average intersections (buy when a shorter moving average penetrates a longer moving average from below). For each rule, the analyst chooses the time horizon over which troughs and peaks are to be identified and moving averages calculated, as well as the threshold before a decision is made.

Most of these technical trading rules are simple and fairly inexpensive to implement. One would therefore not expect such rules to generate excess profits in an efficient market. The evidence on whether they do does not point clearly in one direction. There appeared to be statistically significant excess returns to commonly used technical rules when they were applicd to US dollar exchange rates throughout the past few decades Levich (1993). In the stock market, the evidence is less clear-cut. Some studies report significant excess returns to technical trading rules, although out-of sample performance is less convincing Brock (1992). Others conclude that technical rules do not earn excess profits over a simple buy and-hold strategy Allen (1999). Perhaps more troubling for the efficient market hypothesis is that technical trading analysis exists at all. For reasons previously mentioned, one might expect a marginal role for participants who search for patterns in the historical data to play a marginal role since this information could be of some use and is not completely costless to obtain.

The method of technical analysis that it is used more in this paper is the *moving average method (MA)*. It includes different versions and levels of sophistication. Unlike the diagrammatic technical analysis method, the MA method is easy to quantify and apply in investment decision-making or empirical tests. A moving average is an average of observations from several consecutive time periods. To compute a moving average sequence, we compute successive averages of a given number of consecutive observations. The objective underlying the MA method is to smooth out seasonal variation in the data. This technical-analysis method is intended to provide a decision rule concerning the appropriate investment position. The method involves a comparison of the most recent market price or index with the long MA of the price or index vector. If the current price is higher by a certain buying filter than the long MA, a long investment position should be adopted, and conversely, if the current price is lower by a certain selling filter than the MA, a short position should be adopted. In another variant of the method, the current price or index can be replaced with a short MA, so that the use of the method involves the comparison of the short MA with the long one.

There are three main types of MAs: simple (arithmetic), weighted (linear) and exponential. The simple MA gives equal weight to all the observations of the average. Critics of the simple MA contend that greater weight should be given to more recent observations. The weighted (linear) MA attempts to solve the equal-weight problem of the simple MA. For an MA of n observations, the first observation is multiplied by n, the last observation is multiplied by one, and the total amount is divided by n (n+1)/2, so that the more recent observations are given a greater weight in the average. Both the simple and the weighted MAs share the problem of excluding observations which fall out of the average considered range. This problem is solved by the exponential MA, which considers all the existing observations in the database. In addition, the exponential MA, like the weighted MA, also gives greater weights to more recent observations. It should be emphasized, however, that the differences between the three types of averages noted here do not necessarily imply that one type of MA is superior to the other. As everybody understands, technical analysis has much to offer to our trial analysis of the stock market. But this hardly seems sufficient to explain the extent of technical trading. For example, Allen and Taylor (1990), report that over 90 per cent of foreign exchange dealers in the London market used technical analysis to inform their forecasts one to four weeks ahead. It is hard to make sense of this almost universal usage of technical analysis if the foreign exchange market is an efficient one.

2. Related Work by Neural Networks, Neuro- Fuzzy and Technical Analysis for the Stock Market Prediction

2.1. Neural Networks and Stock Market Prediction

There are many scientists, who have tried to make a model of NN trend analysis. Kim (2000) proposes three genetic algorithms (BPLT, GALT, GAFD) approach to feature discretization and the determination of connection weights for artificial neural networks (ANNs) to predict the stock price index. The research data used in this study is technical indicators and the direction of change in the daily Korea stock price index (KOSPI). The total number of samples is 2928 trading days, from January 1989 to December 1998. Approximated 20% of the data is used for holdout and 80% for training. The training data is used to search the optimal or near-optimal parameters and is employed to evaluate the fitness function. The holdout data is used to test the results with the data that is not utilized to develop the model. The experimental results indicate that GAFD has higher average prediction accuracy than BPLT and GALT by 10 - 11% for the holdout data. It is worth giving attention to the fact that there is a shade of difference of prediction accuracy between the training data and the holdout data for GAFD.

Another paper with many important points is that of Cao et al., (2005). This study uses artificial neural networks to predict stock price movement (i.e., price returns) for firms traded on the Shanghai stock exchange. It compares the predictive power using linear models from financial forecasting literature to the predictive power of the univariate and multivariate neural network models. The results show that neural networks outperform the compared linear models. These results are statistically significant across their sample firms, and indicate that neural networks are a useful tool for stock price prediction in emerging markets, like China. This study covers the time period of January 1, 1999 through December 31, 2002. The data consists of daily closing prices, quarterly book value and common outstanding shares. The ANN is a three-layer feed forward network. The ANN is compared with other non-linear and linear models and calculates three error metrics to measure forecast accuracy (MAD, MAPE, and MSE). Finally, they conclude that ANN forecast models are superior in predicting the stock price returns to the linear predictive model counterparts.

Brownstone (1996) demonstrates that it is possible to predict a stock market to a high degree of accuracy. For this purpose, the Financial Times Stock Exchange (F.T.S.E) 100 Share Index in the UK was selected. Neural network predictions were obtained for the daily market close 5 days ahead and 25 days ahead, as measured in mean square error and in root mean square error. To measure percentage accuracy, each individual test case prediction was compared with the actual market outcome, and the total percentage accuracy for the whole test set was similarly calculated. The results of two neural networks were obtained, together with those from four different modes of a standard statistical alternative, multiple linear regression. Finally, it is obvious from the analysis which took place, that, when relating the predictions of a neural network to the actual rises and falls of a stock market, the percentage accuracy of a prediction versus the actual result more clearly demonstrates the usefulness of neural networks to a potential user.

Another interesting study is the paper of Chenoweth et al., (1996). The proposed stock market prediction system is comprised of two reprocessing components, two specialized neural networks, and a decision rule base. Daily and monthly experiments are conducted and performance is measured by computing the annual rate of return and the return per trade. Comparison of the results achieved by the dual neural network system to that of the single neural network depicts that the dual neural network system gives much larger returns with fewer trades. The system described is used for both daily and monthly S&P 500 stock market buy/sell recommendations. Finally, as it is claimed, comparing the daily to the monthly experimental results, it seems evident that the proposed system yields better returns when using slower data sampling (e.g. monthly rather than daily data).

An interesting stock market study was undertaken in Madrid by Fernandez-Rodriguez et al., (2000). Their results, based on applying this investment strategy to the General Index of the Madrid Stock Market, suggest that, in absence of trading costs, the technical trading rule is always superior to a buy-and-hold strategy for both the ''bear'' market and ''stable'' market episodes. On the other hand, they find that the buy-and-hold strategy generates higher returns than the trading rule based on ANN only for a ''bull'' market sub-period. The ANN that they used is the feed-forward network. Of course, there are many more researchers, who have used artificial neural networks and other soft computing techniques to predict the stock prices or the stock trend such as Enke (2005), Chen (2003), Armano (2004), Chen (2006), Hassan (2007), Kannas (2001), and Lam (2003).

2.2. Neuro-Fuzzy and Stock Market Prediction

The fuzzy inference system has a structural knowledge representation in the form of fuzzy if-then rules. Fuzzy sets were introduced by Zadeh, as a means of representing and manipulating data that is not precise, but rather fuzzy. It is specifically designed to mathematically represent uncertainty and vagueness and to provide formalized tools for dealing with the imprecision intrinsic to many problems.

Kuo et al., (2001) proposed a genetic algorithm based fuzzy neural network (GFNN) to formulate the knowledge base of fuzzy inference rules which can measure the qualitative effect on the stock market. Next, the effect is further integrated with the technical indexes through the artificial neural network (ANN). An example based on the Taiwan stock market is utilized to assess the proposed intelligent system. Evaluation results indicate that the neural network considering both the quantitative and qualitative factors exceeds the neural network considering only the quantitative factors both in the clarity of buying-selling points and buying-selling performance.

Wang (2002) tried to predict the stock price instantly at any given time. One problem with predicting stock prices is that there may be a large or small difference in two continuous sets of data. The other problem is that the volume of stock data is so large that it affects our ability to use it. However, a fuzzy grey prediction, which helped to solve all these problems, was developed. All the data was collected from a stock-broker mainframe in the Taiwan stock market and was recorded every 5 minutes. To simplify the data processing, the data was grouped into hours assuming the trading time is from 9:00am to 14:00pm on weekdays. To demonstrate how effective their system is, they used data from September 2000 to February 2001 as training examples, and data from March 2001 to April 2001 as testing examples.

In addition, most of the neuro-fuzzy systems are either based on Takagi-Sugeno or Mamdani type. Takagi-Sugeno (1986) type based neuro-fuzzy models are widely used for model based applications. The Takagi-Sugeno type combines the advantages of being a general approximator that can reach a high level of accuracy and is easy to interpret, since it can be represented in a natural way. The Mamdani type based neuro-fuzzy systems can be modelled using faster heuristics but with a low performance Abraham (2000).

The neuro-fuzzy model ANFIS was used from Atsalakis and Valavanis (2006). ANFIS uses a hybrid learning algorithm that combines the backprobagation gradient descent and least square methods to create a fuzzy inference system whose membership functions are iteratively adjusted according to a given training set of input and output data. It has a fixed number of layers to represent the FIS structure. The implementation of the proposal system is demonstrated in the National Bank of Greece (ETE), which is listed in the Athens Stock Exchange. More than nineteen years of data have been analyzed for the above mentioned company. The rate of change of these indexes is used as inputs to the ANFIS to predict the trend of next day of the ETE stock. Other researchers, who have been focusing on neuro-fuzzy systems, are Nayak (2004), Jang (1997), Altug (1999), and Lin (2002).

2.3. Technical Analysis and Stock Market Prediction

Technical analysis ignores the EMH totally. The test of weak form of the EMH relies on testing whether excess returns exist by using technical analysis. Because technical analysis has many indicators and theories, the analysts must choose some of them in order to use them as tools for stock price prediction. To decide which indicators an analyst will use depends on the investment strategy that the analyst follows and from their experience. As technical analysis deals with probability, in order to improve the results multiple indicators must be used. Each analyst is familiar with some indicators and these are the most commonly used.

Gunasekarage (2001) analyses the performance of one group of these trading rules using index data for four emerging South Asian capital markets (the Bombay Stock Exchange, the Colombo Stock Exchange, the Dhaka Stock Exchange and the Karachi Stock Exchange), and examines the implications of the results for the weak form of the efficient market hypothesis. The findings indicate that technical trading rules have predictive ability in these markets and reject the null hypothesis stating that the returns to be earned from studying *moving average* values are equal to those achieved from a naive buy and hold strategy; the employment of these techniques generates excess returns to investors in South Asian markets.

Tsang (1999) attempted to explore the potential prediction power of technical analysis. For this reason he presented a genetic programming based system FGP (Financial Genetic Programming), which specialises in taking some well known technical rules and adapting them to prediction problems. FGP uses the power of genetic programming to generate decision trees through an efficient combination of technical rules with self-adjusted thresholds. The generated rules are more suitable for the prediction problem at hand. FGP was tested extensively on historical S&P 500 data through a specific prediction problem. Preliminary results indicate that it outperforms commonly used, non-adaptive, individual technical rules with respect to prediction accuracy and annualised rate of return over two different out-of-sample test periods (three and a half years in each period). Data were taken by the Dow Jones Industrial Average (DJIA) index from 7 April 1969 to 11 October 1976 (1,900 trading days) as training data (or in-sample data). Subsequently, these data were tested on the data (or out-of-sample data) from 12 October 1976 to 5 May 1980 (900 trading days). Finally, they managed to "achieve a 4% return with 63 trading days in the DJIA index".

Wang (2007) examined the potential profit of bull flag technical trading rules using a template matching technique based on pattern recognition for the Nasdaq Composite Index (NASDAQ) and the Taiwan Weighted Index (TWI). The empirical results indicated that all of the technical trading rules correctly predict the direction of changes in the NASDAQ and TWI. This finding may provide investors with important information on asset allocation. Moreover, a better bull flag template price fit is associated with a higher average return. The empirical results demonstrated that the average return of trading rules conditioned on bull flag is significantly better than buying daily throughout the study period, especially for TWI.

Marshall (2005) considers the returns to technical analysis on the New Zealand stock market. The small nature, short-selling constraints, lack of analyst coverage, and loose insider trading regulation suggest that the New Zealand equity market may be less efficient than overseas markets. This raises the possibility that technical analysis is still profitable in New Zealand. A bootstrapping technique was used with common null models for stock returns and 12 popular technical trading rules. Finally, he discovered that the returns to technical analysis in New Zealand follow a similar pattern to those in large offshore markets.

Phylaktis (2004) examined stock market linkages of a group of Pacific-Basin countries with the US and Japan by estimating the multivariate co-integration model in both the autoregressive (AR) and moving average (MA) forms over the period 1980–1998 . The results for the 1980s indicated that the relaxation of foreign ownership restrictions was not sufficient enough to attract foreign investors' attention and those other factors must have affected the portfolio diversification decision. The results of the 1990s suggested that the relaxation of the restrictions might have strengthened international market interrelations. Country Funds have provided access to highly regulated capital markets.

Shachmurove (2001) aimed to examine the efficacy of using technical trading rules in the emerging market of Israel, through the analysis of the Tel-Aviv 25 Index (TA25) and to compare its weak-form market efficiency to the performance of the S&P 500. Two types of moving averages (MA) will be used here, short and long. The short MA consists of one day (the index itself), while the longer MAs will be based on varying ranges of 9, 49, 99 and 149 days. Using no filter, a signal to buy (sell) is received when the short MA crosses the longer MA in an upward (downward) direction. From the results, it is obvious, that the case of TA25 for (relatively moderate) moving averages of 9 and 49 days, the MA method beats the B&H policy, and this holds true for both the long-cash and the long-short strategy. The relatively high success proportion of 78.5% obtained for the MA method further affirms this result. However, for the very long MAs of 99 and 149 days the MA method yields lower returns than those of the B&H policy. In contrast to the TA25, the MA method for the S&P 500 Index yields substantially lower returns than those of the B&H policy. The superiority of the B&H policy over the MA method is higher for short MAs of 1 and 9 days than for the long MAs of 99 and 149 days.

Stock prices are highly nonlinear and many researchers have been focusing on technical analysis to improve the investment returns, Benachenhou (1996), Gately (1996), Simutis (2000), and Azoff (1992).

3. Model Theory

3.1. Theory of Artificial Neural networks (ANN)

An Artificial neural network is a system derived from the field of neuropsychology. The traditional view of an ANN is of a program that emulates biological neural networks and ''learns'' to recognize patterns or categorize input data by being trained on a set of sample data from the domain. ANNs are an assortment of mathematical models that imitate some of the observed phenomena in a biological nervous system, most importantly, adaptive biological learning. ANN models simulate parallel computational structure with highly interconnected simple units, called neurons. In addition, artificial neural network methodology is preferred to alternative non-linear models because it is nonparametric. It offers excellent solutions to a variety of classification problems and prediction system modelling, where the physical processes are not intelligible.

3.2 Theory of Genetic Algorithms (GAs)

GAs are search algorithms based on survival of the fittest among string structures Goldberg (1989). In a broader usage of the term, a genetic algorithm is any population based model that uses selection and recombination operators to generate new sample points in a search space. An implementation of the GAs deals with a population of ''chromosomes'', each representing a potential solution of a target problem, usually in the form of binary strings. GAs have been investigated recently and shown to be effective in exploring a complex space in an adaptive way, guided by the biological evolution mechanisms of reproduction, crossover, and mutation Adelli (1995). GAs often works with a form of binary coding. If the problems are coded as chromosomes, the populations are initialized. Each chromosome within the population is gradually evolved by biological operations. Larger populations ensure greater diversity but require more computational burden. Once the population size is chosen, the initial population is randomly generated Bauer (1994). GAs are usually employed to improve the performance of artificial intelligence techniques. For ANN, GAs are popularly used to select neural network topology such as optimizing a relevant feature subset, determining the optimal number of hidden layers and processing elements. GAs are better than other search algorithms Karr (1995), because they not only consider a single point but many points simultaneously in the search space reducing the chance of converging to local optima, they work directly with strings of characters representing the parameter set, not the parameters themselves, and use probabilistic rules, not deterministic rules, to guide their search.

GAs operate in four stages: problem representation, selection, crossover and mutation. A) The problems must be represented as a suitable form to be handled by GAs. Once the population size is chosen, the initial population is randomly generated. B) Each chromosome is evaluated by the fitness function. The role of the fitness function is to numerically encode the performance of the chromosome. C) Crossover, when combined with selection, yields good components of good structures combining to yield even better structures. Each pair produces two offspring structures to the mutation stage. The offspring are the outcomes of cutting and splicing the parent structures at various randomly selected crossover points. The approaches for selecting crossover points are one-point crossover, two-point crossover, and uniform crossover. D) Mutation creates new structures that are similar to current ones. With a small, pre-specified probability, mutation randomly alters each component of each structure. The reason for using mutation is to prevent missing some significant information during reproduction and crossover. This procedure would avoid the local minimum. GAs are particularly suitable for multi-parameter optimization problems with an objective function subject to numerous hard and soft constraints. One of the ways to make genetic algorithm evolutionary, is to use a feedback rule from the state of the system which modifies a parameter during the search process.

3.3. Moving Average

A price moving average is a method of calculating the average value of a security's price, or indicator, over a period of time. The term "moving" implies, and rightly so, that the average changes or moves. When calculating a moving average, a mathematical analysis of the security's average value over a predetermined time period is made. As the securities price changes over time, its average price moves up or down. Six different types of moving averages have been most often used: simple (also referred to as arithmetic), exponential, time series, triangular, variable, and weighted. Also moving averages of the security's open, high, low, close, median price, typical price, volume, open interest, or indicator can be calculated. The only significant difference between the various types of moving averages is the weight assigned to the most recent data. Once this "weighting" scheme has been determined, it is held static over the range of calculations. The exception is the variable moving average. The variable moving average automatically adjusts its weighting based on market conditions. A variable moving average becomes more sensitive to recent data as volatility increases and less sensitive to recent data as volatility decreases. The equation of simple moving average is:

$$SMA = \frac{Sum of\ x\ day's\ close\ price}{Number of\ x\ days} \tag{1}$$

where x is the number of time periods. The most popular method of interpreting a moving average is to compare the relationship between a moving average of the security's closing price and the security's closing price itself.

The critical element in a moving average is the number of time periods used in calculating the average. When using hindsight, you can always find a moving average that would have been profitable. The key is to find a moving average that will be consistently profitable. The most popular moving average is the 39-week (or 200-day) moving average. This moving average has a good track record in timing the major (long- term) market cycles. The length of a moving average should fit the market cycle that analyst wishes to follow Achelis (1995), Murphy (1986).

In this paper many combinations of moving averages throughout different time periods have been calculated (three, five, seven, nine, eleven thirteen and fifteen days) and used as inputs variables to the neural network model. After trial end error test the three, five and seven days moving averages were chosen as inputs to the model.

4. Model Description

The advantages that neural network have, does not guarantee that the process to building a neural network for a particular forecasting problem will always be successful. The following issues that affect the performance of the model must be considered carefully: the architecture (the number of layers, the number of nodes in each layer and the number of arcs that interconnect with the nodes), activation functions for the processing notes, the training algorithms, data normalization methods, training data and performance measures Zhang (1998).

The architecture of the proposed feedforward neural network is composed of three layers. The first layer corresponds to the length of the input vectors. It has three nodes that correspond to each input vector (the stock price moving average of 3, 5 and 7 days). The number of inputs was determined by trial and error, with large numbers of input vectors (moving average of 9, 11, 13, 15, 17, 19, 21, 23, 25, 27 and 29 days).

The second layer is a hidden layer. It includes three nodes (neurons) which were determined by trial and error with a large number of nodes.

The third layer is the last one which corresponds to the forecasting horizon. It has one node that represents the stock trend one-step-ahead.

The activation or transfer function is the logistic function which determines the relationship between inputs and outputs of a node in the network, and introduces a degree of nonlinearity:

$$f(x) = (1 + \exp^{(-x)})^{-1} \tag{2}$$

Also, genetic evolutionary algorithm is involved, as a learning method. The number of generations of genetic algorithm after many trial-error tests was set at 50.

The data set covers the period from January, 1986 to May, 2006 (4,850 observations). For calculation reasons the rate of input change is calculated as the final inputs to the model.

The data is scaled in order to facilitate the nonlinear estimation process and to avoid the underflow or overflow problems. Helge Petersohn's scaling function is used to scale the data from zero to one, denoted [0, 1], McNelis (2005). To compare the model estimations with the actual values the data is transformed again in a no scaling status.

The data set is divided into training and evaluation data. The training data, which constitute the 80% of the data set, is used to train the model and to carry out the in sample evaluation of the model. The remaining 20 % of the unforeseen data is used for out-of-sample evaluation.

The three inputs to the model are the rate of change of the stock closing price moving average of 3 days, 5 days and 7 days. The output of the model is stock price rate change on the next session.

Performance measures calculated the trading performance of the model and the comparison of returns with the buy and hold strategy.

The buying and selling signals of the model were used to trade each stock. The rate of return (ROR) is calculated according to the trading signals which measured the efficiency of the simulation of the model. These results were compared with the buying and hold strategy (B&H), which is a strategy that depicts, ROR. In the case where the stock is bought at the beginning of the evaluation period, it is held and sold at the end of the evaluation period.The model provides an one step ahead daily trend prediction, so it gives the rate of change of the stock's close price for the next day. Figure 1 depicts the model structure.

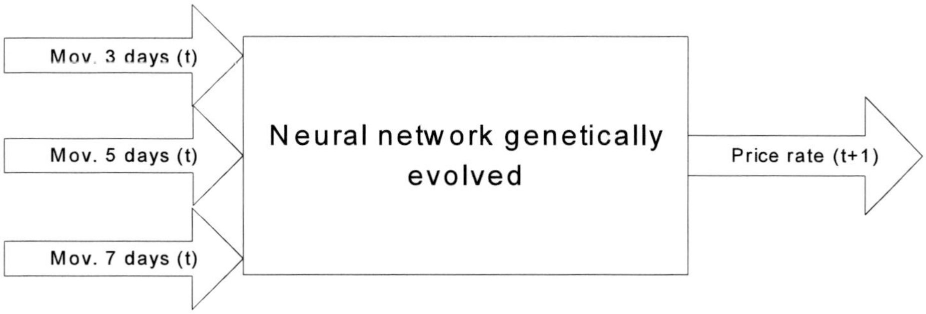

Figure 1. The model structure.

5. EXPERIMENTAL WORK

The five stocks evaluated are the National Bank of Greece (NBG), Alpha Bank (ALPHA), Commercial Bank (CB), Titan (TITAN) and Aluminum of Greece (ALGR) these are all listed in the Athens Stock Exchange, an emerging market. Additional evaluations have been performed for the stocks of General Electric (GE), Caterpillar, General Motors (GM), International Business Machine (IBM) and Kodak stocks, all listed in the NYSE, a well developed market. Also, the following indexes are used for evaluation: Down Jones Industrial Average (DJIA), General Index of ASE (GD) and Financial Times Stock Exchange (FTSE) of ASE.

After training the model an in sample and out of sample evaluation took place. Further evaluation was carried out by using the out of sample results to simulate the system according to the trading signals. The rate of return is compared with the Buy and Hold strategy (B&H). The hit rate (the trend) of a stock is calculated by the following formula:

$$Hitrate = \frac{h}{n} \tag{3}$$

where h denotes the number of correct predictions of the stock trend and n denotes the number of tests. The Rate of return is calculated as follows:

$$ROR = \frac{net gain\ in\ stock}{initialinvestment} \tag{4}$$

The following tables present the model performance. The second row of the table depicts the in sample forecasting accuracy (the same data used for training was used for validation also). The third row presents the model forecasting accuracy using data that was not used for training the model (out of sample). The fourth row presents the rate of return that is given by simulating the model according the buying and selling signals. When the next day forecasting trend is up, the stock is bought and when the trend is down the stock is sold. The last row of the tables depicts the rate of return in case the stock is bought at the begging of the period and is sold in the end of the period (buy and hold strategy). Table 1 - 9 demonstrates the evaluation results for three different periods.

Table 1. Forecasting accuracy of the 1st testing period

1st testing period	GD	FTSE	ETE	CB
Hit rate in sample	52	59	53	56
Hit rate out of sample	49	55	50	55
ROE	1.69	-1.63	3.07	4.16
B&H strategy	2.29	9.37	2.04	-3.45

Table 2. Forecasting accuracy of the 1st testing period

1st testing period	ALGR	ALPHA	TITAN	DJIA
Hit rate in sample	56	65	54	56
Hit rate out of sample	52	55	48	55
ROE	10.51	4.64	5.12	6.06
B&H strategy	8.77	-0.26	4.29	4.83

Table 3. Forecasting accuracy of the 1st testing period

1st testing period	GE	CAT	IBM	EK	GM
Hit rate in sample	58	59	58	59	62
Hit rate out of sample	56	56	57	56	55
ROE	-0.23	4.68	4.97	3.16	-1.63
B&H strategy	-1.24	1.53	-3.38	0.07	9.37

According to Tables 1 to 3, the mean in sample forecasting accuracy of the thirteen stocks and indexes that are depicted in the table is 57.46% while the mean out of sample accuracy is 53.77%. In 9 out of the 13 cases the model gives a higher rate of return than the buying and hold strategy. Tables 4 through 6 demonstrate the forecasting results for the second testing period.

Table 4. Forecasting accuracy of the 2nd testing period

2nd testing period	GD	FTSE	ETE	CB
Hit rate in sample	61	56	65	54
Hit rate out of sample	55	54	58	49
ROE	11.436	12,16	2.14	0.07
B&H strategy	-13.74	8.97	4.88	1.77

Table 5. Forecasting accuracy of the 2nd testing period

2nd testing period	ALGR	ALPHA	TITAN	DJIA
Hit rate in sample	68	53	53	50
Hit rate out of sample	65	52	55	50
ROE	19.23	7.04	-1.56	9.24
B&H strategy	8.61	15.22	2.42	3.349

Table 6. Forecasting accuracy of the 2nd testing period

2nd testing period	GE	CAT	IBM	EK	GM
Hit rate in sample	57	62	61	56	58
Hit rate out of sample	50	55	60	55	50
ROE	4.34	2.62	5.17	9.34	23.45
B&H strategy	-1.24	15.25	-3.38	0.07	9.37

Tables 4 through 6 indicates the mean in sample forecasting accuracy of the thirteen stocks and indexes that are depicted in the table. The mean for in-sample forecasting is 58.00% while the mean for out of sample accuracy is 54.46%. In 8 out of the 13 cases the model provides a higher rate of return than the buying and hold strategy. Table, 7 through 9 depict the forecasting results for the third testing period.

Table 7. Forecasting accuracy of the 3rd testing period

3rd testing period	GD	FTSE	ETE	CB
Hit rate in sample	55	64	61	62
Hit rate out of sample	54	56	55	54
ROE	1.04	-0.17	4.96	-1.52
B&H strategy	-2.74	14.42	2.14	-15.07

Table 8. Forecasting accuracy of the 3rd testing period

3rd testing period	ALGR	ALPHA	TITAN	DJIA
Hit rate in sample	61	66	60	58
Hit rate out of sample	59	55	50	54
ROE	11.43	4.64	4.27	9.34
B&H strategy	-13.74	-0.26	-3.74	4.83

Table 9. Forecasting accuracy of the 3rd testing period

3rd testing period	GE	CAT	IBM	EK	GM
Hit rate in sample	57	58	56	59	52
Hit rate out of sample	55	48	50	55	50
ROE	6.25	3.22	1.37	5.38	-0.17
B&H strategy	-1.24	-6.86	-2.74	0.07	14.42

Tables 7 through 9 depict the mean in sample forecasting accuracy of the thirteen stocks and indexes. The results indicate that the mean is 59.15% while the mean out of sample accuracy is 53.45%. In 10 out of 13 cases the model gives a higher rate of return than the buying and hold strategy.

CONCLUSION

This paper presents a genetically evolved neural network model for one step ahead prediction of the trend of a stock close price. It examined the efficiency of the moving average as input variables to the model. It is approved that the model can predict future stock prices against the efficient market hypothesis.

Reported case studies do not consider commission and tax liabilities; this means that actual returns will be less than those reported. Nevertheless, the proposed system clearly demonstrates the potential of genetically evolved neural network based modeling for financial market prediction. Due to these promising, initial results, it is the author's intention to extend this work to include various input variables from the field of technical and fundamental analysis.

REFERENCES

Abraham, A. and Nath, B. (2000), "Optimal design of neural nets using hybrid algorithms", PRICAI, VIC , (pp.510-520), Melbourne.

Adeli, H. and Hung, S. (1995), "Machine learning: neural networks, genetic algorithms, and fuzzy systems", working paper, New York, Wiley.

Achelis, S.B. (1995), "Technical Analysis from *A to Z",* Probus Publishing Company, Chicago.

Allen, F. and Karjalainen, R. (1999), "Using Genetic Algorithms to Find Technical Trading Rules", Journal of Financial Economics, 51(2), 245–271.

Allen, H. and Taylor, M.P. (1990),"Charts, Noise and Fundamentals in the London Foreign Exchange Market", The Economic Journal, 100(400), 49–59.

Altug, S., Chow, M.Y. and Trussel, H.J. (1999), "Fuzzy inference systems implemented on neural architectures for motor", IEEE Trans Ind Electron, 46(6), 1069-1079.

Armano, G., Marchesi, M. and Murru, A. (2004), "A hybrid genetic-neural architecture for stock indexes forecasting", Information Sciences, Elsevier, 170(12), 3–33.

Atsalakis, G. and Valavanis, K. (2006), "Technical Analysis and Neuro-fuzzy based stock forecasting system". Working paper, department of management and production engineering, Technical University of Crete.

Azoff, M.E. (1992), "Neural Network Time Series Forecasting of Financial Markets", New York, Wiley.

Bauer, R..J. (1994), "Genetic algorithms and investment strategies", New York, Wiley.

Benachenhou, D. (1996), "Smart trading with FRET. Trading On The Edge", New York, Wiley.

Brock, W., Lakonishok, J., and LeBaron, B. (1992), "Simple Technical Trading Rules and the Stochastic Properties of Stock Returns", Journal of Finance, 47(5), 1731–1764.

Brownstone, D. (1996), "Using percentage accuracy to measure neural network predictions in Stock Market movements", Neurocomputing, 10(2), 237-250.

Cao, Q. , Karyl, B.and Schniederjans, M..J. (2005), "A comparison between Fama and French's model and artificial neural networks in predicting the Chinese stock market", Computers & Operations Research, vol. 32, 2499–2512.

Chen, A., Leung, M.T. and Daouk, H. (2003), "Application of neural networks to an emerging financial market: forecasting and trading the Taiwan Stock Index", Computers & Operations Research, vol. 30, 901–923.

Chen, Y. ,Yanga, B. and Abraham, A. (2006), " Flexible neural trees ensemble for stock index modelling", Neurocomputing, vol. 70, 697–703.

Chenoweth, T, and ObradoviC, Z. (1996), "A multi-component nonlinear prediction system for the S&P 500 Index", Neurocomputing, vol. 10, 275-290.

Ehrentreich, N. (2006), "Technical trading in the Santa Fe Institute Artificial Stock Market revisited", Journal of Economic Behavior & Organization, vol. 61, 599–616.

Enke, D. and Thawornwong, S. (2005), "The use of data mining and neural networks for forecasting stock market returns", Expert Systems with Applications, vol. 29, 927–940.

Fama, E. (1991), "Efficient capital markets: II", The Journal of Finance, vol. 46, 1575–1617.

Fama, E., Fisher, L., Jensen, M. and Roll, R. (1969), "The Adjustment of Stock Prices to New Information", International Economic Review, 10(1), 1–21.

Fernandez-Rodrıguez, F., Gonzalez-Martel, C. and Sosvilla-Rivero, S. (2000), "On the profitability of technical trading rules based on artificial neural networks: Evidence from the Madrid stock market", Economics Letters, vol. 69, 89–94.

Gately, E. (1996), "Neural Networks for Financial Forecasting", New York, Wiley.

Goldberg, D. E. (1989), "Genetic algorithms in search, optimization, and machine learning", Reading, MA: Addison-Wesley.

Gunasekarage, A. and Power, D.M. (2001), "The profitability of moving average trading rules in South Asian stock markets" Emerging Markets Review, vol.2, 17-33.

Hassan, R., Nath, B., and Kirley, M. A. (2007), "Fusion model of HMM, ANN and GA for stock market forecasting", Expert Systems with Applications, vol. 33, 171–180.

Jang, J-S.R.. Sun, C., and Mizutani, E. (1997), "Neuro-fuzzy and soft computing: a computational approach to learning and machine intelligence", Prentice Hall.

Kanas, A., and Yannopoulos, A. (2001), "Comparing linear and nonlinear forecasts for stock returns", International Review of Economics and Finance, vol. 10, 383–398.

Karr, C. (1995), "Adaptive control of an exothermic chemical reaction system using fuzzy logic and genetic algorithms, in: L.R. Medsker (Ed.)", Hybrid Intelligent Systems, Kluwer Academic Publishers.

Keane, S. (1991), "Paradox in the current crisis in efficient market theory", Journal of Portfolio Management, vol. 17, 30–34.

Kim, K. and Ingoo, H. (2000), "Genetic algorithms approach to feature discretization in artificial neural networks for the prediction of stock price index", Expert Systems with Applications, vol. 19, 125–132.

Kuo, R.J., Chen, C.H. and Hwang, Y.C. (2001), "An intelligent stock trading decision support system through integration of genetic algorithm based fuzzy neural network and artificial neural network", Fuzzy Sets and Systems, Elsevier, vol. 118, 21-45.

Lam, M. (2003), "Neural network techniques for financial performance prediction: integrating fundamental and technical analysis", Decision Support Systems, vol. 37, 567–581.

Levich, R.M. and Thomas, L.R. (1993), "The Significance of Technical Trading- Rule Profits in the Foreign Exchange Market: A Bootstrap Approach". Journal of International Money and Finance, 12(5), 451–474.

Li, J. and Tsang, E. (1999), "Improving Technical Analysis Predictions: An Application of Genetic Programming", Proceedings of Florida Artificial Intelligence Research Symposium, USA.

Lin,. C.-S., Khan, H.A. and Huang, C. (2002), " Can the Neuro Fuzzy Model Predict Stock Indexes Better than its Rivals?", Discussion Papers of University of Tokyo CIRJE-F-165.

Marshall, B. and Cahan, R.H. (2005), "Is technical analysis profitable on a stock market which has characteristics that suggest it may be inefficient?", Research in International Business and Finance, vol.19, 384–398.

Murphy, J. J. (1986), "Technical Analysis of the Futures Markets, NY", Institute of Finance, New York.

McNelis, D.P. (2005), "Neural Networks in Finance: Gaining predictive edge in the market", Elsevier, Academic Press.

Nayak, P.C., Sudheer, J.K., Rangan, D.M. and Ramasastri, K.S. (2004), "A neuro-fuzzy computing technique for modeling hydrological time series", Journal of Hydrology, vol. 291, 52-66.

Phylaktis, K. and Ravazzolo, F. (2004), "Stock market linkages in emerging markets: implications for international portfolio diversification", Int. Fin. Markets, Inst. and Money, vol.15, 91–106.

Pring, MJ. (1985), "Technical Analysis Explained: the Successful Investor's Guide to Spotting Investment Trends and Turning Points", 2nd edition, McGraw Hill,New York.

Shachmurove, Y., BenZion, H.,Klein, P. and Yagil, J. (2001),"A Moving Average Comparison of the Tel-Aviv 25 and S & P 500 Stock Indices", Working paper, Pennsylvania.

Simutis, R. (2000), "Fuzzy logic based stock trading system", Proc. IEEE/IAFE Conference on Computational Intelligent of Financial Engineering, New York.

Sugeno, M.. and Kang, G. (1986), "Fuzzy modeling and control of multilayer incinerator", Fuzzy Sets System, vol.18, 329-346.

Takagi., T. and Sugeno, M. (1985), "Fuzzy identification of systems and its application to modeling and control", IEEE Transactions on Systems. Man and Cybernetics, 15(1), 116-132.

Zhang, G., Patuwo, B.E. and Hu, M.Y. (1998), "Forecasting with the artificial neural networks: the state of the art", International Journal of Forecasting, vol. 14, 35-62.

Wang, J. and Chan, C.H. (2007), "Stock market trading rule discovery using pattern recognition and technical analysis", Expert Systems with Applications, vol.33, 304–315.

Wang, Y.F. (2002), "Predicting stock price using fuzzy grey prediction system", Expert systems with Applications, vol. 22, 33-39.

In: Computational Techniques in Economics and Finance
Editor: Constantine Zopounidis
ISBN: 978-1-61324-558-3

Chapter 9

A MEMETIC ALGORITHM FOR THE IDENTIFICATION OF FIRMS RECEIVING QUALIFIED AUDIT REPORTS

Magdalene Marinaki[1]*, Yannis Marinakis[2] and Constantin Zopounidis[3]

[1] Industrial Systems Control Laboratory
[2]Decision Support Systems Laboratory
[3]Financial Engineering Laboratory, Department of Production Engineering and Management, Technical University of Crete, University Campus, Chania

ABSTRACT

In this paper, a new procedure for solving the Feature Subset Selection problem is presented. This procedure utilizes a memetic algorithm, which is based on the concepts of Genetic Algorithms (GA) and Particle Swarm Optimization (PSO). Contrary to genetic algorithms, in the proposed algorithm the evolution of each individual of the population is performed using a PSO algorithm. The proposed memetic-based classification algorithm is combined with a number of nearest neighbour based classifiers and is tested in a very significant financial classification task, involving the identification of qualified audit reports. The algorithm is compared with a classic genetic algorithm and other metaheuristic algorithms, like Ant Colony Optimization and Particle Swarm Optimization.

Keywords: Memetic Algorithms, Particle Swarm Optimization, Genetic Algorithms, Feature Selection Problem, Qualifications in Audit Reports.

1. INTRODUCTION

Genetic algorithms are a particularly attractive approach for problems like feature subset selection since they are generally very effective in solving large-scale problems. The first GA

* Corresponding Author - Industrial Systems Control Laboratory, Department of Production Engineering and Management, Technical University of Crete, University Campus, 73100 Chania, E-mail: magda@dssl.tuc.gr

was developed by John H. Holland in the 1960s to allow computers to evolve solutions to difficult search and combinatorial problems, such as function optimization and machine learning (Holland, 1975). Genetic Algorithms (GAs; Goldberg, 1989) are search procedures based on the mechanics of natural selection and natural genetics. They are based on an imitation of the biological process in which new and better populations among different species are developed during evolution. Thus, unlike most standard heuristics, GAs use information of a population of solutions, called individuals, when they search for better solutions. A GA is a stochastic iterative procedure that maintains the population size constant in each iteration, called a generation. Their basic operation is the mating of two solutions in order to form a new solution. To form a new population, a binary operator called crossover, and a unary operator, called mutation, are applied (Reeves, 1995; Reeves, 2003). Crossover takes two individuals, called parents, and produces two new individuals, called offspring, by swapping parts of the parents. Usually in a genetic algorithm each individual of the population is used in discrete phases. Some of the individuals are selected as parents and by using the crossover and mutation operator they produce the offspring which can replace them in the population. But this is not what really happens in real life. Each individual has the possibility to evolve in order to optimize its behaviour as it goes from one phase to the other during its life. The evolution of each individual of the population is realized with the use of a PSO algorithm in the proposed algorithm. Thus, the reason that a memetic algorithm, i.e. a genetic algorithm with a local search phase (Moscato and Cotta, 2003), is used instead of a classic genetic algorithm is that it is very difficult for a pure genetic algorithm to effectively explore the solution space. Thus, a combination of a global search optimization method with a local search optimization method usually improves the performance of the algorithm. In this paper instead of using a local search method to improve each individual separately we use a global search method, like Particle Swarm Optimization algorithm, and thus each individual does not try to improve its solution by itself but it uses knowledge from the solutions of the whole population. In each generation, all the individuals (parents and offspring) are considered as a single swarm and they try to improve their solution (i.e., the offspring to learn from their parents) by following the physical movement of the best particle of the whole swarm. Thus, in this paper, we focus on how each individual can be evolved with the use of the Particle Swarm Optimization (PSO) algorithm. At the end of each phase of the Particle Swarm Optimization the fittest of the whole swarm survive and move to the next phase of the genetic algorithm, i.e. in the selection of the parents phase of the genetic algorithm. The main advantage of the application of a PSO algorithm in the evolutionary part of the algorithm is that, in contrary to others metaheuristics, there are only two variables for each individual of the population that will have to be calculated in each iteration, the position and the velocity.

The proposed memetic algorithm for the feature subset selection problem is combined with a number of nearest neighbour based classifiers in order to solve an auditing task regarding the identification of firms that receive qualified audit reports. It should be noted that the verification of whether the financial statements of a firm represent its actual position is of major importance for auditors, who should provide a qualified report if they conclude that the financial statements fail to meet this requirement.

The rest of the paper is organized as follows: In the next section, a brief review of some feature selection algorithms is presented. In section 3, a detailed description of the proposed algorithm is given. In section 4, the application of the proposed algorithm to the audit qualifications problem is presented. In section 5, the computational results of the proposed method are presented while the last section concludes the paper and proposes some future research directions.

2. Algorithms for the Feature Selection Problem

Selecting the right set of features for classification is one of the most important problems in designing a good classifier. The basic feature selection problem is an optimization problem, with a performance measure for each subset of features to measure its ability to classify the samples. The problem is to search through the space of feature subsets to identify the optimal or near-optimal one with respect to the performance measure.

In the literature, many successful feature selection algorithms have been proposed. These algorithms can be classified into two categories based on whether features are selected independently of the learning algorithm used to construct the classifier. If feature selection depends on learning algorithm, the approach is referred to as a wrapper model. Otherwise, it is said to be a filter model. Filters, such as mutual information criterion (MI), are based on statistical tools. Wrappers assess subsets of features according to their usefulness to a given classifier.

Unfortunately, finding the optimum feature subset has been proved to be NP-hard (Kohavi and John, 1997). Many algorithms are, thus, proposed to find the suboptimal solutions in comparably smaller amount of time (Jain and Zongker, 1997), branch and bound approaches (Narendra and Fukunaga, 1977), sequential forward/backward search (Aha and Bankert, 1996; Cantu-Paz et al., 2004) and filters approaches (Cantu-Paz, 2004) deterministically search for the suboptimal solutions. One of the most important of the filter approaches is the Kira and Rendell's Relief algorithm (Kira and Rendell, 1992). Stochastic algorithms, including simulated annealing (Siedlecki and Sklansky, 1988), scatter search algorithms (Lopez et al., 2006), ant colony optimization (Al-Ani, 2005a; Al-Ani, 2005b; Parpinelli et al., 2002; Shelokar et al., 2004) and genetic algorithms (Cantu-Paz et al., 2004) are of great interest recently because they often yield high accuracy and are much faster.

3. The Proposed Memetic Algorithm

3.1. General Outline

In this paper, an algorithm for the solution of the feature selection problem based on a memetic algorithm is presented. A memetic algorithm is a genetic algorithm with a local search procedure (Moscato and Cotta, 2003). This algorithm is combined with three nearest neighbour based classifiers, the 1-nearest neighbour, k-nearest neighbour and the wk-nearest neighbour classifier. A pseudocode of the proposed algorithm is presented. A more detailed description of the components of the proposed memetic based classification algorithm will be given below.

Initialization
Generate the initial population

Evaluate the fitness of each individual using 1-nearest neighbour or k-nearest neighbour or wk-nearest neighbour
Main Phase
***Do while** stopping criteria are not satisfied*
***Select** individuals from the population to be parents*
***Call** crossover operator to produce offspring*
***Call** mutation operator*
***Evaluate** the fitness of the offspring using 1-nearest neighbour or k-nearest neighbour or wk-nearest neighbour*
***Call** Particle Swarm Optimization for the Evolution phase of the population*
***Replace** the population with the fittest of the whole population*
Enddo
***Return** the best individual (the best solution).*

3.2. Encoding

Each individual in the population represents a candidate solution to the feature subset selection problem. Let m be the total number of features. The individual (chromosome) is represented by a binary vector of dimension m. If a bit is equal to 1, then the corresponding feature is selected (activated); otherwise the feature is not selected. This is the simplest and most straightforward representation scheme.

3.3. Initial Population

The initial population is generated randomly. Thus, in order to explore subsets of different numbers of features, the number of 1's for each individual is generated randomly. Only different individuals are allowed. Thus, in the initial population there are no individuals with the same characteristics. In this way we gain the diversity of the initial population.

3.4. Fitness Function

The fitness function measures the quality of a solution. In this study, we implement the overall classification accuracy (OCA; see below for a complete description). In the fitness function we would like to maximize the OCA.

3.4.1. Nearest Neighbour Classifiers

The nearest neighbour classifiers (Duda and Hart, 1973) are selected as they are methods very easy to be implemented and they do not need any optimization procedure as for example it is necessary in support vector machines and in neural networks. Assume a training sample of M_{train} vectors $\mathbf{y}_j = (y_{j1}, \ldots, y_{jd})$, $j = 1, \ldots, M_{train}$, where d is the number of selected features and y_{jl} is the description of observation j on feature l.

In the 1-nearest neighbour classifier (1-nn), the classification of an unknown observation $\mathbf{x}_i = (x_{i1}, \ldots, x_{id})$ is based on its Euclidean distance D_{ij} from each training observation j, which is defined as follows:

$$D_{ij} = \sqrt{\sum_{l=1}^{d} |x_{il} - y_{jl}|^2} \quad (1)$$

Then $\mathbf{x}_i$ is classified in the class to which its nearest training observation belongs to.

The previous approach may be extended to the k-nearest neighbour (k-nn) method, where the k-nearest training observations are used to classify the test case through majority voting scheme.

The k-nn algorithm can be extended by assigning weights to each of the nearest neighbours. The weights are defined in terms of the closeness of the corresponding training observations to the unknown case $\mathbf{x}_i$. This extension is called the weighted k-nearest neighbour (wk-nn). In particular, assuming that the neighbours are sorted in descending order according to their distance from $\mathbf{x}_i$, the weight of the ith neighbour is defined as:

$$w_i = \frac{i}{\sum_{i=1}^{k} i} \quad (2)$$

Thus, the following hold:

$$w_k \geq w_{k-1} \geq \ldots \geq w_1 > 0 \quad (3)$$

$$w_k + w_{k-1} + \ldots + w_1 = 1 \quad (4)$$

3.4.2. Performance Measure

In a 2-class problem if the actual class of a sample is the 1, the estimated class is denoted by T_1 (True 1) if the sample is classified in its actual class and F_2 (False 2) if the model misclassifies the sample. On the other hand, the estimated class is denoted by T_2 (True 2) when the sample is classified correctly in class 2 and by F_1 (False 1) if the sample is misclassified in the class 1. In Table 1 the definitions are presented.

Table 1. Definitions of the classified and misclassified observations

Estimated Class	Actual Class	
	1	2
1	T_1	F_1
2	F_2	T_2

Thus, the overall classification accuracy (OCA) can be easily obtained as:

$$OCA = \frac{T_1 + T_2}{T_1 + F_2 + T_2 + F_1} 100 \tag{5}$$

where $T_1\% = \frac{T_1}{T_1 + F_2} 100$ is the accuracy for group 1 and $T_2\% = \frac{T_2}{T_2 + F_1} 100$ is the accuracy for group 2. This is the evaluation criterion that is used in this study to evaluate the quality of a model.

3.5. Selection of the Parents

The selection mechanism is responsible for selecting the parent chromosome from the population and forming the mating pool. The selection mechanism emulates the survival of-the-fittest mechanism in nature. It is expected that a fitter chromosome has a higher chance of surviving on the subsequent evolution. In this work, we are using the roulette wheel selection which is one of the most common and easy to implement selection mechanism. Basically, it works as follows: each individual in the population is associated with a sector in a virtual wheel. According to the fitness value of the individual, the sector will have a larger area when the corresponding individual has a better fitness value while a lower fitness value will lead to a smaller sector.

3.6. Crossover Operator

The most classic crossover operator, the 1-point crossover, is used in the crossover phase of the algorithm. In the 1-point crossover, the two parents are separated in two parts in a specific point. Then, the two offspring takes the 1-part from the one parent and the second part of the other parent. Afterwards, for each offspring its fitness function is calculated.

For example:

Parent 1: 1 0 0 1 | 1 0 1 0 1
Parent 2: 1 1 1 1 | 0 0 0 0 0

The two parents are separated between the fourth and the fifth feature and the two produced offsprings are the following:

Offspring 1: 1 0 0 1 0 0 0 0 0
Offspring 2: 1 1 1 1 1 0 1 0 1

3.7. Mutation Operator

In a specific percentage of the offspring (25% in our case) a mutation phase is applied. Mutation operates on a single string and generally changes a bit at random. Afterwards, for each offspring its fitness function is calculated.

For example:

Before mutation: 1 1 1 **1** 1 0 1 0 1
After mutation: 1 1 1 **0** 1 0 1 0 1

3.8 Evolution of the Population – Particle Swarm Optimization

In the evolution phase of the population, a PSO algorithm is used. PSO is a population-based swarm intelligence algorithm. It was originally proposed by Kennedy and Eberhart (1995) as a simulation of the social behaviour of social organisms such as bird flocking and fish schooling. PSO uses the physical movements of the individuals in the swarm and has a flexible and well-balanced mechanism to enhance and adapt to the global and local exploration abilities. The swarm of particles in PSO is, usually initialized at random but here the individuals of the population take the place of the particles in the swarm. The basic PSO algorithm and its variants have successfully operated for continuous optimization functions. In each iteration, the swarm is updated by the following equations (Kennedy and Eberhart, 1997) applied for the discrete binary version of PSO:

$$\upsilon_{id}(t+1) = w\upsilon_{id}(t) + c_1\, rand1\, (p_{id} - s_{id}(t)) + c_2\, rand2\, (p_{gd} - s_{id}(t)) \tag{6}$$

$$sig(\upsilon_{id}) = \frac{1}{1+\exp(-\upsilon_{id})} \tag{7}$$

$$s_{id}(t+1) = \begin{cases} 1, & \text{if } rand3 < sig(\upsilon_{id}) \\ 0, & \text{if } rand3 \geq sig(\upsilon_{id}) \end{cases} \tag{8}$$

where $s_{id} \in \{0, 1\}$ is the current solution; υ_{id} is the corresponding velocity; p_{id} is the best position encountered by ith particle so far; p_{gd} represents the best position found by any member in the whole swarm population; t is iteration counter; *rand1*, *rand2* and *rand*3 are three uniform random numbers in [0, 1]; c_1 and c_2 are acceleration coefficients.

The acceleration coefficients control how far a particle will move in a single iteration. Low values allow particles to roam far from target regions before being tugged back, while high values result in abrupt movement towards, or past, target regions. Typically, these are both set to a value of 2.0, although assigning different values to c_1 and c_2 sometimes leads to improved performance.

As in the basic PSO algorithm, a parameter V_{max} is introduced to limit υ_{id} so that $sig(\upsilon_{id})$ does not approach too closely 0 or 1 (Kennedy et al., 2001). Such implementation can ensure that the bit can transfer between 1 and 0 with a positive probability. In practice, V_{max} is often set at ±4. The proposed algorithm is established based on the standard PSO algorithm, namely basic PSO with inertia weight developed by Shi and Eberhart (1998). The inertia weight w controls the impact of previous histories of velocities on current velocity, which is often used as a parameter to control the trade-off between exploration and exploitation. The particle adjusts its trajectory based on information about its previous best performance and the best performance of its neighbours. The inertia weight is also used to control the convergence behaviour of the PSO algorithm. In order to reduce this weight over the iterations, allowing the algorithm to exploit some specific areas, the inertia weight w is updated according to the following equation:

$$w = w_{\max} - \frac{w_{\max} - w_{\min}}{iter_{\max}} \times t \tag{9}$$

where w_{max}, w_{min} are the maximum and minimum values that the inertia weight can take and $iter_{max}$ is the maximum number of iterations (generations).

3.9. Next Generation – Survival of the Fittest

In the next generation, the fittest from the whole population survives. With the term whole population we mean the initial population and the offspring from mutation, crossover and evolution phases. Thus, the population is sorted based on the fitness function of the individuals and in the next generation the fittest individuals survived. It must be mentioned that the size of the population of each generation is equal to the initial size of the population.

3.10. Stopping Criteria

There are two stopping criteria for the memetic algorithm. The one is the maximum number of generations, which is a variable of the problem, and the other is the convergence (whenever the solutions of the genetic algorithm converge to one solution the genetic algorithm stops).

4 Application

4.1. Data

The proposed algorithm is applied to a financial classification problem. The financial problem studied is an auditing task regarding the identification of firms that receive qualified audit reports. The verification of whether the financial statements of a firm represent its actual position is of major importance for auditors, who should provide a qualified report if they conclude that the financial statements fail to meet this requirement. The sample is taken from Doumpos et al. (2005); it consists of 1754 large UK firms over the period 1998–2003, which correspond to 6048 firm-year observations, from which 859 received a qualified audit report.

Previous studies have used various financial variables (features) to formulate audit opinion expectations (Doumpos, et al., 2005). The use of financial variables is justified by the fact that auditors express their opinion based on the examination of the financial statements. Therefore, we consider an initial set of 14 financial variables covering all aspects of firms' performance, such as liquidity, leverage, profitability, managerial activity and annual changes in basic accounts (Table 2 presents a list of the initial set of financial variables along with their definitions). In addition to the financial variables, one more attribute is used, which indicates the overall financial strength of the firms. The use of such a variable is justified on the basis of previous studies indicating that firms with a high probability of default are more likely to receive qualified reports because their ability to continue is in greater doubt. Thus, a five-group rating (secure, stable, normal, unstable/caution and high-risk, Doumpos and Pasiouras, 2005) is used as a proxy of the performance of the firms and their likelihood of failure. The credit risk variable is modelled using three levels: high, caution, and at least normal (e.g. normal, stable or secure). To introduce this variable in the analysis, two dummy 0–1 variables are used. The first dummy variable (caution rating) indicates whether a firm belongs in the caution risk group (caution rating 1) or not (caution rating 0), whereas the second (at least normal rating) indicates whether a firm belongs in one of the normal, stable and secure groups (at least normal rating 1) or not (at least normal rating 0). A high-risk firm is represented by zero values in both these dummy variables.

4.2. Parameters of the Proposed Algorithm

The algorithm was implemented in Fortran 90 (Lahey f95 compiler) on a Centrino Mobile Intel Pentium M750/1.86GHz, running Suse Linux 9.1. To test the efficiency of the proposed methods a 10-fold cross validation procedure is utilized. Initially, the data set is divided in 10 disjoint parts containing approximately *M*/10 observations each, where *M* is the total number of sample observations. Next, each of these parts is systematically removed from the data set, a model is built from the remaining parts (the training set) and, then, the accuracy of the model is calculated using the excluded parts (the test set).

Table 2. Financial features for the audit task

Feature number	Financial Ratio	Feature number	Financial Ratio
1	Current ratio	9	Fixed assets turnover
2	Quick ratio	10	Fixed assets change
3	Solvency ratio	11	Current assets change
4	Return on total assets	12	Current liabilities change
5	EBIT margin	13	Stock change
6	Stock turnover	14	Turnover change
7	Debtors' ratio	15	Caution rating variable
8	Creditors' ratio	16	At least normal rating variable

As it has already been mentioned, three approaches that use different classifiers, the 1-nn, k-nn and the wk-nn, are used. In the memetic-based classification algorithm the value of k is changed dynamically depending on the number of iterations. Each generation uses different k. The reason why k does not have a constant value is that we would like to ensure the diversity of the population in each iteration of the memetic algorithm, respectively. The determination of k is done by using a random number generator with a uniform distribution (0,1) in each iteration. Then, the produced number is converted to an integer k (e.g., if the produced number is in the interval 0.2 - 0.3, then k = 3. If k is an even number then the random generator is called again until an odd number of k is found). The value of k was selected between 1 and 10 as this selection led to better results.

The parameter settings for the proposed memetic-based classification algorithm is:

1. The population size is equal to 1000.
2. The number of generations of the memetic algorithm is set equal to 50.
3. The probability of crossover is set equal to 0.8.
4. The probability of mutation is set equal to 0.25.
5. The number of swarms is set equal to 1.
6. The number of particles is set equal to the number of individuals.
7. The number of generations of PSO is set equal to 50.
8. The coefficients of PSO are $c_1 = 2$, $c_2 = 2$, $w_{max} = 0.9$ and $w_{min} = 0.01$.

For comparison purposes, four other metaheuristic algorithms were used, namely tabu search (Glover, 1989; Glover, 1990), a genetic algorithm (Goldberg, 1989), ant colony optimization (Dorigo and Stützle, 2004) and particle swarm optimization (Kennedy and Eberhart, 1995). These methods use in the classification phase the 1-nn, the k-nn and the wk-nn classifiers. In the genetic, ACO and PSO based metaheuristics with the k-nn and w-knn classifier the value of k is changed dynamically depending on the number of iteration. The parameter settings for the genetic based metaheuristic (namely, the population size, the number of generations, the probability of crossover, and the probability of mutation) and the PSO based metaheuristic (namely, the number of swarms, the number of particles, the number of generations and the coefficients c_1, c_2, w_{max} and w_{min}) are the same as those used in the proposed algorithm. The maximum number of iterations for the tabu based metaheuristic is equal to 1000 and the size of the tabu list is equal to 10. For the Tabu metaheuristic the value of k was selected equal to 5 after thorough testing. The parameter settings for the ACO based metaheuristic are:

1. The number of ants used is set equal to the number of features (16).
2. The number of iterations that each ant constructs a different solution, based on the pheromone trails, is set equal to 50.

4.4. Results

The selection of a set of appropriate input feature variables is an important issue in building a good classifier. Because of the curse of dimensionality, it is often necessary and beneficial to limit the number of input features in a classifier in order to have a good predictive and less computationally intensive model. In the classification problem analysed in this paper, there are 2^{16}-1 possible feature combinations. As the main task when solving the feature subset selection problem is to find the smallest set of features that can result in satisfactory predictive performance, the objective of the computational experiments is to show the performance of the proposed algorithm in searching for a reduced set of features with high accuracy.

In Table 3, the optimal solution of each of the algorithms the average number of features that each algorithm selects and the accuracies of each algorithm are presented. The best results are denoted in bold. As it can be seen from this Table, the proposed algorithm performs better in terms of overall classification accuracy compared to the other methods. Memetic 1-nn provides the best results on the evaluation criteria followed by Memetic k-nn. In terms of the number of features used in the final model, Memetic wk-nn gives the better results (compared to Memetic 1-nn and Memetic k-nn). It should be noted, however, that concerning the average number of features, the Tabu w5-nn algorithm gives the best results with an average of 8.3 features. It should, also, be noted that the results of the memetic based classification algorithm are much better in terms of overall classification accuracy than those obtained when the simple genetic based classification algorithm.

In Table 4, the frequency that each feature is selected (the % percentage in the parenthesis) in the optimal solutions of all algorithms are presented. As it can be seen, the two variables involving the credit rating level are the most important features, followed by the creditors' ratio and the fixed assets turnover (both features have been selected 103 times, *i.e.* in 68.66% in all solutions).

Table 3. Classification results

Methods	Overall classification accuracy (%)	Average No. of features
Memetic 1-nn	*90.31*	10
Memetic k-nn	90.26	10.3
Memetic wk-nn	90.14	9.6
ACO 1-nn	89.02	9.1
ACO k-nn	88.90	10.4
ACO wk-nn	88.98	10.8
PSO 1-nn	89.02	9.1
PSO k-nn	89.81	9.7
PSO wk-nn	89.03	8.9
Gen 1-nn	88.90	9
Gen k-nn	88.78	9.9
Gen wk-nn	88.73	9.4
Tabu 1-nn	88.70	9.8
Tabu 5-nn	88.64	9.7
Tabu w5-nn	88.14	*8.3*

Table 4. Selection frequencies of the features

Features	Frequency		Features	Frequency	
1	73	(48.66)	9	**103**	**(68.66)**
2	85	(56.66)	10	89	(59.33)
3	91	(60.66)	11	90	(60.00)
4	62	(41.33)	12	91	(60.66)
5	65	(43.33)	13	99	(66.00)
6	74	(49.33)	14	82	(54.66)
7	66	(44.00)	15	**132**	**(88.00)**
8	**103**	**(68.66)**	16	**135**	**(90.00)**

CONCLUSIONS AND FUTURE WORK

A memetic-based classification algorithm is proposed in this paper. The feature subset selection problem is used by a memetic algorithm while three different classifiers are used for the classification problem, based on the nearest neighbour classification rule. The performance of the proposed algorithm is tested in the auditing task regarding the identification of firms that receive qualified audit reports.

The obtained results indicate the high performance of the proposed algorithm. Also, a reduced set of features (around 60% of all features) was selected in the final model by the proposed algorithm. Future research is intended to be focused on the use of different machine learning classifiers (SVM, neural networks, etc.).

REFERENCES

Aha, D.W. and Bankert, R.L. (1996), "A comparative evaluation of sequential feature selection algorithms", in D. Fisher, J.-H. Lenx (eds.), Artificial Intelligence and Statistics, Springer-Verlag, New York.

Al-Ani, A. (2005a), "Feature subset selection using ant colony optimization", International Journal of Computational Intelligence, 2(1), 53-58.

Al-Ani, A. (2005b), "Ant colony optimization for feature subset selection", Transactions on Engineering, Computing and Technology, 4, 35-38.

Cantu-Paz, E. (2004), "Feature subset selection, class separability, and genetic algorithms", Genetic and Evolutionary Computation Conference, 959-970.

Cantu-Paz, E., Newsam, S. and Kamath, C. (2004), "Feature selection in scientific application", in: Proceedings of the 2004 ACM SIGKDD International Conference on Knowledge Discovery and Data Mining, 788-793.

Dorigo, M. and Stützle, T. (2004), Ant Colony Optimization, A Bradford Book, The MIT Press, Cambridge, Massachusetts, London, England.

Doumpos, M. and Pasiouras, F. (2005), "Developing and testing models for replicating credit ratings: A multicriteria approach", Computational Economics, 25, 327-341.

Doumpos M, Gaganis C and Pasiouras F (2005). Explaining qualifications in audit reports using a support vector machine methodology. *Intelligent Systems in Accounting, Finance and Management* 13: 197-215.

Duda, R.O. and Hart, P.E. (1973), Pattern Classification and Scene Analysis, John Wiley and Sons, New York.

Glover, F. (1989), "Tabu Search I", ORSA Journal on Computing, 1(3), 190-206.

Glover, F. (1990), "Tabu Search II", ORSA Journal on Computing, 2(1), 4-32.

Goldberg, D.E. (1989), Genetic Algorithms in Search, Optimization, and Machine Learning, Addison-Wesley Publishing Company, INC, Massachussets.

Holland, J.H. (1975), Adaptation in Natural and Artificial Systems, University of Michigan Press, Ann Arbor, MI.

Jain, A. and Zongker, D. (1997), "Feature selection: Evaluation, application, and small sample performance", IEEE Transactions on Pattern Analysis and Machine Intelligence, 19, 153-158.

Kennedy, J. and Eberhart, R. (1995), "Particle swarm optimization", in: Proceedings of 1995 IEEE International Conference on Neural Networks, 4, 1942-1948.

Kennedy, J. and Eberhart, R. (1997), "A discrete binary version of the particle swarm algorithm", in: Proceedings of 1997 IEEE International Conference on Systems, Man, and Cybernetics, 5, 4104-4108.

Kennedy, J., Eberhart, R. and Shi, Y. (2001), Swarm Intelligence, Morgan Kaufmann Publisher, San Francisco.

Kira, K. and Rendell, L. (1992), "A practical approach to feature selection", in: Proceedings of the Ninth International Conference on Machine Learning, Aberdeen, Scotland, 249-256.

Kohavi, R. and John, G. (1997), "Wrappers for feature subset selection", Artificial Intelligence, 97, 273-324.

Lopez, F.G., Torres, M.G., Batista, B.M., Perez, J.A.M. and Moreno-Vega, J.M. (2006), "Solving feature subset selection problem by a parallel scatter search", European Journal of Operational Research, 169, 477-489.

Moscato, P. and Cotta, C. (2003), "A Gentle Introduction to Memetic Algorithms", in: Handbooks of Metaheuristics, F., Glover, and G.A., Kochenberger (Eds.), Kluwer Academic Publishers, Dordrecht, 105-144.

Narendra, P.M. and Fukunaga, K. (1977), "A branch and bound algorithm for feature subset selection", IEEE Transactions on Computers, 26(9), 917-922.

Parpinelli, R.S., Lopes, H.S. and Freitas, A.A. (2002), "An ant colony algorithm for classification rule discovery", in: H. Abbas, R. Sarker, C. Newton (eds.), Data mining: A heuristic approach, London, UK: Idea group publishing, 191–208.

Reeves, C.R. (1995), Genetic Algorithms, in: C.R. Reeves, (ed.), Modern Heuristic Techniques for Combinatorial Problems, McGraw - Hill, London, 151-196.

Reeves, C.R. (2003), Genetic Algorithms, in: F. Glover, G.A. Kochenberger (eds.), Handbooks of Metaheuristics, Kluwer Academic Publishers, Dordrecht, 55-82.

Siedlecki, W. and Sklansky, J. (1988), "On automatic feature selection", International Journal of Pattern Recognition and Artificial Intelligence, 2(2), 197-220.

Shelokar, P.S., Jayaraman, V.K. and Kulkarni, B.D. (2004), "An ant colony classifier system: application to some process engineering problems", Computers and Chemical Engineering, 28, 1577-1584.

Shi, Y. and Eberhart, R. (1998), "A modified particle swarm optimizer", in: Proceedings of 1998 IEEE World Congress on Computational Intelligence, 69-73.

In: Computational Techniques in Economics and Finance
Editor: Constantine Zopounidis
ISBN: 978-1-61324-558-3

Chapter 10

REAL OPTIONS USING MARKOV CHAINS: AN APPLICATION TO PRODUCTION CAPACITY DECISIONS*

***Dalila B. M. M. Fontes*[1,♣], *Luıs Camões*[2], *Fernando A. C. C. Fontes*[3] *and Panos M. Pardalos*[4]**

[1]LIAAD-INESC Porto L.A.,
Faculdade de Economia da Universidade do Porto, Porto, Portugal
[2]Banif – Banco Internacional do Funchal, Porto, Portugal
[3]Departamento de Matemática para a Ciência e Tecnologia,
Universidade do Minho, Guimarães, Portugal
[4]Department of Industrial and Systems Engineering,
University of Florida, Florida, US

ABSTRACT

In this work we address investment decisions using real options. A standard numerical approach for valuing real options is dynamic programming. The basic idea is to establish a discrete-valued lattice of possible future values of the underlying stochastic variable (demand in our case). For most approaches in the literature, the stochastic variable is assumed normally distributed and then approximated by a binomial distribution, resulting in a binomial lattice. In this work, we investigate the use of a sparse Markov chain to model such variable. The Markov approach is expected to perform better since it does not assume any type of distribution for the demand variation, the probability of a variation on the demand value is dependent on the current demand value and thus, no longer constant and it generalizes the binomial lattice since the latter can be modelled as a Markov chain. We developed a stochastic dynamic programming model that has been implemented both on binomial and Markov models. A numerical example

* Research is partially supported by NSF and AirForce grants and by FCT/POCI 2010/FEDER through project POCTI/MAT/61842/2004.

♣ Corresponding author: Dalila B. M. M. Fontes – LIAAD-INESC Porto L.A., Faculdade de Economia da Universidade do Porto Rua Dr. Roberto Frias, 4200-464 Porto, Portugal. Email: fontes@fep.up.pt.

of a production capacity choice problem has been solved and the results obtained show that the investment decisions are different and, as expected the Markov chain approach leads to a better investment policy.

Keywords: Flexible Capacity Investments, Real Options, Markov Chains, Dynamic Programming.

INTRODUCTION

Manufacturing flexibility has become a very important competitive aspect for production oriented companies. Many researchers, e.g. (Fine & Hax 1985) also rank manufacturing flexibility as a competitive priority together with e.g. cost and quality. Several types of flexibility can be evaluated. Here, we are concerned with the sometimes called "volume" flexibility, which can be defined as the ability to operate with profit at different output levels. A possible way of measuring flexibility is to estimate its value, which can be compared with the cost of acquiring it. The Net Present Value (NPV) analysis typically assumes that an immediate accept-or-reject decision must be made and thus, it ignores the flexibility to optimally time project initiation. NPV says that an investment should be made whenever the expected discounted future cash-flows match investment costs. Real Options (RO) on the other hand, require that expected discounted future cash-flows to be significantly above the investment costs. This happens, since making the investment implies the loss of the waiting option and hence, it represents an opportunity cost (Zopounidis, Doumpos & Pardalos 2008, Dalakouras, Kwon & Pardalos 2008).

The term "real options" was coined by Stewart Myers in 1977. It referred to the application of option pricing theory to the valuation of non-financial or "real" investments with learning and flexibility, such as multi-stage R&D, manufacturing plant expansion, and the like (Myers1977). This type of approach is based on three factors, namely: the existence of uncertainty about the project rewards, i.e. future cash-flows; the investment irreversibility, at least partially, i.e. money cannot be fully recovered once an investment decision has been done; and the investment timing, for which there is some flexibility that allows for the arrival of new information. A large and rapidly growing literature on investment under uncertainty interprets the firm as consisting either wholly or in part of a portfolio of options, and uses options-based models and option pricing techniques to study the investment decision. This approach also recognizes the sequential nature of investment decisions as a key feature. The options studied include the option to temporarily shut down (McDonald & Siegel 1985, Brennan & Schwartz 1985), the option to continue or discontinue a planned series of investments (Majd & Pindyck 1987), the option to defer investment (McDonald & Siegel 1986), the option to abandon project earlier (Myers & Majd 1990), the option to increment capacity (Bollen 1999, Pindyck 1988, Kandel & Pearson 2002), amongst others.

Managerial flexibility has been valued by option pricing for almost two decades and during this time different kinds of real options have been treated. Kulatilaka (1988) uses a stochastic dynamic programming model to evaluate the options in a flexible production process and incorporates the effects of switching costs. Andreou (1990) evaluates process flexibility in different configurations of dedicated and flexible equipment when demand of two products is uncertain. Triantis & Hodder (1990) evaluate process flexibility, in a given fixed capacity equipment as a complex option. The profit margins of different products are assumed to be stochastic and dependent on quantity produced. The latter effect is a result of allowing for downward sloping demand curves. In their model there are no switching costs. Capacity constraints are considered and the model allows the firm to temporarily shut down and restart operation. He & Pindyck (1992) examine investments in flexible production capacity. Here, the capacity choice problem is considered, i.e. whether to buy flexible or non-flexible equipment and how much capacity with respect to the fact that investment is irreversible. As in (Tannous 1996) demand is uncertain but in this case differs, via a demand shift parameter depending on whether market is perfectly competitive or not. Kamrad & Ernst (1995) model multi-product manufacturing with stochastic input price, output yield uncertainty and capacity constraints to value multi-product production agreements. During one period, only one product type is produced with respect to the inventory available. Tannous (1996) carries out capital budgeting for volume flexible equipment and compares a non-flexible to a flexible system in a case based on a real company. In his model, demand is uncertain and dependent on price and a stochastic factor. The effect of having inventory available is also considered. Bollen (1999) evaluates the option to switch between production capacities. The demand stochastic process is governed by a stochastic product life cycle which is modeled by using a regime switching process. In his study a comparison between flexible and fixed capacity projects is also made.

In this work, we present a model to evaluate investment decisions based on real options. In the problem considered we incorporate partial reversibility into the model by letting the firm reverse its capital investment at a cost, both fully or partially. Therefore, three options are considered: temporarily shutdown, defer investment, and switch between production capacities. The standard RO approach considers the stochastic variable to be normally distributed and then approximated by a binomial distribution, resulting in a binomial lattice. In this work, we propose to model the discrete stochastic variable by means of a sparse Markov chain, which is derived from the demand data previously collected. The main advantages of the proposed approach are: i) the Markov chain does not assume any type of distribution for the stochastic variable, ii) the probability of a variation is not constant, actually it depends on the current value, and iii) it generalizes current literature using binomial distributions since they can be modelled by a Markov chain. Nevertheless, the Markov approach is computationally more demanding. However, the sparsity of the Markov matrix, that naturally results from data streamslike ours, can be exploited to improve the computational performance of the algorithm.

PROBLEM DESCRIPTION AND FORMULATION

Following the approach outlined in Dixit & Pindyck (1994) and Trigeorgis (1996), the opportunity of adopting a specific value of production capacity can be viewed as representing a real option to the firm. This type of investment decisions can be casted as a sequence of embedded decisions since the current capacity decision has implications on future decisions.

Our starting point is the irreversible investment model by Pindyck (1988), which is a flexible and tractable example of the options-based models, and can be readily generalized to allow for partial reversibility. In his model, a monopolist faces a demand function that shifts stochastically, towards and away from the origin, over time as given by

$$Q = \theta - \lambda P, \tag{1}$$

where Q is the industry output and θ models the dynamics of demand. Of course, for the case of monopoly (1) is also the demand curve faced by the firm. (In financial options it is standard to assume that the underlying security is traded in a perfectly competitive market. However, many real asset markets are monopolistic or oligopolistic, rather than perfectly competitive.)

The total variable production costs are assumed to be a quadratic function of quantity produced, which is a standard assumption, see for example (Pindyck 1988, Trigeorgis 1996, Bollen 1999). Thus, the total production costs are

$$C(Q, m) = c_1 Q + \frac{c_2}{2m} Q^2 + c_3 m, \tag{2}$$

where the fixed and variable coefficients of the marginal cost function are c_1 and $c_2/(2m)Q$, m is the installed production capacity, and the fixed component c_3m represents the overhead costs.

The operating profit of period t, given the demand and production capacity installed, is then computed as

$$\pi\left(\theta_t, m_{t-1}\right) P(Q_t) - C(Q_t, m_{t-1}) = \left(\frac{\theta_t}{\lambda} - c_1\right) Q_t - \left(\frac{1}{\lambda} + \frac{c_2}{2m_{t-1}}\right) Q_t^2 - c_3 m_{t-1}. \tag{3}$$

(It should be noticed that we are assuming that the capacity in place at period t is the capacity chosen in the previous period. This is not a limitation since the reasoning and formulae given can be applied with any number of installation periods.)

The firm maximizes operating profit over produced quantity and hence,the optimum quantity Q^*, which is obtained by solving $\partial\pi/\partial Q=0$, is given by

$$Q^*(\theta_t) = \frac{\theta_t - \lambda c_1}{2 + \lambda c_2/m_{t-1}}. \tag{4}$$

Furthermore, the quantity to be produce in each period Q_t is bounded from above by the production capacity and from below by zero, thus it is given as

$$Q^{**}(\theta_t) = max\left(0, min\left(Q^*(\theta_t), m_{t-1}\right)\right) \tag{5}$$

and therefore, the optimal operating profit is

$$\pi^*(\theta_t, m_{t-1}) = P(Q^{**}(\theta_t)) - C(Q^{**}(\theta_t), m_{t-1}) \tag{6}$$

We also consider partial reversibility,which is incorporated into the model by letting the firm reverse its capital investment at a cost. The ability to partially reverse the capital investment is modeled through capacity sell out, which allows for recovering a fraction of the purchase price for each unit sold. More specifically, following the work by Bollen (1999), we use $S(m_1,m_2)$ to represent additional investment or recovered investment associated with changing capacity level from m_1 to m_2:

$$\begin{aligned} S(m_1, m_2) &= s_1 c_4 (m_2 - m_1) + s_3, & \text{if } m_2 > m_1, \\ S(m_1, m_2) &= s_2 c_4 (m_1 - m_2) + s_3, & \text{otherwise.} \end{aligned} \tag{7}$$

where s_1 and s_2 are percentages of the initial capacity cost c_4 and s_3 is a fixed switching capacity cost. Here the switching costs, equation (7), are given by a fixed-charge cost function; however they may have any other form, i.e. piecewise concave in order to incorporate economies of scale. It should be noticed, that although in the example solved in this work we set $s_1 = 1$ and $0 < s_2 < 1$, they could assume any positive or negative value. Moreover, the switching costs could also be time dependent.

Solution Methodology

To solve the problem it is necessary to find the optimal sequence of capacity choices, namely: invest in additional capacity, sell out excessive capacity, keep exactly the same capacity; and the optimal production in each period given the capacity decision previously made. These two types of decisions must be addressed simultaneously since the existence of switching costs implies that a capacity decision made in a period alters future switching costs and future profits and thus, future switching decisions. Therefore, the project value must be determined simultaneously with the optimal production capacity policy.

The standard RO approach is to consider a continuous stochastic variable and then discretize it through the use of a binomial lattice as explained in Section 3.1. Here, we propose a Markov chain approach that makes use of the discrete data, available for the stochastic variable, to set up a sparse one-step transition probabilities matrix. This is further explained in Section 3.2.

The solution approach we used is to set up a discrete-valued lattice or grid for which a dynamic programming model is derived and then solved by backward induction.

3.1. The Binomial Lattice

A standard assumption in the real options literature is that the underlying stochastic variable is governed by a geometric diffusion, which implies that at each period there is only one constant growth/decay rate. If this is assumed then a natural way of obtaining a valued-lattice for the stochastic variable is to discretized it through a standard binomial lattice, see Figure 1.

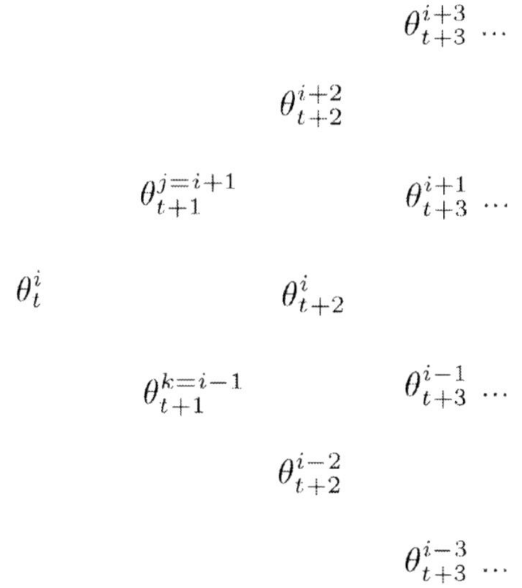

Figure 1. A lattice discretizing selling price.

A node of value θ_t^i can lead to two nodes with their values being given by $\theta_{t+1}^j = u\theta_t^i$ and $\theta_{t+1}^k = d\theta_t^i$ with probability q_u and $q_d = 1 - q_u$, respectively. The probability of reaching each of these nodes is the usual equivalent martingale measure used in the binomial option pricing model of Cox, Ross & Rubinstein (1979):

$$q_u = \frac{(1 + r_f) - d}{u - d} \quad \text{and} \quad q_d = 1 - q_u, \tag{8}$$

where r_f is the risk free rate over the interval Δt, $u = \exp(\sigma\sqrt{\Delta t})$, and $d = \exp(\sigma\sqrt{\Delta t})$.

3.2. The Markov Grid

If the stochastic variable under consideration is the demand, it seems unrealistic to assume it to be governed by a geometric diffusion, since this implies that at each period demand grows/decays at a constant rate. The implication of the constant rate of growth assumption are twofold.

On one hand, it undervalues the option to contract or abandon project, since it underestimates the probability of low demand in future. On the other hand, it overvalues the option to expand capacity as demand is able to increase forever.

We propose the use of a Markov chain. This way, not only we allow for demand variations dependent on demand current value, but we also allow for probability values dependent on demand current value. Moreover, the grid obtained by a Markov chain, generalizes the binomial lattice approach since it can be used to model a binomial lattice. We obtain the Markov chain from the data previously collected.

A Markov chain is defined by a one step transition probability matrix. The levels of demand can be easily described by a square grid of all possible states i =1,2,...,n, see Figure 2, where the planning horizon is discretized in Δt intervals and the state variable in Δθ.

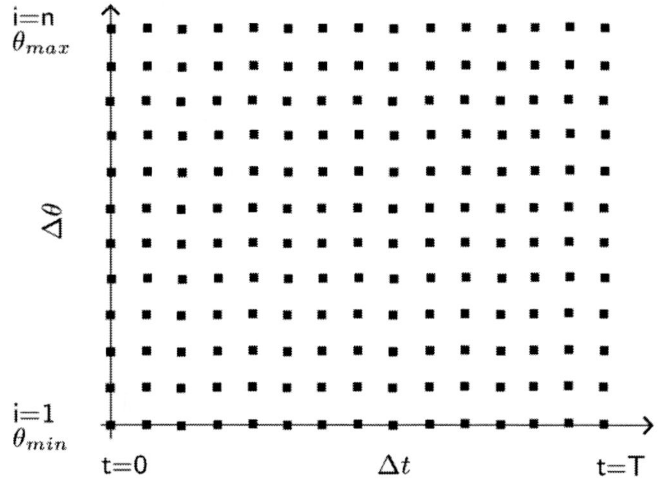

Figure 2. A grid for the Markov discretization of demand.

The Markov matrix of transition probabilities can be obtained from the data as follows. The probability of reaching state j in some period of time being in state i in the previous time period is given by the ratio between the number of transitions from demand value θ_i to demand value θ_j in consecutive periods and the total number of transitions out of demand value θ_i to all other possible demand values in consecutive periods, which can be written as

$$Prob(\theta_i, \theta_j) = \frac{\sum_{t=1}^{T}\left(\theta_i^{t-1}, \theta_j^t\right)}{\sum_{t=1}^{T}\sum_{k=1}^{n}\left(\theta_i^{t-1}, \theta_k^t\right)} \tag{9}$$

where $(\theta_i^{t-1}, \theta_j^t)$ denotes a transition from state i in period t-1 to state j in period t. Note that these probabilities are time invariant.

3.3. The Decision Process

Recall that, we have defined to have three options, namely temporarily shutdown, defer investment, and switching capacity. The temporarily shut down option is a reversible option that is only taken if we are better off not producing, which in our problem is done implicitly. Such a decision is reached whenever the optimal quantity to be produced is determined to be zero. The defer investment option corresponds to a capacity switch to the same value and thus, it can be simultaneously addressed with the capacity switching option. This way, we only have to explicitly address the capacity switching option. In each period the firm must make two decisions,one regarding the quantity to be produce Q_t and another regarding the production capacity m_t that is to be in place for the following period. The decision on the quantity to be produced is given by maximizing the operating profit and hence, the optimal quantity $Q^{**}{}_t$ to be produced in period t is given as in equation (5). The decision about the production capacity is related to the profit of the future periods since the chosen capacity will be available from the next period. Recall that an increase in installed capacity requires an investment, while a sell out of capacity leads to a partial recover of investment, as given in equation (7). Therefore, at each period the project value is dependent on the level of demand and production capacity and is obtained by maximizing the sum of the optimal current period's profit with the optimal continuation value for each possible capacity. The latter value is given by the discounted expected future profits net of switching costs.

Before proceeding let us review the notation:

- $\pi^*(\theta_t, m_{t-1})$ represents the optimal operating profit in state (demand value) θ_t when the installed production capacity is m_{t-1}. Recall that π^* is computed as in equation (6).
- $f(\theta_t, m_{t-1}, t)$ represents the optimal value of the project in state θ_t when the installed production capacity m_{t-1}, assuming optimal future switching decisions.
- m_t represents the optimal production capacity value to be installed and working in period t +1 given that in period t state θ_t is entered with production capacity m_{t-1}.
- E[] is the expectation operator.
- $S(m_1, m_2)$ represents the cost to be paid for to switch production capacity from m_1 to m_2.

The optimal project value at period t given the demand θ_t and available production capacity m_{t-1} is then given by

$$f(\theta_t, m_{t-1}, t) = \pi^*(\theta_t, m_{t-1}) + \max_{m_t} \left\{ \frac{E\left[f(\theta_{t+1}, m_t, t+1)\right]}{1+r_f} + S(m_{t-1}, m_t) \right\}. \quad (10)$$

As said before, and in order to allow for earlier exercise, the valuation procedure begins in the last stage and works backwards to initial time. In the final period t = T, for each demand value and capacity available, the project value is given by the final operating profit plus the capacity salvage value

$$f(\theta_T, m_{T-1}, T) = \pi^*(\theta_T, m_{T-1}) + S(m_{T-1}, 0). \quad (11)$$

The implementation of the Dynamic Programming recursion,given by equation (10), on a standard binomial lattice computes expected value of future profits as

$$E\left[f(\theta_t, m_{t-1}, t)\right] = q_u f(u\theta_t, m_t, t+1) + q_d f(d\theta_t, m_t, t+1), \quad (12)$$

where q_u, q_d, u, and d are as explained in Section 3.1, while the implementation on a Markov grid is computed as

$$E\left[f\left(\theta_t, m_{t-1}, t\right)\right] = \sum_{i=1}^{n} P_{\theta_t,\theta_i} f\left(\theta_i, m_t, t+1\right), \tag{13}$$

where P_{θ_i,θ_j} is the transition probability from demand value θ_i to demand value θ_j in consecutive periods.

RESULTS

In order to test our methodology we have implemented, in MATLAB, the dynamic programming model on the binomial lattice and on the Markov grid, both derived from the collected data. These models differ only in the way of taking the expectation of future profits. The binomial lattice model takes the expectation by considering that from each node only two nodes can be reached in the following period, as given in equation (12), while the Markov model considers that regardless the current node, i.e. demand value, all possible demand values can be reached in the following period, as given in equation (13). As we have considered the initial production capacity also to be decided we have to solve

$$Project\ Value = \max_{m_0} \left\{f\left(\theta_1, m_0, 1\right)\right\} / \left(1 + r_f\right) - c_4 m_0 \tag{14}$$

using the dynamic programming recursion given in equation (10) and the terminal conditions of equation(11).

Both the Binomial and Markov models have been used to find out an optimal capacity investment policy, which we call apriori solution. The quality of these models is then tested by evaluating the policy performance on specific data realization sets, which we call a posteriori solution.

We have collected monthly sales data for a 48 months period, given in the Appendix. The first 24 months of data are used to set up both the Binomial and the Markov models. These models are then used to obtain the optimal capacity policy and the predicted project value.

It follows the description of the specific problem solved. The values for the parameters associated with selling price, production and switching costs, and production capacity have been taken from Bollen (1999). The demand data collected has been scaled in order to be of the same magnitude of demand values used in (Bollen1999). The initial demand was set to the average demand over the first 24 months period.

Production costs: $c_1 = 0.1$, $c_2 = 0.5$, and $c_3 = 0.1$.
Capacity and capacity switching costs: $c_4 = 2$, $s_1 = -1$, $s_2 = 0.85$, and $s_3 = 0.05$.
Production capacity values: ranging from 0 up to 2.5 with capacity step values varying between 0.05 and 0.5.
Price parameter: $\lambda = 1$.

Annual risk free rate. rf =10%.

The binomial lattice parameters have been computed by using the first 24 months of data, as given in Section 3.1: u =1.695, d =1/u, q_u =0.378, and q_d =1/qu. The Markov grid was computed as in equation (9) also by using the first 24 months of data, see Appendix.

Several tests have been performed in order to compare the results obtained by each methodology. For these tests we have used both the collected data and randomly generated data.

4.1. Comparing the Accuracy of the Models

To evaluate project value accuracy, we compare the predicted project value (or model value) to the value obtained by applying the policy found to the data used to derive the model (months 1 to 24), see Table 1. For each possible value of capacity changing step, we report the model value, i.e. the predicted project value which is computed as given in equation (14), and the corresponding initial capacity. We also give the data value, which is the value obtained by applying the optimal capacity changing policy to the data set used to set up the model.

From the results reported it can be concluded that the strategies proposed by the two models are different since the initial capacity values are different. As expected, the better values for the predicted project value are obtained for smaller capacity steps, in both models. Furthermore, the predicted project value is larger for the Binomial model, which although might seem to be an advantage is actually a drawback since in both cases the project value tends to be an overestimation. This can be observed in the columns giving the model to data project value ratio, where we have computed the ratio between the predicted project value and the project value obtained by applying the optimal capacity policy to the data which was used to set up the model. The project value obtained for the first 24 months period data, is better if the capacity changing policy used is the one provided by the Markov model. The Markov model provides values between 37% and 40% better than the Binomial model, as can be seen in the Mark/Bin Ratio column.

Table 1. Predicted project value for binomial and Markov models (months1-24)

	Binomial Lattice				Markov Grid				Data
Cap. Step	Model Value	Init. Cap.	Data Value	Mod/Data Ratio (%)	Model Value	Init. Cap.	Data Value	Mod/Data Ratio (%)	Mark/Bin Ratio (%)
0.5	7.91	0.5	4.80	165.03	5.63	1.0	5.28	106.63	140.48
0.4	7.93	0.8	5.13	154.93	5.78	0.8	5.45	106.11	137.12
0.3	7.94	0.6	5.10	155.94	5.74	0.6	5.44	105.67	138.16
0.2	7.94	0.6	4.97	160.16	5.78	0.8	5.45	106.11	137.30
0.1	7.94	0.7	5.13	155.20	5.79	0.7	5.47	105.87	137.12
0.05	7.95	0.65	4.90	162.58	5.79	0.75	5.47	106.00	137.15

4.2. Comparing the Performance of the Models on Real Data

To test the efficiency of the models we used the capacity policies of each model on 7 different sets of data as given in Tables 2 and 3. Data sets 1 and 2 correspond to, respectively, the first and the last 24 months of the collected data. The remaining data sets were randomly generated between the minimum and maximum values of the data collected having demand averages of 1.4, 1.5, 1.6, 1.7, and 1.8.

Table 2. Project values for specific data realizations using the Binomial model policy

	Binomial - Project Value						
Step	Set 1	Set 2	Set 3	Set 4	Set 5	Set 6	Set 7
0.5	4.804	6.729	5.573	5.835	7.357	7.852	9.078
0.4	5.130	7.304	6.075	6.168	8.296	8.600	10.353
0.3	5.101	7.075	5.895	6.011	7.881	8.416	9.744
0.2	4.969	7.075	5.895	6.011	7.881	8.416	9.744
0.1	5.131	7.246	6.052	6.147	8.182	8.734	10.153
0.05	4.900	7.178	5.992	6.097	8.058	8.602	9.978

As it can be seen, the real project values are higher when the Markov policies are used. Onlyin1 outof the42 values computed theBinomial modelperformsbetter. Furthermore,the project values obtainedby using theMarkov model varyfrom99.99% to114.95% of theproject values obtained by using the Binomial model.

Table 3. Project values for specific data realizations using the Markov model policy

	Markov - Project Value						
Step	Set 1	Set 2	Set 3	Set 4	Set 5	Set 6	Set 7
0.5	5.280	7.230	5.939	6.037	8.271	8.866	10.435
0.4	5.449	7.304	6.075	6.168	8.296	8.862	10.353
0.3	5.435	7.075	5.895	6.011	7.881	8.416	9.744
0.2	5.449	7.304	6.075	6.168	8.296	8.862	10.353
0.1	5.473	7.246	6.052	6.147	8.181	8.734	10.153
0.05	5.467	7.287	6.077	6.168	8.257	8.816	10.275

4.3. Comparing the Effect of Project Duration on the Models Performance

In order the analyze the impact of project life in the models performance, we have considered horizons of 12, 36, 48, and 60 months in addition to the 24 months horizon previously considered. In Tables 4 and 5, project values are reported for data sets 3 to 7 considering capacity steps of 0.5 and 0.1, respectively . Data sets 1 and 2 cannot be considered for horizons larger than 24 months since they consist of 24 demand values only.

Again, it can be observed that the performance of the Markov model is better. For a capacity changing value of 0.5, the Binomial project value is never better than the Markov project value and the latter one can be up to 15.8% better. When comparing the project values by considering 0.1 and 0.5 as the capacity changing steps, the Binomial model improves more than the Markov model. Nevertheless, project values given by using the Markov policy are still larger.

Table 4. Project value for varying time horizon using a 0.5 capacity changing step

	Binomial Lattice					Markov Grid				
T	Set 3	Set 4	Set 5	Set 6	Set 7	Set 3	Set 4	Set 5	Set 6	Set 7
12	1.749	2.639	4.407	4.521	4.598	1.749	2.639	4.407	4.521	4.598
24	5.573	5.835	7.357	7.852	9.078	5.939	6.037	8.271	8.866	10.435
36	8.567	10.162	9.947	11.151	12.734	9.390	10.364	11.058	12.578	14.610
48	10.112	12.803	12.661	15.211	16.588	10.913	13.226	14.133	17.352	19.110
60	12.221	15.387	15.215	18.342	20.242	13.198	16.145	16.938	20.936	23.444

Only in 2 out of the 25 values computed the Binomial model produced a better value. The Markov project values are now between 99.91% and 113.72% of the Binomial project values. It should be noticed that except for a capacity changing value of 0.4, the best performance of the Binomial model was observed when it was 0.1, see Table 2 above, which is not the case for the Markov model.

Table 5. Project value for varying time horizon using a 0.1 capacity changing step

	Binomial Lattice					Markov Grid				
T	Set 3	Set 4	Set 5	Set 6	Set 7	Set 3	Set 4	Set 5	Set 6	Set 7
12	1.802	2.744	4.760	4.872	4.942	1.800	2.766	4.966	5.075	5.161
24	6.052	6.147	8.182	8.734	10.153	6.052	6.147	8.181	8.734	10.153
36	9.436	10.338	10.979	11.675	14.219	9.436	10.338	10.979	12.363	14.219
48	11.053	13.182	14.002	15.276	18.559	11.053	13.182	14.002	16.951	18.559
60	13.342	16.057	16.777	18.291	22.717	13.432	16.239	16.995	20.800	23.184

CONCLUSIONS

In this work, we address the problem of making investment decisions on a flexible production capacity firm. The problem involves deciding not only the optimal quantity to be produced at every single period but also the in place production capacity policy throughout the whole planning period. We consider the investments to be, at least, partially reversible since capacity sell out allows for partial investment recovering.

We propose to address this problem by using dynamic programming implemented on a Markov grid rather than on the standard binomial lattice. The Markovian approached was expected to perform better since it is a generalization of the binomial lattice in the sense that is can be used to model the latter one. Furthermore, the binomial approach assumes that demand varies according to normal distribution and the lattice is constructed based on demand constant growth rates at constant probabilities. Moreover, the Markov grid takes into account the current value of demand not only into the growth rate but also into the probabilities. An example using real data for th estochastic variable (demand) has been solved, using both approaches. It has been shown that the Markov approach is more reliable and leads to a better decision policy. The computational tests performed, also allowed for the conclusion that the Markov model is less sensitive to project time horizon and to capacity changing steps.

APPENDIX

In this Appendix we give the demand data collected and also the one step transition probability Markov matrix.

Collected data Markov transition probability matrix

$$\begin{bmatrix}
0 & 0 & 0 & 0 & 0 & 1 & 0 & 0 & 0 & 0 & 0 \\
0 & 0 & 0 & 0 & 0 & 0 & 0 & 0 & 1 & 0 & 0 \\
0 & 0 & 0 & 0 & 1 & 0 & 0 & 0 & 0 & 0 & 0 \\
0 & 0 & 0 & 0 & 0 & 0 & 1/4 & 0 & 1/2 & 0 & 1/4 \\
0 & 0 & 0 & 0 & 0 & 0 & 1/2 & 1/2 & 0 & 0 & 0 \\
0 & 0 & 0 & 0 & 0 & 0 & 0 & 0 & 1 & 0 & 0 \\
1/2 & 0 & 0 & 0 & 0 & 0 & 0 & 0 & 0 & 1/2 & 0 \\
0 & 0 & 0 & 0 & 0 & 0 & 0 & 0 & 1 & 0 & 0 \\
0 & 0 & 0 & 2/7 & 1/7 & 1/7 & 0 & 0 & 2/7 & 1/7 & 0 \\
0 & 0 & 1/2 & 1/2 & 0 & 0 & 0 & 0 & 0 & 0 & 0 \\
0 & 1 & 0 & 0 & 0 & 0 & 0 & 0 & 0 & 0 & 0
\end{bmatrix}$$

Table 6. Collected data – monthly demand

	Monthly Demand			
Month	2000	2001	2002	2003
January	1117	1288	1342	1566
February	1520	1558	1767	1696
March	1758	1656	1724	1608
April	1099	1105	1630	1473
May	1669	1675	1851	1480
June	1345	1148	1717	1241
July	1456	1872	2322	1763
August	611	726	867	536
September	1363	1657	1951	1409
October	1664	1703	2152	1549
November	1811	1734	1981	1110
December	1033	1388	1465	998

REFERENCES

Andreou, S. A. (1990), 'A capital budgeting model for product-mix flexibility', Journal of Manufacturing and Operations Management 3, 5–23.

Bollen,N.P.B.(1999), 'Real options and product lyfe cycles', Management Science 45, 670–684.

Brennan, M. & Schwartz, E. (1985), 'Evaluating natural resource investments', Journal of Business 58, 135–157.

Cox, J., Ross, S. & Rubinstein, M. (1979), 'Option pricing: a simplified approach', Journal of Financial Economics 12, 229–263.

Dalakouras, G.V., Kwon, R.H. & Pardalos, P.M.(2008), Computational Methods in Financial Engineering, Springer, Berlin, Germany, chapter Semidefinite Programming Approaches for Bounding Asian Option Prices.

Dixit, A. K. & Pindyck, R. S. (1994), Investment under Uncertainty, Princeton, NJ: Princeton Univ. Press.

Fine, C.H. & Hax, A. (1985), 'Manufacturing strategy: A methodology and an illustration', Interfaces 15, 28–46.

He, H. & Pindyck, R.S. (1992), 'Investment in flexible production capacity', Journal of Dynamics and Control 16, 575–599.

Kamrad, B. & Ernst, R.(1995), In Real options in Capital Investment: Models, Strategies, and Application, Praeger, chapter Multiproduct manufacturing with stochastic input prices and output yield uncertainty.

Kandel, E. & Pearson, N.D. (2002), 'Option value, uncertainty, and the investment decision', Journal of Financial and Quantitative Analysis 37, 341–374.

Kulatilaka, N. (1988), 'Valuing the flexibility of flexible manufacturing system', IEEE Transaction in Engineering Management 35, 250–257.

Majd, S. & Pindyck, R. (1987), 'Time to build, option value,and investment decisions', Journal of Financial Economics 18, 7–27.

McDonald, R. & Siegel, D. (1985), 'Investment and the valuation of firms when there is an option to shut down', International Economic Review 26, 331–349.

McDonald, R. & Siegel,D. (1986), 'The value of waiting to invest', Quarterly Journal of Economics 101, 707–727.

Myers, S.C. (1977), 'Determinants of corporate borrowing', Journal of Financial Economics 5, 147–175.

Myers, S.C. & Majd, S. (1990), 'Abandonment value and project life', Advances in Futures and Options Research 4, 1–21.

Pindyck, R. (1988), 'Irreversible investment, capacity choice and the value of the firm', American Economic Review 78, 969–985.

Tannous, G. F. (1996), 'Capital budgeting for volume flexible equipment', Decision Sciences 27, 157–184.

Triantis, A. & Hodder, J. (1990), 'Valuing flexibility as a complex option', The Journal of Finance 45, 549–565.

Trigeorgis, L. (1996), Real Options: Managerial Flexibility and Strategy in Resource Allocation, MIT Press.

Zopounidis, C., Doumpos, M. & Pardalos, P.M., eds (2008), Handbook of Financial Engineering, Applied Optimization, Springer, Berlin, Germany.

In: Computational Techniques in Economics and Finance ISBN: 978-1-61324-558-3
Editor: Constantine Zopounidis

Chapter 11

INVESTMENT DECISIONS AND CAPITAL ADJUSTMENT COSTS: ESTIMATION OF A DYNAMIC DISCRETE CHOICE MODEL USING PANEL DATA FOR GREEK MANUFACTURING FIRMS

Athanasios Lapatinas*

Department of Economics

University of Ioannina and FEIR[19], Greece.

ABSTRACT

In this paper we estimate a dynamic structural model of capital investment at the firm level. Our dataset consists of a balanced panel of 1419 Greek firms. Two important features are present in our dataset. There are periods in which firms decide not to invest and periods of large investment episodes. This empirical evidence of infrequent and lumpy investment is in favour of irreversibilities and non-convex capital adjustment costs. We consider a dynamic discrete choice model of a general specification of adjustment costs including convex and non-convex components. We also assume total irreversibility of investment. We use an indirect inference procedure to estimate the structural parameters. Our goal is to investigate the nature of the capital adjustment process at the firm level for Greek data.

Keywords: Investment, Capital Adjustment Costs, Indirect Inference, Panel Data.

---

* I am grateful to Plutarchos Sakellaris and Apostolis Philippopoulos for their support and advice. I am also grateful to Russell Cooper for giving me the simulated annealing algorithm in Matlab. Financial support from "Bank of Cyprus" is acknowledged. Any errors are my own.

Correspondence: Athanasios Lapatinas, Department of Macroeconomic Analysis and Policy, Foundation for Economic and Industrial Research, 11 Tsami Karatasi street, GR 117 42 Athens, Greece. E-mail address: alapatin@aueb.gr (Athanasios Lapatinas)

[19] Foundation for Economic and Industrial Research.

1. Introduction

1.1. Motivation

Investment is very important to macroeconomics. As one of the main components of aggregate demand, investment plays a central role in both the cyclical and long run performance of any economy. Economists have long been trying to understand the components of investment activity and much effort has been dedicated to this direction. Although a voluminous literature concerning investment at macro level exists, it has been in the last years when investment literature had shown an increasing concern about the modeling of investment decisions at micro level.

The neoclassical theory and Tobin's Q theory with strictly convex adjustment costs have been the workhorse of modern investment research. The Jorgenson's (1963) neoclassical model –with no capital adjustment costs- yielded a static decision rule for capital stock. Jorgenson's approach compares the marginal product of capital with its user cost. The optimal level of capital stock results from the equivalence between the marginal product of capital and the user cost of capital. Tobin's (1969) approach compares the capitalized value of marginal investment with the replacement cost of one unit of capital. The capitalized value of marginal investment is the market value of one unit of capital. The ratio of the market value of one unit of capital to its replacement cost is called Tobin's q and conditions the decision of undertaking or not an investment project (Tobin, 1969). Empirical evidence has shown the failure of these models to explain investment behavior. The estimates of investment responsiveness to fundamentals have been very low.

For analytical and econometric convenience, the literature adopted a quadratic-strictly convex function for the adjustment costs. Strictly convex adjustment costs imply that it is always optimal to make a continuous, non-zero adjustment (there are no periods of time with zero adjustment). This feature is strongly at odds with data on investment. Empirical research reveals that firms tend to concentrate the adjustment of capital in relatively short periods of time, which alternate periods of no adjustment. In other words, the adjustment process of capital can be characterized as intermittent and lumpy. The assumption of strictly convex adjustment costs and the resulting linear dynamic models are unable to explain the infrequent and lumpy dynamic pattern of investment activity.

Doms and Dune (1998) using data for 12000 US manufacturing firms, for the period 1972-1989, find that over the half of the firms increase their capital stock more than 35 percent in a single year. Nilsen and Schiantarelli (2003) report similar findings for Norwegian firms' panel data. They note that, in every year, about 30 percent of the firms undertake no investment at all, at disaggregate level.

The above evidence of intermittent and lumpy adjustment of capital can be supported by non-convex adjustment cost function. One way of explaining the periods of no adjustment is the inclusion of a linear (piecewise) adjustment cost to the model. Zero adjustment (inactivity) entails non-differentiability and in general, the linear adjustment cost component is interpreted as the reflection of the (partially) irreversible nature of investment. Total irreversibility means that gross investment cannot be negative. Partial irreversibility appears when the sale price of capital is lower than its replacement cost. Although linear adjustment cost explains the infrequent adjustment of capital, it cannot suitably explain the lumpiness.

To capture the lumpy character of adjustment, Hamermesh (1989) first proposed the introduction of a fixed component in the adjustment costs function. Incorporating this non-convexity, a firm decides whether to invest in capital or not. This decision depends on whether the expected gains of the investment are high enough to overcome the fixed costs. If fixed costs are substantial, firm will invest infrequently, and when it does, it will carry out a large investment.

Abel and Eberly (1994) extend the Q model incorporating quadratic, piecewise and fixed adjustment costs in their model. They show that for critical values of marginal q three potential regimes for investment occur: positive, zero and negative gross investment. In an empirical application of this model, Barnett and Sakellaris (1998) and Abel and Eberly (2002) reach the conclusion that non-linearities are important in explaining investment behavior.

Caballero, Engel and Haltiwanger (1995) and Caballero and Engel (1998, 1999) consider the gap between actual and desired capital stock to be the fundamental of investment, in order to interpret the non-linearities in the investment process. They implement the adjustment hazard function. This function is defined as the difference between the log of actual and the log of desired level of capital, where the latter is the optimum level of capital obtained under zero adjustment costs. The model predicts that the larger the gap is, the higher the probability of investment to be recorded is.

Cooper and Willis (2001) criticize the "gap methodology" arguing that the results are particularly sensitive to mis-specification of the target level to which the actual capital stock is assumed to adjust.

Cooper and Haltiwanger (1993) and Cooper, Haltiwanger and Power (1999) investigate the machine replacement problem in the presence of non-convex adjustment costs. They find that, however low the level of current capital stock is (thus, the older the capital is), the higher the probability of investment to occur is. Furthermore, the longer you wait for the replacement of capital, the larger the adjustment of capital will be.

Cooper and Haltiwanger (2006), in their influential work, compare models with alternative adjustment costs: quadratic, fixed adjustment costs and adjustment costs associated with irreversibility of investment. They show that the models with only one type of adjustment cost are not successful in matching the dynamic nature of investment. On the other hand, the mixed model of non-convex and convex costs of adjustment matches satisfactorily the features of investment. In order to estimate the structural parameters of the model, Cooper and Haltiwanger use the simulated method of moments so as to match key moments of the plant level capital adjustment dynamics.

Bayraktar (2002) and Bayraktar, Sakellaris and Vermeulen (2006) extend Cooper and Haltiwanger's (2006) model incorporating the existence of financial market imperfections.

1.2. This Work

Our approach specifies a dynamic structural model of investment at the firm level in order to get a better understanding of microeconomic investment decisions and the nature of capital adjustment costs Greek firms face when they decide to undertake an investment project. The aim of this paper is to investigate the effects of both convex and non-convex adjustment costs of capital on Greek firms' investment activity. Moreover its target is to look into the dynamic nature of capital adjustment process at the firm level. In addition to this, we monitor if the Greek micro data supports the presence of both convex and non-convex components of adjustment costs and more specifically to find the structural estimates of the convex and non-convex adjustment costs that are consistent with the micro evidence for the Greek economy. Our work, as far as we know, constitutes the first attempt of studying the investment behavior of Greek economy at micro level. As a result, we hope that this work not only contributes to the better understanding of the complex dynamics of investment, but it also constitutes an essential tool for the evaluation of different policies regarding Greek economy.

In this paper a dynamic structural model of capital investment at the firm level is estimated. We inquire about the investment behavior of a balanced panel of 1419 Greek firms (9933 observations) for the period 1996-2002. The evidence of infrequent and lumpy investment is present in our dataset. Based on these empirical facts, we introduce a dynamic discrete choice model with a general specification of adjustment costs including both convex and non-convex components. We also assume total irreversibility of investment. We use an indirect inference procedure as in Gourieroux, Monfort and Renault (1993) and Smith (1993), in order to estimate the structural parameters of the model. The reason for not using analytical tools is the presence of non-convex adjustment costs that cause the dynamic problem to be discontinuous. Firms need to choose between undertaking and not an investment project. The structural parameters determining the magnitude of convex and non-convex adjustment costs are chosen to reproduce the econometric relationship between the investment rate and the profitability shocks with their square term. The square term of profitability shocks captures the non-linearities in the investment process.

The rest of the paper is organized as follows. In section 2 we describe the dataset used in this study. Section 3 formulates the dynamic structural model of investment. In section 4 we describe the estimation of the model: the methodology (section 4.1), the estimation method we implement (section 4.2) and the estimation results (section 4.3). Section 5 gives the main policy and modeling implications of our findings and section 6 concludes.

2. Features of the Data

Data Set

The main data source in this paper is the ICAP firm-level database. The ICAP is the largest company providing economic data and consultative services in Greece and is a member of the international network INFOALLIANCE and participant of the European economic and business information network EUROGATE. The company is also a member of Federation of Business Information Services (FEBIS), European Association of Directory and Database Publishers (EADP), European Federation of Management Consulting Association and a member of the international research organization GALLUP INTERNATIONAL. Our data are a balanced panel of 2097 active Greek manufacturing firms over the period 1996-2002 containing 14679 observations. These are the data we get after filtering all the manufacturing firms that are registered in the ICAP databank, depending on the availability of the plant, property and equipment data. We delete firms with missing data points between 1996 and 2002. Since net profits are an essential variable to our analysis, we only keep manufacturing firms that have positive profits information. This leads to 1690 firms on 11830 observations.

The definition of capital includes plant, property, and equipment. ICAP provides fixed assets items for each firm which represent the book value of all fixed assets of the firm, including building, land and structures, machinery and equipment, intangible fixed assets and financial fixed assets such as share ownership in other companies. For this paper, the book value of the capital stock, (T) counts land and estates, buildings and structures, and machinery and equipments (for more details on sample selection see the Appendix). Our investment measure, t , is calculated by applying a perpetual inventory procedure with a depreciation of 8 percent per annum for all years (this value is proposed by previous studies at micro-level, see for example Bond et al., 1999):

$$F(t) = \Pr(T < t) \Rightarrow S(t) = 1 - F(t) = \Pr(T \geq t) \tag{1}$$

Real investment, I_t, is constructed as investment at current prices, $p_t I_t$, deflated by the investment price deflator, with 1995 to be the base year. Real capital stock, K_t , is constructed in the same way. The investment rate is then defined as the ratio of real investment to the real capital stock, $\frac{I_t}{K_t}$.

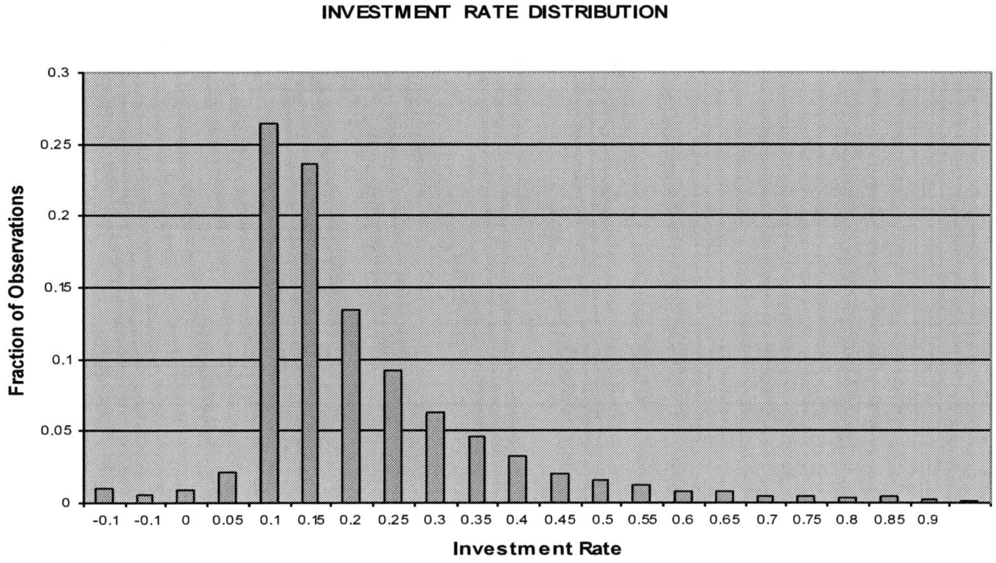

Figure 1. Investment rate distribution.

The dataset of 1622 firms on 11354 observations is not our final dataset. Following Bayraktar, Sakellaris and Vermeulen (2006), we assume that investment rates higher than 90 percent are measuring a merger or acquisition. All the firms that display investment rate over

90 percent in any year among the period 1996-2002 are excluded from our panel. This leads to our final panel dataset of 1419 firms on 9933 observations for the period 1996-2002. The dataset is balanced and each firm has exactly 7 observations (6 observations for investment). The 1419 manufacturing firms comprise a considerable portion of the active Greek manufacturing firms. For the year 2000 the 1419 firms of our dataset represent about 6.6 percent of the private investment in Greece. They had a total investment expenditure of 1.26 billion euros, where the total private fixed investment (excluding stockbuilding) in Greece was 19 billion euros in 2000 (this is taken from the OECD data source).

Summary Statistics

Table 1 shows summary statistics of the data, Table 2 shows some features of the investment rate and Figure 1 represents the distribution function of the investment rate for the period 1996-2001.

Table 1. Summary statistics

	Mean	median	std. dev	min	max
I_{it}/K_{it}	0.18	0.14	0.16	-0.92	0.92
K_{it}	3.8	0.8	22.4	0	719

Note: capital stock is in million euros measured in 1995 prices

Table 2. Features of the distribution of the investment rate

Variable	Fraction of obs.
$\lvert I_{it}/K_{it}\rvert < 0.01$	0.55%
$\lvert I_{it}/K_{it}\rvert < 0.02$ (inaction region)	1.04%
$I_{it}/K_{it} < 0$	2.5%
$I_{it}/K_{it} > 0.2$ (positive investment spike)	31.7%
$I_{it}/K_{it} < -0.2$ (negative investment spike)	0.6%
$I_{it}/K_{it} < -0.02$	2.02%
corr($(I/K)_{it}, (I/K)_{it-1}$)	0.17

Note: all statistics are calculated for 1419 firms and for the period 1996-2002

All statistics are calculated by pooling data for 1419 Greek manufacturing firms and for the period of 1996-2002. In that period, the median firm had a capital stock of 0.8 million euros (in 1995 prices) and an investment rate at 0.14. The average value of the capital stock is 3.8 million euros and the average value of the investment rate is 0.18. The statistics of the investment rate are quite close to the statistics found by Cooper and Haltiwanger (2006), Bayraktar (2002) and Bayraktar, Sakellaris and Vermeulen (2006). The first order autocorrelation of investment rate is 0.17. It is a quite large number when it is compared to 0.058 and 0.008, which are found by Cooper and Haltiwanger and Bayraktar, Sakellaris and Vermeulen respectively, and it is about the same with that found by Bayraktar. The inaction region is defined as less than 2 percent investment rate in absolute value. The fraction of observations in this region is 1.04 percent. Around 2.5 percent of the investment rates are negative (as a comparison it is 1.8 percent in Cooper and Haltiwanger, 8.68 percent in Bayraktar, and 4.7 percent in Bayraktar, Sakellaris and Vermeulen). This number is crucial as it concerns the structure of our model. The small fraction of negative investment rates comprises the basic motivation of considering investment, total irreversible –and not partial irreversible- in our model. In contrast with other studies, our formulation emphasizes the feature that a firm has only two options, of investing and not investing, and not a third one of selling capital (disinvesting). The investment rate is more than 20 percent for 31.7 percent of observations (positive investment spike). The latter number is 18.6 percent in Cooper and Haltiwanger, 17.34 percent in Bayraktar and 38 percent in Bayraktar, Sakellaris and Vermeulen. The fraction of observations that corresponds to investment rate less than -20 percent (negative investment spike) is only 0.6 percent. The presence of huge asymmetries between positive and negative investment is apparent in our dataset, since the last fraction is compared very low to the fraction of investment rate points that exceed 20 percent.

There is a huge empirical literature highlighting the importance of inaction and lumpiness in microeconomic investment datasets. Doms and Dune (1998) use data on American firms from 1972 to 1989. They find that more than half of them increase their capital stock over than 35 percent in some of the years considered. Nilsen and Schiantarelli (2003), using information on Norwegian plants, find that about 30 percent of them present zero investment in an average year. Similar findings are reported concerning different countries in Barnett and Sakellaris (1998), Caballero, Engel, and Haltiwanger (1995), Abel and Eberly (2002), Eberly (1997).

The empirical evidence reported in this section stresses two important stylized facts: there are periods in which firms decide not to invest (periods of inaction) and periods of large investment episodes (lumpiness). These empirical findings clearly back up the adoption of an investment model which accounts for irreversibilities and non-convex capital adjustment costs.

3. Model and Implications

The specifications of the model are from Cooper and Haltiwanger (2006). We assume a large and fixed number of firms. Firm i begins to period t with the inherited real capital stock, K_{it}, which has been adjusted in the previous period. Before making any investment decision, the firm observes the current period profitability shock. Given this state variable, the firm makes a decision on investment, depending on the nature of adjustment costs.

The most general specification of the dynamic optimization problem of the firm is given by:

$$V(A_{it},K_{it}) = \max_{\{I_{it}\}} \Pi(A_{it},K_{it}) - C(I_{it},K_{it}) - pI_{it} + \beta E_{A_{it+1}/A_{it}} V(A_{it+1},K_{it+1}) \tag{2}$$

subject to the following constraint:

$$I_{it} = K_{it+1} - (1-\delta)K_{it} \tag{3}$$

where the profit function $\Pi(A_{it},K_{it})$ is parameterized in the following way:

$$\Pi(A_{it},K_{it}) = A_{it}K_{it}^{\theta} \tag{4}$$

where $0<\theta<1$, is the parameter for the curvature of the profit function. A_{it} is the current period profitability shock that contains both an idiosyncratic component, as well as an aggregate one. It is assumed that capital is the only quasi-fixed factor of production and all variable factors have already been maximized out of the problem. p is the constant cost of capital. δ is the depreciation rate of capital, which is constant too. The costs of adjustment are given by the function $C(I_{it},K_{it})$. I_{it} is the level of investment that the firm's manager chooses. The function $C(I_{it},K_{it})$ is general enough to have components of both convex and non-convex costs of adjustment. The discount factor, β, is fixed and equals $(1+r)^{-1}$, where r is the risk-free market interest rate.

3.1. Adjustment Cost Structures

Much attention has been given in investment literature to the adjustment costs component. As Hamermesh and Pfann (1996) mention, this component was introduced into investment models so as to provide an explanation for the observation that firms change their demand for capital more slowly than the shocks to capital demand warrant. Adjustment cost functions are not empirically observable. However, simulation results provide a better clue as to how different functional forms for adjustment costs imply different adjustment patterns. Therefore, as suggested by e.g. Cooper and Haltiwanger (2006) and Abel and Eberly (1994, 2002), attention is given to the estimation of a unified model that incorporates different types of adjustment costs. The adjustment cost functions incorporate both convex and non-convex adjustment costs.

Convex Capital Adjustment Costs

Traditionally, a symmetric convex adjustment cost function is assumed, usually quadratic, like:

$$C(I_{it}, K_{it}) = \frac{\gamma}{2}\left[\frac{I_{it}}{K_{it}}\right]^2 K_{it} \tag{5}$$

This is the standard specification in the literature. The parameter γ affects the magnitude of total and marginal adjustment costs. The higher the γ is, the higher the marginal cost of investing is and thus the lower the responsiveness of investment to variations in the underlying profitability of capital is. The maintenance and gradual capital adjustments can be considered as examples of convex adjustment costs. Given this adjustment cost function and the assumption of a constant factor price [illegible], the first order condition of the dynamic optimization problem (2) produces the following equality between the marginal benefit of investment and its marginal cost:

$$\gamma I_{it} + p = \beta E_{A_{it+1}/A_{it}} V_{K_{it+1}}(A_{it+1}, K_{it+1}) \tag{6}$$

where $V_{K_{it+1}}(A_{it+1}, K_{it+1})$ is the derivative of the value function with respect to capital. In fact, this derivative is not observable. The conditional expectation in (6) is the marginal q of the Q theory. It represents the marginal value of an additional unit of future capital. This term is unobservable, so equation (6) cannot serve for estimation. However, Hayashi (1982) shows, that under the additional assumption of proportionality of profits to the capital stock ($\theta = 1$), the problem of marginal q being unobserved can be overcome. Under the given assumptions, marginal q equals average q (Tobin's q) which in turn can be determined -at least for publicly traded firms- from stock market information. Of course, given that the estimate of the curvature of the profit function is significantly less than 1, any Q theory is misspecified.

The convex adjustment cost function implies that the investment rate is a linear function of the fundamentals. This suggests continuous investment activity.

NON-CONVEX CAPITAL ADJUSTMENT COSTS AND TOTAL IRREVERSIBILITY

Convex capital adjustment costs cannot match the findings of recent empirical studies for lumpiness of investment adjustment. Firms tend to concentrate their capital adjustment into short periods of time. Consequently, firms exhibit frequent periods of no adjustment (inaction). Therefore, it has been suggested to add fixed costs and irreversibility components to the adjustment cost function. Here, we allow the case of a component of costs being fixed when investment is undertaken regardless of the investment's magnitude. In order for this cost to be relevant at all stages of a firm's life we assume that it is proportional to firm's size as measured by its capital stock: : FK_{it}. The structural parameter F determines the magnitude of fixed costs. The fixed adjustment costs represent plant restructuring, worker retraining and organizational restructuring. Generally, these costs capture indivisibility in capital and increasing returns to the installation of capital. We should emphasize that when there are no fixed costs associated with capital adjustment, the value function is continuous and concave. The introduction of fixed adjustment costs breaks the concavity (Slade, 1998 and Aguirregabiria, 1999, characterize the optimal decision rule for problems with non-concave value functions. The role of fixed costs was stressed by Abel and Eberly, 1994, 2002, Caballero and Leahy, 1996, Caballero and Engel, 1999, among others).

In a model of total irreversible investment (total irreversibility does not allow capital to be sailed in a second-hand market), the firm should decide on making investment or not. While deciding regarding this issue, the firm compares the value function in case of capital adjustment (V^a) to the value function in case of non-adjustment (V^{na}), and chooses the maximum:

$$V(A_{it},K_{it}) = \max\left\{V^a(A_{it},K_{it}),V^{na}(A_{it},K_{it})\right\} \tag{7}$$

This formulation, occuring from the assumption of total irreversibility, emphasizes the feature that a firm has two options. The dynamic optimization problem in the case of capital adjustment is:

$$V^a(A_{it},K_{it}) = \max_{\{I_{it}\}} \Pi(A_{it},K_{it}) - C(I_{it},K_{it}) - pI_{it} + \beta E_{A_{it+1}/A_{it}} V(A_{it+1},K_{it+1}) \tag{7a}$$

subject to the constraint

$$I_{it} = K_{it+1} - (1-\delta)K_{it}$$

The value function in the case of no adjustment, on the other hand, is defined as follows:

$$V^{na}(A_{it},K_{it}) = \Pi(A_{it},K_{it}) + \beta E_{A_{it+1}/A_{it}} V(A_{it+1},(1-\delta)K_{it}) \tag{7b}$$

In this framework, there will be periods of inaction when fundamentals are not favorable and periods of bursts of investment when fundamentals are high or low enough. The firm invests when its capital stock is less than its optimal level, otherwise prefers to avoid adjustment costs and remains inactive.

3.2. Value Maximization

The firm manager's dynamic program can be written as follows:

$$V(A_{it},K_{it}) = \max\left\{V^a(A_{it},K_{it}),V^{na}(A_{it},K_{it})\right\} \tag{8}$$

The manager needs to choose optimally between investing (adjusting capital), with value $V^a(.)$, or undertaking no investment at all, with value $V^{na}(.)$. Both of these two alternative options have a value, given by:

$$V^a(A_{it},K_{it}) = \max_{\{I_{it}\}} \Pi(A_{it},K_{it}) - \frac{\gamma}{2}\left[\frac{I_{it}}{K_{it}}\right]^2 K_{it} - FK_{it} - I_{it} + \beta E_{A_{it+1}/A_{it}} V(A_{it+1},K_{it+1}) \tag{8a}$$

subject to the constraint $I_{it} = K_{it+1} - (1-\delta)K_{it}$

$$V^{na}(A_{it},K_{it}) = \Pi(A_{it},K_{it}) + \beta E_{A_{it+1}/A_{it}} V(A_{it+1},(1-\delta)K_{it}) \tag{8b}$$

In more detail, the value of investment given by (8a) implies that investing (buying capital) incurs two sources of costs. The first is the investment outlay, I_{it}, in which the cost of capital is normalized to one. The second is the adjustment cost, which in turn has a fixed and a convex component. The value of investment is defined as the profits minus total costs under the optimal decision, plus the discounted future value, given this period's decision and optimal behaviour in subsequent periods. Equation (8b) gives the value of no adjustment (inaction), which of course does not involve any costs or maximization.

Due to the presence of non-convexities, which cause discontinuity in the investment process, the model cannot be solved analytically. The model is solved using a numerical method known as the Value Function Iteration method. This method can be summarized as follows. Let V be the value function. The value function iteration starts with some initial value V_0 and then evaluates $V_{j+1} = T(V_j)$ for $j = 0,1,2.....$ (where T is a mapping operator). The desired value function is obtained when the difference between V_{j+1} and V_j is less than some predetermined threshold value (see Rust, 1987a, b, for details).

The set of the structural parameters is given as $\{\beta,\delta,\theta,\gamma,F\}$. These together with the transition matrix for the profitability shocks determine the behavior of the model.

4. Estimation of the Model

4.1. Methodology

4.1.1. Estimation of the Profit Function

The profit function is given by

$$\Pi(A_{it},K_{it}) = AK_{it}^{\theta}$$

where A_{it} is the profitability shock, θ is the curvature of the profit function and K_{it} is the firm level capital stock. In this model, it is assumed that capital is the only quasi-fixed factor of production and all the variable factors have already been maximized out of the problem. We estimate θ by regressing the natural log of net profit (net of cost of production) on the natural log of the replacement value of the capital stock using firm level Greek panel data. Although θ is assumed to be the same for each firm at each period, we remove fixed effects in order to take into account the structural differences across firms (in order to fix the structural heterogeneity problem). If θ is less than one, this shows the decreasing marginal profitability of capital. This might be caused by some degree of monopoly power or decreasing returns in the technology. From our data θ is estimated as 0.7, with a standard error of 0.006. This estimate of θ is not at variance with other estimates in the literature. Cooper and Ejarque (2001) find the same estimation in their work and a curvature of between 0.5 and 0.8 is estimated by Gilchrist and Himmelberg (1999).

4.1.2. The Fundamental of Investment: Profitability Shocks

The investment literature is traditionally relied on neoclassical Tobin's q. Tobin's q is equal to the ratio of the market value of firms to the replacement value of capital. The neoclassical models that take Tobin's q as the fundamental of investment are too simple to explain complex dynamics of investment and rely on very strict assumptions of perfectly competitive product markets and quadratic convex adjustment costs. The quadratic convex capital adjustment costs imply a linear relationship between the investment rate and Tobin's q, therefore neoclassical investment models deal only with the smooth part of the capital adjustment process. In recent years, this feature is strongly at odds with the empirical studies which reveal that at the micro level, firms tend to concentrate the adjustment of capital in relatively short periods of time, pointing the lumpy, infrequent and sunk nature of investment. These facts have stimulated the introduction of new empirical fundamentals in order to explain investment behaviour.

Caballero and Engel (1999) introduce the gap between the desired and actual capital stock, which, until today, is the most commonly used fundamental of investment in the studies. In their model, once the gap reaches a threshold level, the adjustment process starts at once. The empirical investigation of this fundamental by Caballero, Engel and Haltiwanger (1995) shows that the response of investment to the gap is nonlinear, supporting therefore the existence of non-convex adjustment costs. In parallel with the development of the literature arguing that non-convexities and irreversibilities play a central role in investment, a literature relating the empirical failure of the neoclassical model to possible measurement errors in Tobin's q evolved. This literature focuses on correcting possible mismeasurement of Tobin's q in order to explain the inadequate results of the "traditional" literature. The idea behind is that the presence of measurement errors prompts fundamentals to be insufficient determinants of investment. Since the main indicator of firms' investment opportunities is expected profitability and since it is not easy to be directly calculated, it is generally approximated by current profitability measures. Abel and Blanchard (1986) first proposed present value of marginal revenue flows of capital to be one of these measures and Gilchrist and Himmelberg (1995, 1999) constructed this "Fundamental Q" measure pooling U.S firm level data. The last and most recently worked up alternative fundamental of investment is profitability shocks. Profitability shocks are defined as changes in firms' profits that cannot be attributed to changes in their factors of production.

4.1.3. Calculation of the Profit Shocks

There are two alternative ways of calculating the profitability shocks, A_{it}. The first way calculates A_{it} indirectly through the first order condition for profit maximization with respect to employment. The second way of calculating A_{it} is through regressing profits on capital, and taking the residuals. Cooper and Haltiwanger (2006), Bayraktar (2002), Bayraktar, Sakellaris and Vermeulen (2006) use the first way because the standard deviation of the shocks using this way is low compared to the standard deviation calculated using the second way. Low standard deviation of the shocks causes the transition matrix to be more informative. Although we fully appreciate the fact that using profit data instead of employment data might raise measurement errors, since employment data is not available we compromise on the second way. We regress the log of profits on the log of capital including time dummies, after removing the fixed effects, and the residuals of this regression represent the idiosyncratic profitability shocks, a_{it} (i denotes the firm and t the period): ince we remove fixed effects, include time dummies, and the variables are taken in log form, the residual shocks are the firm specific idiosyncratic shocks in log form (time dummies capture the aggregate component of the profitability shocks). Table 3 shows some features of the idiosyncratic profitability shocks.

Table 3. Features of the idiosyncratic profitability shocks, a_{it}

minimum:	-0.72
maximum:	0.34
std. dev.:	0.1
autocorrelation:	0.693

4.1.4. The Relationship between Investment and Profitability Shocks

Throughout this paper we study the following relationship between investment and profitability shocks

$$\tilde{i}_{it} = \Psi_0 + \Psi_1 a_{it} + \Psi_2 (a_{it})^2 + u_{it}$$

where $\tilde{i}_{it}$ is the deviation of the investment rate of firm i in period t from the firm specific mean, a_{it} is the idiosyncratic profitability shock, $(a_{it})^2$ is the square term of a_{it}. The square term is included in order to test for our dataset the argument that the investment process is a non-linear function of the fundamentals.

Table 4. Summary Statistics of the regression variables

	mean	std. dev	min	max
$\tilde{i}_{it}$	0.00	0.154	-1.07	0.7
a_{it}	0.00	0.1	-0.72	0.34
$(a_{it})^2$	0.01	0.02	0.00	0.52

Table 5. Correlation matrix of the regression variables

	$\tilde{i}_{it}$	a_{it}	$(a_{it})^2$
$\tilde{i}_{it}$	1		
a_{it}	0.187	1	
$(a_{it})^2$	-0.016	-0.376	1

Table 6. Actual Data: Regression Results

Coefficients	Estimated values
a_{it}	0.322* (0.017)
$(a_{it})^2$	0.443* (0.08)

* significant at the 1 percent level. Rsquared adjusted = 0.04.

Note: data was pooled for 1419 Greek firms and for the period 1996-2002. The estimation technique is the least square. The dependent variable is the deviation of the investment rate from the firm specific mean. Standard errors are reported in the parentheses.

Table 4 shows some summary statistics of the regression variables. Table 5 gives the correlation matrix of the regression variables. Notice that the investment rate is positively correlated with the contemporaneous profitability shock (correlation = 0.187). The least square estimated coefficients are reported in Table 6. The regression results show that both the level and the square term of the profitability shocks are important in explaining investment. Thus, we could say that these results support the argument of non-linear response of investment to its fundamentals.

4.1.5. Simulations

The coefficients $\{\beta, \delta, \theta\}$ and the profitability shocks are calibrated using the ICAP Greek firm-level database. We fix the discount factor β at the empirically reasonable value 0.97 (r is set approximately at 3 percent which is the average real interest rate on government bonds in Greece). We have also estimated the model with different values of β (0.95 and 0.99) obtaining similar results. Following the relevant micro-level studies we pin down the depreciation rate, δ, at 0.08. The curvature of the profit function, θ, is estimated as 0.7 by regressing the log of profit on the log of capital using Greek firm-level data.

The profitability shocks, A_{it}, contain both an aggregate and an idiosyncratic component. The aggregate shocks are assumed to have a high and low value: $\{0.9, 1.1\}$. The serial correlation between the aggregate shocks is calculated as 0.8. We represent the aggregate shock process as a two-state Markov process with a symmetric transition matrix in which the probability of remaining in either of the two aggregate states is 0.8. The details of calculating the idiosyncratic shocks, a_{it}, are in section 4.1.3. We assume that the idiosyncratic profitability shocks follow an AR(1) process:

$$a_{it+1} = \rho a_{it} + \varepsilon_{it+1} \quad \text{where } \varepsilon_{it} \sim iid\ N(0, \sigma_{\varepsilon}^2) \tag{9}$$

We approximate this process by a discrete Markov process using the method outlined in Tauchen (1986). A time invariant Markov chain is defined by (Z, T), where $Z \in \mathbb{R}^n$ is a vector describing the states possible of the Markov process, and T is an $n \times n$ dimensional transition matrix with elements (i, j) that express the probability of transition from state Z_i to state Z_j. Thus, the rows of T sum to unity. The method proposed by Tauchen (1986) is used to create a discrete state space representation of the stochastic AR(1) process for the firm specific shocks. The idiosyncratic shocks take 11 different values. The serial correlation of the idiosyncratic shocks is 0.69. The standard deviation is 0.1. Table 7 presents the idiosyncratic shocks and the transition matrix of these shocks.

Table 7. Idiosyncratic shocks and their transition matrix

idiosyncratic shocks	-0.1815	-0.1114	-0.0757	-0.0478	-0.0232	0	0.0233	0.0478	0.0757	0.1115	0.1815	sum
-0.1815	0.4478	0.2159	0.1303	0.0824	0.0524	0.0328	0.0197	0.011	0.0054	0.002	0.0003	1
-0.1114	0.2159	0.2046	0.1652	0.1291	0.0983	0.0724	0.0509	0.0333	0.0194	0.0089	0.002	1
-0.0757	0.1303	0.1652	0.1571	0.1396	0.1188	0.0971	0.0757	0.0553	0.0363	0.0194	0.0054	1
-0.0478	0.0824	0.1291	0.1396	0.137	0.1273	0.1131	0.0957	0.0762	0.0553	0.0333	0.011	1
-0.0232	0.0524	0.0983	0.1188	0.1273	0.1278	0.1221	0.1113	0.0957	0.0757	0.0509	0.0197	1
0	0.0328	0.0724	0.0971	0.1131	0.1221	0.1251	0.1221	0.1131	0.0971	0.0724	0.0328	1
0.0233	0.0197	0.0509	0.0757	0.0957	0.1113	0.1221	0.1278	0.1273	0.1188	0.0983	0.0524	1
0.0478	0.011	0.0333	0.0553	0.0762	0.0957	0.1131	0.1273	0.137	0.1396	0.1291	0.0824	1
0.0757	0.0054	0.0194	0.0363	0.0553	0.0757	0.0971	0.1188	0.1396	0.1571	0.1652	0.1303	1
0.1115	0.002	0.0089	0.0194	0.0333	0.0509	0.0724	0.0983	0.1291	0.1652	0.2046	0.2159	1
0.1815	0.0003	0.002	0.0054	0.011	0.0197	0.0328	0.0524	0.0824	0.1303	0.2159	0.4478	1

The transition matrix for the idiosyncratic shocks is computed from the empirical transitions observed at the firm-level and reproduces statistics from the idiosyncratic profitability shock series.

4.2. Estimation Method: Indirect Inference

The vector of remaining structural parameters to be estimated is $\Theta \equiv (\gamma, F)$. The approach is to estimate these parameters by matching the implications of the structural model with key features of the data. The methodology that is used for this purpose is the structural empirical approach called indirect inference method. This method is explained by Gourieroux et al. (1993), Smith (1993), Gourieroux and Monfort (1996) and works as follows.

With an arbitrary set of parameter values and by using the Value Function Iteration method we solve the firm's dynamic programming problem (see section 3.2). After the model is solved for given Θ values, a 500 firms and 100 periods simulated panel data are obtained using the created policy functions. This simulated data set is used to calculate the model analogues of the coefficients and/or moments we obtained using actual data. The reduced form equation we estimate using both the simulated and actual data is

$$\tilde{i}_{it} = \Psi_0 + \Psi_1 a_{it} + \Psi_2 (a_{it})^2 + u_{it}$$

where $\tilde{i}_{it}$ is the deviation of the investment rate of firm i in period t from the firm specific mean, a_{it} is the idiosyncratic profitability shock, $(a_{it})^2$ is the square term of a_{it}. The square term is included in order to take into account the non-convexities in the adjustment process. Denoting as Ψ^d the vector of moments from the actual data and as $\Psi^s(\Theta)$ the vector of moments from data simulated given Θ, the indirect inference routine looks for the structural parameter estimates that minimize the weighted distance between the two vector of moments (as pointed by Gourieroux and Monfort, 1996, minimizing the distance between the simulated data moments and the actual data moments will emerge consistent estimates of the structural parameters). More formally, the statistic we try to minimize with respect to Θ in order to find the structural parameter values is the following quadratic function:

$$J(\Theta) = (\Psi^d - \Psi^s(\Theta))' W (\Psi^d - \Psi^s(\Theta))$$

where W is a weighting matrix (we implement the 2x2 identity matrix). The vector of true moments is $\Psi^d = [\Psi_1, \Psi_2] =$ [0.322, 0.443]. Given the discontinuities in the model and the discretization of the state space, as it is the case in related studies, we use the method of simulated annealing in order to minimize $J(\Theta)$ with respect to Θ. As Bayraktar (2002) and Bayraktar, Sakellaris and Vermeulen (2006) notice, simulated annealing is the ideal algorithm for dealing with complex functions, first because it explores the function's entire surface and can escape from local optima by moving uphill and downhill and second, because the assumptions required with respect to functional forms are quite relaxed.

4.3. Estimation Results

Using the indirect inference method, the structural parameters of the model proposed in section 3 are estimated. Table 8 gives the estimated values.

Table 8. Estimated Structural Parameters

Coefficients	Estimated values
γ	0.5164 (0.0130)
F	0.1557 (0.0035)

Note: standard errors are reported in parentheses.

The structural parameters γ and F are significantly different from zero, indicating the importance of convex and fixed adjustment costs. It is essential to bring to reader's notice that the estimation results are affected by the fact that we are only exploiting the binary choice between zero investment and positive investment. In this sense, our results are not directly comparable with the results obtained by Cooper and Haltiwanger (2006), Bayraktar (2002), and Bayraktar, Sakellaris and Vermeulen (2006).

The estimated value of the coefficient determining the magnitude of the convex adjustment cost, γ, is 0.5164. Cooper and Haltiwanger (2006) estimate γ as 0.455, Bayraktar (2002) finds an estimated γ at 0.311 and Bayraktar, Sakellaris and Vermeulen (2006) estimate γ as 0.532. The estimated value of the coefficient determining the magnitude of the fixed adjustment cost, F, is 0.1557. This implies that a firm that undertakes an investment project faces a fixed adjustment cost of 15.57 percent of installed capital. The estimated value of the coefficient F is high compared to the estimates found by relevant studies (Cooper and Haltiwanger, 2006, Bayraktar, 2002, Bayraktar, Sakellaris and Vermeulen, 2006, estimate F at 0.069, 0.029 and 0.031 respectively).

Now we focus on the comparison of the simulated data results with the actual data results. Table 9 shows the regression coefficients of the reduced form regression of investment rate on the profitability shocks using the actual data and the simulated data (the simulated data regression coefficients were obtained using the simulated data that were generated using the estimated values of Table 8).

Table 9. Actual Data versus Simulated Data: Regression Results

Coefficients	Actual Data	Simulated Data
a_{it}	0.322	0.322
$(a_{it})^2$	0.443	0.443

Note: The estimation technique is the least square. The dependent variable is the deviation of the investment rate from the firm specific mean.

Table 10. Moments of actual data versus moments of simulated data

Moments	Actual Data	Simulated Data
mean of investment rate	0.18	0.10
correlation ($\tilde{i}_{it}$, a_{it})	0.187	0.39
autocorrelation of inv. rate	0.17	-0.03
investment rate (> 0.2)	31.7%	13.8%
investment rate < 0	2.5%	16.9%

The estimated coefficients using the actual and simulated data are exactly the same. In Table 10 we also compare some moments of actual data and simulated data. The dynamics of the simulated data seems to be different than the dynamics of the actual data. The weakest result produced by the model compared to the actual results is the autocorrelation of the investment rate. While the actual value is 0.17, it is estimated as -0.03 by the model. One possible explanation for such a low estimated value might be related to the presence of financial frictions. The model is not working well in terms of the estimated autocorrelation of the investment rate due to the omission of financial market imperfections. Furthermore, it is possible that measurement error in the profit data is the cause of some of the difference in dynamics. Despite this, the overall investment rate is captured quite well by the model. The actual value of the average investment rate is 0.18 and it is estimated as 0.1 by the model. With regard to the contemporaneous correlation of the investment rate with the profitability shocks, while the correlation in the actual data is 0.19, we have a comparable estimation of 0.39. Now, with regard to the fraction of the observations corresponding to the different values of the investment rate, we think that the nonlinear effect of the profitability shocks is not perfectly captured as evidenced by a somewhat different fraction of firms having investment bursts. In parallel, the fraction of observations with a negative investment rate is estimated as 16.9 percent, while its actual value is 2.5 percent.

5. Policy and Modeling Implications

Firm's changes in input demands are liable to adjustment costs and economists are concerned of what those costs look like. This is for a wide range of reasons, many having to do with the ability to predict the effects of factor market policies at external shocks and furthermore, aggregate investment sums firms' changes in their capital stock and measures responses that are determined by the structure and size of the adjustment costs. Therefore, GDP is partly determined by adjustment costs, as are labor productivity and total factor productivity. In addition, knowledge of structures of adjustment costs is crucial for predicting the possibly long and complex path of responses of capital demand to shocks, therefore should be a basic input into debates over the long run effects of policies that concern investment.

Specifically, to predict the effects of proposed policies or the possible impact of external shocks, we need to know (as Hamermesh and Pfann (1996) mention): 1) the source of the adjustment cost the firm is facing. Is it adjustment costs that generate slow adjustment, or does stickiness arise from other aspects of a firm's behavior or market environment? 2) The structure of these costs. Without knowing the structure of the costs, the path of firm's capital demand in response to shocks cannot be predicted, and 3) the size of adjustment costs. Higher costs associated with investment reduce the firms' long-run demand for capital.

Elaborating these questions, we have found that slow adjustment is generated –and can be explained – by costs associated with changing capital demand. Adjustment costs are found to be statistically important, thus firms change their demand for capital more slowly than the shocks to capital demand warrant, due to the interference of these costs. As far as the structure of the costs is concerned, the estimation results reported in Tables 8 and 10 indicate that a model which mixes both convex and non-convex adjustment processes can match the moments calculated from firm-level data quite well. The conclusion that adjustment costs are not characterized by a symmetric quadratic structure (as is usually assumed) affects aggregate behavior.

Finally, with regard to the size of the adjustment costs, our findings indicate high costs associated with investment in the Greek (micro) economy. The estimated value of the coefficient determining the magnitude of the convex adjustment costs (γ) is found to be 0.5164, which is higher than the values structurally estimated by other authors for other countries. Cooper and Ejarque (2001) estimate γ to be 0.149 in their study for USA. Cooper and Haltiwanger (2006), Bayraktar (2002) and Bayraktar, Sakellaris and Vermeulen (2006) estimate the value of γ to be very close to the value found here (namely, 0.5164). The estimated value of the coefficient determining the magnitude of the fixed adjustment has been found to be high (higher than in most of the literature). A Greek firm that undertakes an investment project faces a fixed adjustment cost of 15.57 percent of installed capital. The variation of our results compared to other studies most likely arises from differences in specification, as is discussed in section 4.3.

With respect to economic modeling, Wilcoxen (1993, p.96) argues that it is important to understand the nature of adjustment costs because it determines the medium- and long-run supply elasticity: "...since the elasticity is sensitive to even small departures of the adjustment cost parameter from unity, it is clearly inappropriate to assume adjustments costs are zero without considerable empirical evidence. This suggests that a fruitful area for future research is the empirical determination of adjustment cost parameters at the industry level. In addition, such research would help identify the underlying source of adjustment costs and would indicate whether these costs would be influenced by policy". Goyal (1994) takes a step ahead and argues that it is important to know the structure of adjustment costs because it determines the long-run elasticity, which is one of the most vexed questions in satisfactory modeling of dynamic Applied General Equilibrium Models.

Regarding policy issues, recent discussions stress that firm-specific aspects are not the unique determinants of capital adjustment. Government's fiscal activity is also important. Public policy plays an important role in the firm's capital investment decision and the cognizance of adjustment cost's source, structure and size has been shown to have a significant bearing on the effectiveness of fiscal policy. Turnovsky (1996), for example, picks up the argument that firm-specific aspects are not the unique determinants of capital adjustment and develops a one-sector endogenous growth model in which capital investment incurs adjustment costs that are related to governmental activity. He shows that the presence of adjustment costs causes a reduction in the equilibrium growth rate. In addition, he demonstrates that adjustment costs reduce the effects of capital taxes on the equilibrium growth rate and cause an expansion in productive government expenditure.

Closing this section it should be noted that the results we obtain here will allow us to improve the predictions of the paths of aggregate investment based on the knowledge of the dispersion of underlying shocks. Furthermore, knowing that costs are not always symmetric and convex guides us to a better understanding of the likely impacts of changes in capital-market policies than we obtain if we rely on the standard assumption. Last, but not least, this paper gives incipient clues and hints of how (stochastic) aggregation maps microeconomic behavior into macroeconomic relations.

CONCLUSIONS

In this paper a dynamic model of investment for Greek manufacturing firms is estimated. A balanced panel dataset of 1419 firms on 9933 observations for the period 1996-2002 has pointed strong evidence of inaction and lumpy investment. On account of these empirical observations, and since descriptive statistics should be taken as a "guide", we have adopted a model that takes into consideration total irreversibility of investment and includes not only convex but also non-convex adjustment costs. The adjustment cost function we assumed included both quadratic and fixed components.

We have estimated the structural parameters of the model using the indirect inference method. The indirect inference procedure works as follows. First, we solve the firm's dynamic programming problem for arbitrary values of the structural parameters and generate the corresponding optimal policy functions. Second, we use these policy functions and arbitrary initial conditions to generate simulated data. Third, this simulated data set is used to calculate the analogues coefficients obtained from the regression of the actual data. Finally, using the simulated annealing algorithm we estimate the structural parameters.

The results indicated that the structural model suits the data adequately. The structural parameters γ and F are significantly different from zero, indicating the importance of both convex and fixed adjustment costs. This rejects the neoclassical model with convex adjustment costs only and buttresses up the argument that adjustment costs are more complex than we once thought. Our estimates imply that frictions are important in determining firm's investment dynamics: traditional representative agent models with convex costs of adjustment only seem to be incapable of capturing the dynamics of investment and capital accumulation.

One of the gains to structural estimation presented in the present paper is to use the estimated parameters for policy analysis. Our next work will be the evaluation of the estimated model in terms of its predictions of the (dis)aggregate effects of an investment tax credit.

An issue that we plan to explore further is whether the presence of non-convexities at microeconomic level matters for aggregate investment. Whether, for example, the aggregation of individual agents facing non-convex (lumpy) adjustment costs generates differences in the paths of aggregate investment to external shocks and whether linearity in the underlying adjustment cost structure determines the paths of business cycles. This issue of aggregate implications has already drawn considerable attention in the literature. Caballero, Engel and Haltiwanger (1995) find that introducing the nonlinearities created by non-convex adjustment processes can improve the fit of aggregate investment models for sample periods with large shocks. Cooper, Haltiwanger and Power (1999) find that there are years where the interaction of an upward sloping hazard and the cross sectional distribution of capital vintages matters in accounting for aggregate investment.

Whereas the analysis has taken labour as flexible factor of production and already being maximized out of the problem, the adjustment cost function could be augmented to include interactions between labour and capital inputs. In future, our study will gravitate to this interesting topic too.

Data Appendix

Sample Selection

The source of the data set used in this paper is the ICAP databank, which is a database providing financial, statistical and market information for the publicly traded companies in Greece. The data set covers, not only the big manufacturing firms, but almost all the Greek manufacturing sector. For our analysis we pooled all the active Greek manufacturing firms that ICAP database had available information for the period 1996-2002. The elimination of firms is conducted following a number of steps:

1. We filter the data depending on the availability of the plant, property and equipment data points. We delete firms with missing data points for the book value of capital stock on plant, property and equipment. The total number of firms after this elimination is 2097. These firms comprise a balanced panel of 14679 observations over the period 1996-2002.
2. We only keep firms if they have profits information. This leads to 1690 firms on 11830 observations.
3. We do not accept this as our final dataset. We need to delete the firms which have involved in significant acquisitions or mergers. There are different ways to eliminate these firms. Bayraktar (2002) adopts the method that Gilchrist and Himmelberg (1995) propose and excludes the firms whenever

$$|G_t - G_{t-1} - I_t + R_t| > 0.15G_{t-1}$$

where G_t is the book value of the capital stock, I_t is nominal capital expenditure and R_t is the retirement of capital. We do not use this formula. Following Bayraktar, Sakellaris and Vermeulen (2006), practically we assume that investment rates higher than 90 percent are measuring a merger or acquisition. We exclude from our panel all the firms that display investment rate over 90 percent in any year among the period 1996-2002. This leads to our final balanced panel dataset of 1419 firms on 9933 observations for the period 1996-2002. Every firm has exactly 7 observations (6 observations for investment).

Description of the Variables

Raw Variables from the ICAP CD-Rom:

- LAND AND ESTATES
- BUILDINGS AND STRUCTURES
- MACHINERY AND EQUIPMENT
- NET PROFITS: the nominal book value of net profits (net of cost of production).

Constructed Variables

Book value capital stock, $p_t K_t$: the book value of the capital stock was constructed by the calculation LAND AND ESTATES + BUILDINGS AND STRUCTURES + MACHINERY AND EQUIPMENT + INTANGIBLE FIXED ASSETS

Investment at current prices, $p_t I_t$: since gross investment is not directly available from ICAP database, it has to be constructed using depreciation and capital stock observations. We use the accounting identity $p_t I_t = p_{t+1} K_{t+1} - p_t K_t (1-\delta)$.

Investment price deflator: was taken from OECD data source ("deflator for total investment"), (based year 1995)

Real investment, I_t: is constructed as investment at current prices deflated by the investment price deflator.

Real capital stock, K_t: constructed as book value capital stock deflated by the investment price deflator.

Investment rate, $\left(\frac{I}{K}\right)_t$.

Greek GDP deflator: was taken from OECD data source (based year 1995)
Real net profits: constructed as net profits deflated by the Greek GDP deflator.

REFERENCES

Abel, A.B. and Blanchard, O.J. (1986), "The Present Value of Profits and Cyclical Movements in Investment", *Econometrica,* 54, 249-273.

Abel, A.B. and Eberly, J.C. (1994), "A Unified Model of Investment under Uncertainty", *American Economic Review*, 84, 1369-1384.

Abel, A.B. and Eberly, J.C. (2002), "Investment and q with Fixed Costs: An Empirical Analysis", mimeo, *The Wharton School, University of Pennsylvania.*

Aguirregabiria, V. (1999), "The dynamics of markups and inventories in retailing firms", *Review of Economic Studies*, 66, 275-308.

Barnett, S.A. and Sakellaris, P (1998), "Non Linear Response of Firm Investment to Q: Testing a Model of Convex and Non Convex Adjustment Costs", *Journal of Monetary Economics,* 42, 261-288.

Bayraktar, N. (2002), "*Effects of Financial Market Imperfections and Non Convex Adjustment Costs in the Capital Adjustment Process*," mimeo, University of Maryland.

Bayraktar, N., Sakellaris, P. and Vermeulen, P. (2006), "Real versus Financial Frictions to Capital Invcstmcnt", *ECB Working Paper* No 566.

Bond, S.R., Harhoff, D and Van Reenen, J. (1999), "Investment, R&D and Financing Constraints in Britain and Germany", Working Paper, W99/5, *The Institute for Fiscal Studies, London.*

Caballero, R.J. and Engel, E. (1998), "Nonlinear Aggregate Investment Dynamics: Theory and Evidence," *National Bureau of Economic Research Working Paper* No. 6420 (Feb.).

Caballero, R.J. and Engel, E. (1999), "*Explaining Investment Dynamics in U.S Manufacturing: A Generalized (S,s) Approach*", Econometrica, 67, 783-826.

Caballero, R.J., and Leahy, J.V. (1996), "Fixed Costs: The Demise of Marginal q," *National Bureau of Economic Research Working Paper* No. 5508.

Caballero, R.J., Engel, E. and Haltiwanger, J. (1995), "Plant-Level Adjustment and Aggregate Investment Dynamics," *Brookings Papers on Economic Activity*, 2, 1-39.

Cooper, R.W. and Ejarque, J. (2001), "Exhuming Q: Market Power vs. Capital Market Imperfections," *National Bureau of Economic Research Working Paper*, 8182.

Cooper, R.W. and Haltiwanger, J. (1993), "The aggregate Implications of Machine Replacement: Theory and Evidence" *The American Economic Review*, 83(3), 360-382.

Cooper, R.W. and Haltiwanger, J. (2006), "On the Nature of Capital Adjustment Costs", *Review of Economic Studies*, 73(3), 611-633.

Cooper, R.W., Haltiwanger; J. and Power, L. (1999), "Machine Replacement and the Business Cycle: Lumps and Bumps." American Economic Review, 89(4), 921-946.

Cooper, R.W. and Willis, J.L. (2001), "The Economics of Labor Adjustment: Mind the Gap", *National Bureau of Economic Research Working Paper*, 8527, forthcoming in American Economic Review.

Doms, M. and Dunne, T. (1998), "Capital Adjustment Patterns in Manufacturing Plants", *Review of Economic Dynamics*, 1(2), 409-429.

Eberly, J.C. (1997), "International Evidence on Investment and Fundamentals", *European Economic Review*, 41, 1055-1078.

Gilchrist, S. and Himmelberg, C.P. (1995), "Evidence on the Role of Cash Flow for Investment." *Journal of Monetary Economics*, 36, 541–72.

Gilchrist, S. and Himmelberg, C.P. (1999), "Investment, Fundamentals, and Finance", in: B.S. Bernanke and J.J. Rotemberg (Eds.), *NBER Macroeconomics Annual*, pp. 223-62. Cambridge: MIT Press.

Gourieroux C; and Monfort, A. (1996), Simulation Based Econometric Methods, *Oxford University Press.*

Gourieroux, C. Monfort; A. and Renault, E. (1993), "Indirect Inference." *Journal of Applied Econometrics,* 8, S85-S118.

Goyal, A. (1994), "Growth Dynamics in a General Equilibrium Macroeconomic Model for India", *Journal of Policy Modeling*, 16(3), 265-289.

Hamermesh, D.S. (1989), "Labor Demand and the Structure of Adjustment Costs", *American Economic Review,* 79, 674-689.

Hamermesh, D.S. and Pfann, G. (1996), "Adjustment Costs in Factor Demand", *Journal of Economic Literature,* 34, 1264-1292.

Hayashi, F. (1982), "Tobin's Average q and Marginal q: a Neoclassical Interpretation", *Econometrica,* 50, 213-224.

Jorgenson, D.W. (1963), "Capital Theory and Investment Behaviour", *American Economic Review,* 53, 247-259.

Nilsen, A.O. and F. Schiantarelli (2003), "Zeroes and Lumps in Investment: Empirical Evidence on Irreversibilities and Non Convexities", *Review of Economics and Statistics*, 85(4), 1021-1037.

Rust, J. (1987a), "Optimal Replacement of GMC Bus Engines: An Empirical Model of Harold Zurcher" *Econometrica,* 55(5), 999-1033.

Rust, J. (1987b), "A Dynamic Programming Model of Retirement Behavior", *National Bureau of Economic Research Working Paper,* No 2470.

Slade, M. (1998), "Optimal Pricing with Costly Adjustment: Evidence From Retail Grocery Prices", *Review of Economic Studies*, 65, 87-107.

Smith, A.A., Jr. (1993), "Estimating Nonlinear Time-series Models Using Simulated Vector Autoregressions", *Journal of Applied Econometrics*, 8, S63-S84.

Tauchen, G. (1986), "Finite State Markov-Chain Approximations to Univariate and Vector Autoregressions", *Economics Letters*, 20, 177-81.

Tobin, J. (1969), "A General Equilibrium Approach to Monetary Theory", *Journal of Money, Credit and Banking,* 1, 15-29.

Turnovsky, S.J. (1996), "Fiscal Policy, Adjustment Costs, and Endogenous Growth", *Oxford Economic Papers*, 48, 361-381.

Wilcoxen, P. (1993), "Supply Elasticities in the Presence of Adjustment Costs", *Journal of Policy Modeling,* 15(1), 91-97

In: Computational Techniques in Economics and Finance
Editor: Constantine Zopounidis
ISBN: 978-1-61324-558-3

Chapter 12

COMPARATIVE PERFORMANCE EVALUATION OF BRANCHES OF A LARGE GREEK COMMERCIAL BANK

***Dimitris I. Giokas*[1] *and Ioannis E. Tsolas*[*2]**
[1] Department of Economics, National and Kapodistrian University of Athens, 8 Pesmatzoglou Street, 105 59 Athens, Greece
[2] School of Applied Mathematics and Physics, National Technical University of Athens, Zografou Campus, 157 80 Athens, Greece.

ABSTRACT

This paper evaluates the performance of a sample of branches of a large commercial bank in Greece by means of data envelopment analysis (DEA). A multi-input multi-output model that is geared towards senior management is considered in this country-wide evaluation. In this model the targets on sales of loans and deposits are proxied by the difference between average values of loans and deposits in two consecutive years. A variable returns to scale DEA input oriented model analyzed here led to valuable results pertaining to the performance of individual branches and moreover, useful information has also been obtained from the examination of the effects of selected branch characteristics and location to branch performance.

Keywords: Banking; Bank branches; Efficiency; Data envelopment analysis.
JEL Classification: C60, G21.

1. INTRODUCTION

The landscape of the Greek banking system has changed substantially in recent years. Greek banks benefit from a stable macroeconomic environment thanks to membership of the European Monetary Union (EMU), and a strong economic performance that has resulted in a rapid improvement of wealth standards. Since 2001, when Greece joined the EMU, its

[*] Corresponding author: E-mail: itsolas@central.ntua.gr

average real growth has been 4%, almost doubling the average in the Eurozone during the same period.

The transformation from a heavily regulated into an outward looking sector started in the last decade with radical structural and operational changes. The deregulation process, that started in the 1990s and was completed in 2003 when the last restrictions on consumer credit were abolished, gave rise to stronger competition and attracted new entrants to the market. Greek banks have become attractive targets for mergers and acquisitions (M&A) (Pasiouras and Zopounidis, 2008), and for entering into strategic alliances or co-operation agreements with foreign credit institutions. The merger and acquisition activity has been helped by the privatization process and the diminishing participation of the state in state-controlled banks. The number of directly or indirectly state-controlled banks has been reduced from 10 a decade ago to 2 today (Agricultural Bank, Postal Savings Bank). In 2006 the participation of the Greek state in the Greek banking system was reduced to 5% from 23% in 2005, following the acquisition of Emporiki Bank by Crédit Agricole. The merger and acquisition activity will more likely continue, either between domestic players or with the participation of banking institutions from abroad, so that banks acquire a critical size that will allow them to effectively compete with their European peers. Mergers and acquisitions have resulted in larger banking institutions that are able to reap the benefits of possible economies of scale and scope and compete more effectively. They are enlarging their products and services offerings, improving service quality, modernizing and expanding their distribution networks (including branches and alternative distribution channels), investing heavily in new technology, and improving their internal processes (i.e. by centralizing their back office functions). Competition among the major Greek banks has intensified over the recent years. The focus has been on retail banking, where, following a period of strong market expansion related to the underbanked state of the retail sector, market conditions have begun to tighten. Banks offer clients a great variety of specialized products to fit retail customer needs, intensively promote their products, and sell their products through different channels of sale.

The Greek banking market currently (at the end of 2006) comprises 62 credit institutions. Twenty- one are Greek commercial banks, which dominate the banking sector as they hold 86.5% of total assets. Twenty four are foreign banks, which are much smaller than their Greek peers as they garner 10.1% of total assets and their market share in traditional banking operations such as lending and deposits is rather small. There are also 16 very small cooperative banks and one specialised credit institution (Consignments and Loans Fund).

The degree of concentration of the Greek banking system in terms of assets is higher than both the EU and the euro area averages as measured by the market share of the five largest banks (2006: Greece 66.4%, EU 42%, Euro area 43%) though considerably lower compared to some individual member countries such as Belgium and the Netherlands. However, there is still room for further concentration as the size of Greek banks is relatively small compared with EU banks' average size (Bank of Greece, 2006).

The Greek banking system is underbanked by european standards. Various key indicators, such as loans to gross domestic product, assets per employee, population per branch, are below the euro area average. Hence, there is apparent scope for further growth. However, over the last years considerable progress has been made towards converging with the euro area. Strong credit and deposit growth have allowed for a substantial rise in the loans/GDP and deposits/GDP ratios. At the end of 2006, the deposits to GDP ratio has risen to the euro area level (89.6%). The loans to GDP ratio stands at 84.7%, much higher than five years ago (56%), but still quite lower than the euro area average (109.4%). Nevertheless, the lower level of activity in the Greek banking sector is set to increase, as loan growth rates remain higher than the euro area average. Corporate loans increase at rates close to the euro area average. However, housing loans grow at rates three times and consumer loans grow at rates five times the respective euro area rates. Hence, total household indebtedness, currently at 44% of GDP, is expected to further converge to the euro area average (54%). Expansion in Southcastcrn Europe with special emphasis on retail banking, especially in the Balkans, has been a basis strategic objective of major Greek banks. The aim is to enhance their activities abroad, so that in the coming years these activities become a major profitability driver which will more than offset the negative effects arising from the increased pressure on domestic interest rate margins.

Prospects for the Greek banking market are positive. Banks operate in a favourable macro-economic environment that is conducive to the further development of banking activities. Competition is expected to further intensify both in terms of the quality and range of products offered and in pricing policies. The ability to offer a broad range of financial products and services at competitive prices is a crucial parameter for the Greek banks' effective operation in the domestic market and especially at an international level. Also, the scale of operations and the investment in new technology will continue to be key factors for determining competitiveness. Loan growth rates are expected to remain at high levels but following a downward trend. In particular, growth rates of loans to enterprises may decelerate but remain above nominal GDP growth. The deceleration in the growth of housing and consumer loans is expected to be more pronounced. In any case, ratios of all types of loans to GDP are set to further converge to the euro area average.

Profitability should remain adequate over the medium term on the back of rising lending volumes both in the domestic market and in Southeastern Europe where Greek banks have significant presence. At the same time, efforts to control operating costs should continue in the light of intensifying competition. A big challenge for Greek banks remains the containment of operating costs. Substantial progress has been made in cutting down on expenses and the expenses to total assets ratio is close to the European Union average. As competition among individual banks gets increasingly stiffer, it becomes even more important for them to manage (i.e. measure, monitor and improve) their performance. Operating performance measurement is usually carried out on the basis of branch profitability by means of ratio analysis. Relevant measures are also alternative conventional indicators of performance (i.e. partial productivity measures such as unit or monetary output per staff member; measures by product type; total operating expenses by unit output etc.). Greek banks have based their performance improvement through tighter cash management and the introduction of new products and services but operations management is another area where improvements can be achieved with positive effects on profitability.

The limitations of ratio analysis (Sherman and Gold, 1985; Foster, 1986; Zopounidis et al., 1995; Athanassopoulos and Ballantine, 1995), together with recent advances in the management science field, have led to the development of multivariate models for assessing bank branches' efficiency, such as Data Envelopment Analysis (DEA; Charnes et al., 1978). DEA models are related with the degree at which each branch makes use of its resources and not only they are considered complementary to the ratio analysis models but they also provide useful information to decision makers.

The major contribution of this paper is the development of an efficiency production model adapted to the branch network of a large Greek commercial bank where the use of a set of variables in the output side of DEA reflect the main operational objectives of bank branches under study, i.e. to increase sales of the products the branches have to offer. Moreover, compared to previous works that have also used from Greek banks, it focus on issues of scale economies and return to scales and examines the effects of selected branch characteristics (i.e. size, profitability) and location (i.e. branches located in urban and rural areas) on variations of efficiency.

The remainder of the paper is organised as follows. Section 2 briefly introduces the literature relevant to bank branches efficiency estimation by means of DEA. Section 3 describes the methodology. Section 4 describes the sample, presents the results of the analysis and discusses some of the implications and, finally, some concluding remarks are given in Section 5.

2. Literature Review

Assessing bank branch performance is a very complicated process that can be accomplished with various methods such as ratio analysis, frontier estimation methodologies, i.e. Stochastic Frontier Analysis as described in Aigner et al. (1977), sometimes referred to as the econometric frontier approach and DEA introduced in banking by Sherman and Gold (1985).

Ratio analysis has traditionally been employed for assessing performance in banking, primarily based on the use of financial ratios (return on assets, loans to assets, loans per employee, deposits per employee, cost to income, etc). Ratio analysis by means of financial ratios has on one hand the advantage to measure the relationship between two numbers in the financial statements. On the other hand, ratio analysis for assessing performance in multi-input multi-output systems, a common fact for banking activities, has many limitations mainly because ratios take into account only one input and only one output (Sherman and Gold, 1985). Moreover, these financial ratios are partial, and short term, and may not convey a consistent picture of the long term financial viability of the branch branches (Pastor et al., 2006). As the branch bank assessment is the objective of this paper what is needed is a description of the overall performance of branch branches, as measured by their ability to convert the resources at their disposal into services and this is not provided by a narrow focus on short term financial ratios. Ratios also provide little help when considering the effects of economies of scale. See also Foster (1986); Lawder (1989); Athanassopoulos and Ballantine (1995); Kosmidou et al. (2004); Pastor et al. (2006); Giokas (2008a).

Developments of econometric frontier approach are summarized in Ferrier and Lovell (1990), Resti (1997), Berger and Mester (1997); applications to banking are discussed in Kumbhakar and Lovel (2000).

The assessment of performance of the branch networks of banks traditionally based on ratio analysis models has changed to more comprehensive benchmarking programs. Frontier estimation methodologies such as DEA have been used to evaluate the relative performance of financial units, assessing how close they are to a best-practice frontier.

By taking into account many inputs and outputs simultaneously, DEA models have the ability to detect the branches with the same resources (inputs) and, under the same conditions, either produce higher outcome or produce the same outcome but of higher quality and using fewer resources. Using DEA the relation of inputs-outputs between each branch and the others is identified and the efficiency of the bank's branches can be examined under several perspectives. The use of DEA has found widespread application, particular in the areas of banking and finance.

The research literature concerning the efficiency of banking institutions using DEA both at thc aggrcgate level (bank efficiency studies) and at the branch level (branch efficiency studies) has experienced a phenomenal growth in the nineties, which was translated into a considerable volume of theoretical and empirical research (see special issue of the Journal of Productivity Analysis (1993); Journal of Banking and Finance (1993); European Journal of Operational Research (1997); Interfaces (1999)). The DEA studies examine branch performance by assuming various behavioral objectives that are categorised into three approaches (Paradi et al., 2004b; Giokas, 2008a): production approach, intermediation approach, and profitability approach.

In the production approach, branches are regarded as using resources (e.g. labor, capital) to produce deposits, loans, and other revenue-generating financial products.

In the intermediation approach, it is examined the ability of a branch to take in deposits and lend the money to worthy and profitable borrowers. In this case, branches play an intermediate role since they buy capital, which they sell in the form of loans and other income-earning activities.

In the profitability approach branches are regarded as using inputs (i.e. expenses) to produce revenues.

Most of the DEA studies analyse bank branch efficiency from a production perspective using small sample sizes, e.g. Sherman and Gold (1985), Parkan (1987), Vassiloglou and Giokas (1990), Giokas (1991), Athanassopoulos and Giokas (2000), and Giokas (2008a); or large sample sizes, e.g. Drake and Howcroft (1994), Schaffnit et al. (1997), Giokas (2008b). Other studies are those of Oral and Yolalan (1990), Al-Faraj et al. (1993), Tulkens (1993), Haag and Jaska (1995), Sherman and Ladino (1995), Athanassopoulos (1997, 1998), Berger et al. (1997), Lovell and Pastor (1997), Camanho and Dyson (1999, 2005), Zenios et al. (1999), Soteriou and Zenios (1999), Golany and Storbeck (1999), Avkiran (1999), Kantor and Maital (1999), Soteriou et al. (1999), Cook et al. (2000), Cook and Hababou (2001), Dekker and Post (2001), Hartman et al. (2001), Bala and Cook (2003), Portela et al. (2003, 2004), Paradi and Schaffnit (2004) and Portela and Thanassoulis (2005, 2007).

Depending upon behavioral goals, analysts should select an approach to analyse efficiency (e.g. production approach), choose the input and output variables, and build a model based on CCR (Charnes et al., 1978), BCC (Banker et al., 1984) or non-radial (e.g. additive) models to achieve the desired answers for decision makers who will have to implement the findings.

3. METHODOLOGY

The original model of DEA is the CCR model. For the present study, the BCC input oriented model is employed. The primary difference between the BCC and the CCR model is the treatment of returns to scale. The CCR version is based on the assumption of constant returns to scale, while the BCC version is more flexible and allows variable returns to scale (VRS).

Given a set of n decision making units (DMUs), i.e. bank branches, j=1,…, n, utilising quantities of inputs $X \in \Re^{m}_{+}$ to produce quantities of outputs $Y \in \Re^{k}_{+}$, we can denote x_{ij} and y_{rj} the amount of the ith input and rth output respectively used by the jth DMU.

The following VRS input oriented value-based model (Thanassoulis, 2001) can be used to assess efficiencies.

$$
\begin{aligned}
&Max \quad h = \sum_{r=1}^{k} \mu_r y_{rj_o} + \omega \\
&s.t \\
&\sum_{i=1}^{m} v_i x_{ij_o} = 1 \\
&\sum_{r=1}^{k} \mu_r y_{rj} - \sum_{i=1}^{m} v_i x_{ij} + \omega \le 0 \quad j = 1, 2, \ldots, j_o, \ldots, n \qquad (1) \\
&\mu_r \ge \varepsilon \qquad\qquad r = 1, 2, \ldots, k \\
&v_i \ge \varepsilon \qquad\qquad i = 1, 2, \ldots, m \\
&\omega \textit{ free on sign}
\end{aligned}
$$

where

$\varepsilon > 0$, a convenient small positive number (non-Archimedean), see also Charnes et al. (1994)

μ_r = output weights estimated by the model

v_i = input weights estimated by the model.

We can use the model (1) to identify the nature of returns to scale holding locally at DMU j_o in case that j_o is Pareto-efficient:

- If ω takes negative values in all optimal solutions to model (1) then locally at DMU j_o decreasing returns to scale hold.
- If ω takes a zero value in some optimal solutions to model (1) then locally where DMU j_o lies or is projected on the efficient frontier constant returns to scale hold.
- If ω takes positive values in all optimal solutions to model (1) then locally at DMU j_o increasing returns to scale hold.

The radial efficiency *h* derived from model (1) shows the rate of reduction to the input levels of branch under evaluation. The dual of model (1) provides the slack values of inputs (see Thanassoulis, 2001).

4. Data, Analyses and Results

4.1. Data

Our data set is comprised of bank branch data of a large Greek commercial bank and covers the 2001-2002 period. It is a large sample size as it consists of 156 branches spread across Greece.

The data included for the particular period are the amount of different types of services proxied by the difference in average value of loans, the difference in average value of deposits and the total number of transactions (i.e. deposit based transactions, loan based transactions and remaining transactions) and cost categories (i.e. personnel cost, running cost, and other operating expenses) and the number of ATMs for each branch.

Five output variables were used in this study: the difference in average value of loans and deposits, and the total number of transactions for the particular year. Although most previous studies on branches' efficiency included in the output set the total value of loans and deposits, in this study we chose to use the difference between average values of loans and deposits in two consecutive years, than the total value. While the various transactions may not generate income streams, branches are nevertheless expected to process these transactions and hence they should be part of the multiple output set in order to fully evaluate the operational efficiency of bank branches.

Three transaction outputs were also used: Deposit based transactions, loan based transactions and remaining transactions. Regarding transaction specific variables, it is necessary to make clarifications concerning their composition. That is, each of the categories included as final outputs was made of a number of subcategories composing the whole range of branch-customer transactions. To accommodate the differences in degree of complexity and difficulty in handling the branch's transactions, we have used information regarding the time required for each type of transaction at the bank level. However, the reliability of such time measurement is not as straightforward especially in the case of banks lacking detailed Activity Based Costing (ABC) system integrated with the Management Information System of the bank.

Regarding specific variables included in the input set, the first input is the personnel cost which include also overtime salary costs; labour is the major input in banking operations in terms of its effect on both the level of production and costs and the contribution of labour to branch production was measured by personnel cost.

A variety of supplies (e.g. stationery) used at the branches is also related to the level of production and, for simplicity of aggregation, was measured in terms of monetary value at standard costs. The corresponding two other inputs used are "running costs" and "other operating expenses". Running costs of the buildings include rents for bank branches' space, electricity etc. For branches that are owned by the bank an estimate of the market value for the rent of the space occupied by the branch was used. Other operating expenses reflect the consumption of a range of inputs by the bank branch and cover all the operating expenses of the branches, such as those for telephone, insurance, advertising expenses, stationery and other supplies. Only those inputs, which directly concern bank branches, were used, ignoring bank overheads, since the objective of this analysis was to evaluate the use of inputs consumed directly by the branch.

Finally, the number of ATMs at each branch was introduced as a fourth input in order to explore possible variations in output volumes due to automation.

Table 1 presents the descriptive statistics of the variables used.

Table 1. Descriptive statistics of inputs and outputs (000 euros if otherwise stated)

Variable	Average	Median	Q1*	Q3	Min value	Max value	CV%
Inputs							
Personnel costs	175.3	162.9	138.4	208.9	71.2	423.3	30.6
Running costs	24.0	18.6	12.6	27.0	4.2	182.9	92.6
Other operating expenses	35.5	34.4	27.1	41.5	4.8	87.1	36.9
ATMs, number	2.1	2.0	2.0	2.0	1.0	5.0	23.2
Outputs							
Difference in average value of loans	526.3	392.5	184.8	643.1	-897.2	3616.1	98.8
Difference in average value of deposits	4691.6	3786.5	2273.7	6354.2	-1284	24236.1	74.4
Deposit based transactions	87337.9	89536.5	56263.8	114531.0	16189.0	182553.0	41.8
Loan based transactions	13005.3	11025.0	8434.5	15633.5	1176.0	40627.0	54.4
Other transactions	19566.7	17873.0	9582.8	26542.3	2690.0	60120.0	61.2

*Q1 = first quartile; Q3 = third quartile; CV = coefficient of variation.

4.2. Input-Output Model Building and Efficiency Rating

Various alternative cases of DEA method can be employed for estimating efficiency giving emphasis either to the reduction of inputs or the increase in outputs, under constant or variable returns to scale. In this study the input oriented BCC model is employed. Input oriented is consistent with management's objective of improving resource efficiency at the current level of outputs (Schaffnit et al., 1997; Sowlati and Paradi, 2004). BCC model is employed under the assumption that the production process in the branch is characterized by variable returns to scale.

This was supported using the Kolmogorov-Smirnov test (Banker, 1996). The null hypothesis was rejected, at a 5% significant level (DN=0.25, critical value=0.15), which means that constant returns to scale and variable returns to scale inefficiencies cannot be assumed to come from the same distribution. It should be noted that the DEA algorithm cannot use negative values for all inputs and outputs. However, in our case some of the outputs (value of loans and deposits) take on and negative values. It is necessary to transform these outputs by adding the most negative value among all branches. This transformation requires that the analysis is restricted to use input oriented DEA model. Since only the outputs were transformed efficiency scores based on comparing inputs were not affected (Stanton, 2002; Emel et al., 2003; Paradi et al., 2004a).

We further investigated the scale economies issue by considered two types of ratios similar to those used by Sherman and Gold (1985): number of transactions per personnel (A1) and operating expenses per transaction (A2). The calculation of the rank order correlation (Spearman) between the total weighted number of transactions (A3) and each of A1 and A2, confirmed that there is significant correlation between any of the ratios and the size (in terms of total weighted transactions) of the branch. The rank correlation between the size of the branch and transactions per personnel is 0.80 (significance level=0.000). Thus, labour economies due to size appear to explain inefficiencies, as the correlation coefficient suggests that larger branches process more transactions per personnel than smaller branches. The rank order correlation between the size of the branch and operating expenses per transaction is – 0.65 (significance level=0.000). This means that smaller branches are more costly, suggesting that bank branch size may have influence on the supplies used per transaction. Based on these ratios, it appears that some of the inefficiencies identified with DEA may be due to scale economies related to personnel and supply usage.

Furthermore, the analysis focuses on examining the relation among size, efficiency by DEA and profitability. Branch profitability is obtained dividing profit before indirect costs by total costs (interest and non-interest) and branch size by capital used. Figure 1 shows the relation between efficiency (CRS and VRS) and size and figure 2 shows the relation between the profitability and size. From these graphs it can be derived that larger branches have higher efficiency and profits, which can be also an indication of the existence of economies of scale in branches' activities.

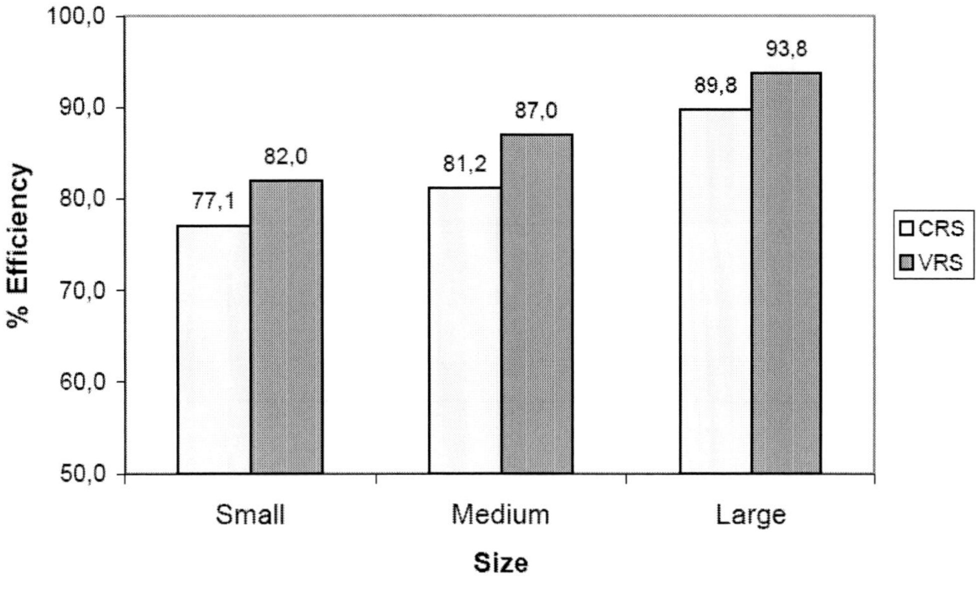

Figure 1. Efficiency and size.

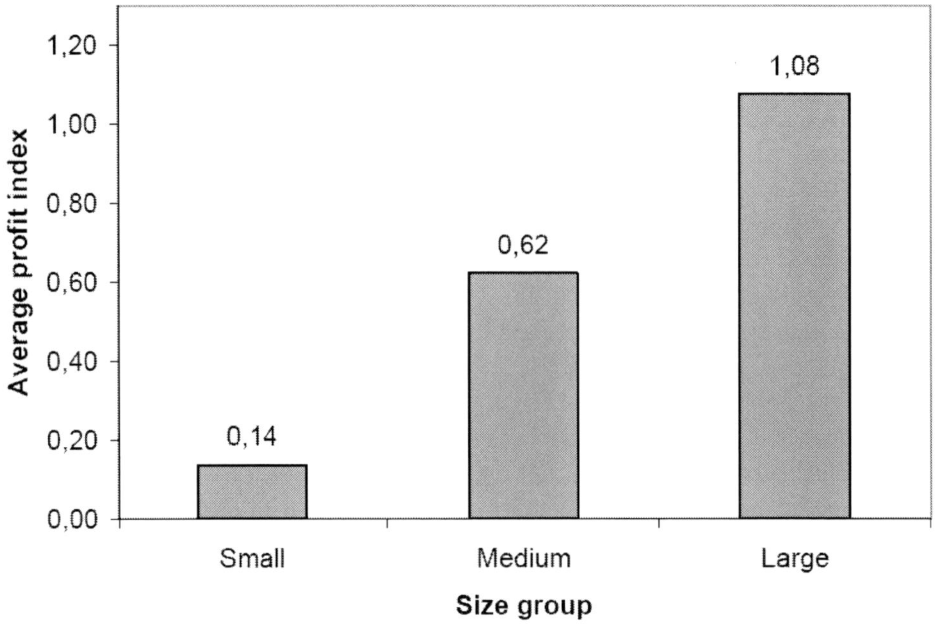

Figure 2. Profit index and size.

4.3. Efficiency by Size and Geographical Area

The efficiency results can also be displayed in terms of branch size categories as in table 2. Results concerning the distribution of the efficiency of the bank branches in terms of branch size categories are presented in figure 3. A gradual increase in average efficiency with size, as well as in percentage of efficient branches, is observed. Large branches have an average efficiency of 93.8%. The category of medium size branches follow (87.0%) on average, whilst the small size branches are the least efficient in comparison with the other categories (82.0%) on average.

These differences are significantly different from one another in the three pair-wise comparison, large branches having the highest percent of efficient branches (40%) and the small branches, the lowest (17%). The general increase in efficiency with size can be attributed to economies of scale. These findings will be further examined later when the issue of economies of scale will be addressed seeking to match the elements of branch size with the size of activities that are undertaken by the branches.

The efficiency results can also be displayed in terms of location (table 2). Results concerning the distribution of the efficiency of the bank branches in terms of location are presented in figure 3.

It is evident that urban branches are superior on their efficiency results as compared to the rural branches. Urban branches have on average efficiency of 84.3%, whilst the total percentage of efficient branches is 28%. Rural branches have on average efficiency 81.3% with a lower percentage of efficient branches, and a quite high dispersion in the efficiency ratios (coefficient of variation: urban branches=16.8%, rural branches=18.3%).

Table 2. Descriptive statistics of the ratio of relative efficiency split by size category and location

	Split by size			Split by location		Significant t- tests			
	Large (47)[a] (1)	Medium (62) (2)	Small (47) (3)	Urban (65) (4)	Rural (91) (5)	(1)-(2)	(1)-(3)	(2)-(3)	(4)-(5)
Average	93.8 (7.63)[b]	87.0 (9.7)	82.0 (10.6)	84.3 (14.2)	81.3 (14.9)	4.1*	6.2*	2.5*	1.30
Median	97.6	87.5	79.5	85.8	80.1				
1st Quartile (Q1)	87.4	79.3	73.4	74.8	69.5				
3rd Quartile (Q3)	100.0	95.9	89.4	100.0	96.5				
Minimum value of the ratio (%)	71.3	65.2	65.6	47.7	41.2				
Number and % of efficient branches	19 (40)	11 (18)	8 (17)	18(28)	21 (23.1)				

[a] Indicates the number of branches per size category.

[b] Standard deviation

* Means statistically significant at 5% level.

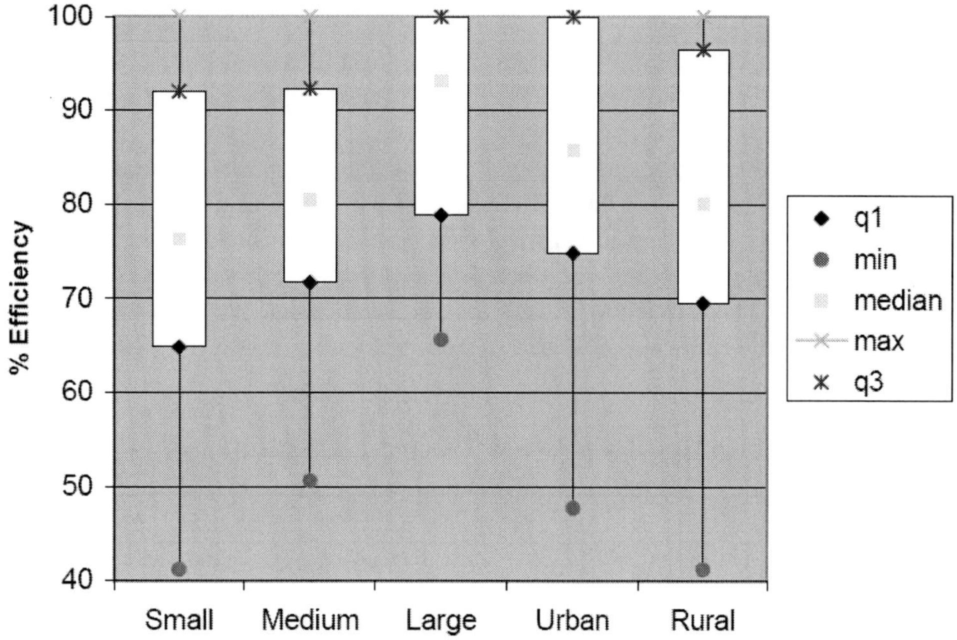

Figure 3. Efficiency by size and location (Box-plots).

Table 3 provides us with insight into the relationship between urban - rural branches controlled for size. Branch location does not seem to play a differentiating role since no statistical association was verified linking location to efficiency. Although rural small branches are about 3.4% less efficient than urban, the t-test fails to show this difference as significant. The same is true with regard to urban medium branches and their rural counterparts. As shown in table 3, the percentages of efficient urban, and rural branches, respectively, were 27.7% and 23.1%. This difference is not significantly different, urban branches having the highest percentage of efficient and rural branches the lowest. The results exhibited in table 3 show that rural large and medium size branches tend to have higher percentages of efficient branches than urban, while urban small branches show higher percentage of efficient branches than rural branches. What is important to notice from the above results is that these differences do not differ significantly across groups.

Table 3. Urban - rural average efficiency and percentage of efficient branches, split by size

	Urban branches			Rural branches			Tests of significance
	n	% average	% efficient	n	% average	% efficient	(z-test for proportions)
Size							
Small	9	79.8(18.4)[a]	22.2	38	76.4(15.2)	18.4	0.25
Medium	23	78.4(13.8)	13.1	39	82.8(14.0)	20.5	-0.72
Large	33	89.7(11.1)	39.4	14	90.1(12.1)	42.9	0.22
Total	65	84.3(14.5)	27.7	91	81.3(14.9)	23.1	0.81

[a] Standard deviation.

In order to test the hypothesis of statistical significant differences in the performance of the groups split by size and location, ANOVA and Kruskal-wallis tests were used. The results are shown in table 4.

The results indicate, with the exception of DEA efficiency split by location, the presence of statistical association between the different groups and performance indicators (DEA and Profit index). In particular, there is statistical evidence of significant differences in the DEA efficiency between the three size categories. These differences seem not to have statistical significance for the DEA efficiency between the two location categories. In contrary, there is statistical evidence of significant differences in the Profit index between the size and location categories.

Table 4. Statistical assessment (ANOVA and Kruskal-Wallis tests) of different groups of branches and performance

	ANOVA		Kruskal –Wallis (non-parametric test)	
Performance	by size	by location	by size	by location
DEA efficiency	F=10.5*	F=1.68	chi-square=18.0* d.f = 2	chi-square=0.22 d.f. = 1
Profit index	F=9.3*	F=11.5*	chi-square=34.0* d.f = 2	chi-square=11.9* d.f. = 1

* Indicates statistically significant at 5% level.

4.4. Returns to Scale and Efficiency Profile

Furthermore, the analysis focuses on examining the nature of returns to scale of the branches. In this paper the BCC returns to scale method introduced by Banker et al. (1984) is used. The classification of the returns to scale can only be referred to branches located on the VRS frontier. For branches not operating on the frontier, their returns to scale can only be determined after the elimination of pure technical inefficiency through the projections towards the VRS frontier. For example, the classification of increasing returns to scale for an inefficient branch may mean that after the input reduction to achieve efficiency, the size of the branch will be smaller than the most productive scale size, although the branch may at present have the right size. In our study the model suggests that 69.2% of the pure technically efficient branches are operating under constant returns to scale (CRS), 7.7% operate under local increasing returns (IRS) to scale and finally 23.1% of the efficient branches operate under local decreasing returns to scale (DRS). About 63% of the inefficient branches seem to operate under IRS, 27.6% under DRS and 9.4% under CRS. The results indicate that a possible increase in the scale of size of operations of branches that are inefficient will lead to increased levels of volume of financial activities with a rate higher than that used to increase the input level. In other words there is a potential in the branch network to accommodate and manage higher levels of business volumes.

4.5. Target Setting

The solution of DEA model yields input inefficiencies (slack levels) which would render the branch being assessed efficient, if not already so. Input inefficiencies indicate excess in every input used by the inefficient branch being assessed. These inefficiencies can be analyzed to determine which inputs contribute most to a branch's computed efficiency ratios. The average input inefficiencies (for inefficient branches) according to location and size of branches are summarized in table 5. The information in table 5 indicates extensive reduction of all input categories across all categories split by size and location. The reduction of personnel cost, running cost, other operating cost, varies from an average of 20.6% in large sized branches (for operating cost) to 44% for small sized branches (for running cost). Small sized branches were found to have the highest possibility for reducing input resources. The possibility of decreasing the personnel cost of rural and small sized branches at a level of 27.9% and 30.9%, respectively, can be observed. Large sized branches have the smaller possibility for reducing personnel cost (22.6%).

The average excess in personnel cost does decrease with branch size. For example, in inefficient small sized branches there exist an average of Euro 49 thousand excess of personnel cost (-30.9%), whereas, in large size branches this average reduces to Euro 43 thousand (-22.6%). A similar situation exists with running cost and operating expenses, the other components of input resources.

These results for the large sized branches support the theory of scale economies that large sized branches should generate. Looking at the input inefficiencies we see significant differences between urban and rural and between small and large sized branches in operating expenses category (table 6).

Table 5. Average input slack values (inefficiencies) by location and size (standard deviation in parenthesis), amounts in euros

Input slacks	Location		Size			Global
	Urban	Rural	Small	Medium	Large	
	(47)[a]	(70)	(38)	(51)	(28)	(117)
Running cost	12,408 (15,212) -42.2[b]	8,696 (20,697) -41.5	9,907 (26,185) -44.0	8,388 (10,071) -38.7	13,845 (18,862) -43.6	10,187 (18,706) -41.8
Personnel cost	42,578 (27.815) -24.6	49,474 (30,080) -27.9	48,965 (30,810) -30.9	46.802 (29,742) -26.1	43,455 (26,886) -22.6	46,704 (29,267) -26.6
Operating cost	8,467 (6,854) -24,3	12,501 (10,412) -32.3	14,022 (11,899) -35.4	10,346 (7,543) -29,1	7,591 (6,999) -20.6	10,881 (9,331) -29.2

[a] Indicates the number of branches per location. [b] Indicates reduction possibility (%).

Table 6. Statistical assessment (t- tests) of input slack values by location and size

	Running cost	Personnel expenses	Operating expenses
Urban-rural	1.05	-1.25	-2.33*
Small-medium	0.37	0.33	1.78
Small-large	-0.67	0.76	2.55*
Medium-large	-1.68	0.49	1.59

*Indicates statistically significant at 5% level.

Furthermore, the analysis focused on examining the overall cost savings proposed in the empirical results. The reduction in total cost that might be achieved is, on average, 21.6% (observed: euro 36.6 mil, efficient: euro 28.7 mil).

More particularly, the personnel cost could be reduced from 27.4 to euro 21.9 mil (-20%), the running cost from 3.7 to euro 2.6 mil (-30%), whereas the operating cost could be reduced from 5.5 to euro 4.2 mil (-24%), (figure 4).

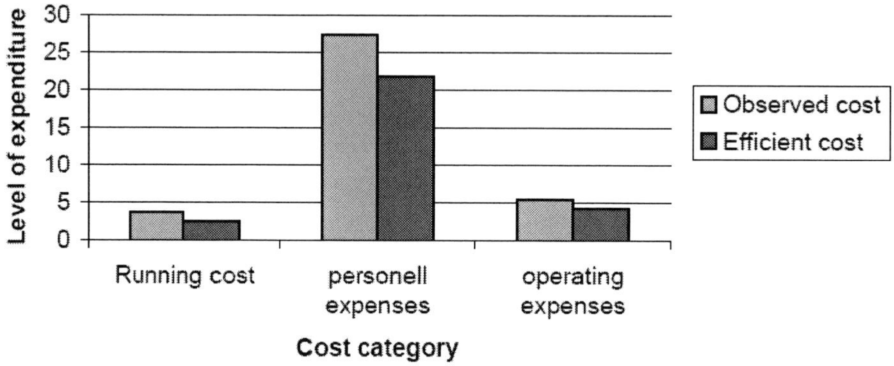

Figure 4. Possible savings in bank branches costs (in mil euros).

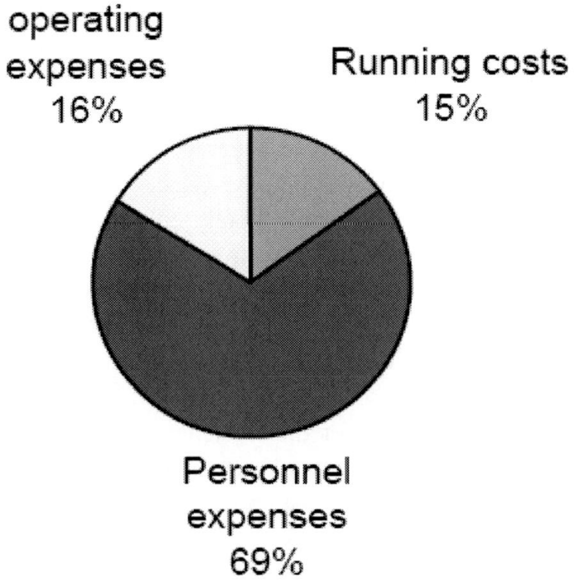

Figure 5. Cost saving contributions (%) from different cost categories.

The most important contributor of the proposed savings is the personnel expenses (personnel expenses represent more than 74% of total cost). The percentage contribution of cost savings from alternative cost categories is presented in figure 5. Cost savings are proposed at a level of 69% from personnel expenses. The remainder 31% is made up in a 15% savings in the running costs category and 16% in operating expenses category.

Non-efficient branches could produce the same outputs if the total cost was reduced by 28.8% (observed: euro 27.8 mil, efficient: euro 19.8 mil). The above indicates that, if these inefficiencies were eliminated by appropriate policies and planning, bank branches could reduce their actual costs to a considerable degree.

Conclusion and Further Direction

The main objective of the study presented in this paper was the comparative performance evaluation of branches of a large commercial bank in Greece in terms of their operating efficiency. This evaluation was realized by means of DEA; the inputs to the model were cost variables (i.e. personnel cost, running cost, and other operating expenses) and a proxy for the introduction of automation (i.e. number of ATMs) and the outputs were the difference in average value of loans and deposits in two consecutive years and three transaction outputs (deposit based transactions, loan based transactions and remaining transactions).

Efficiency estimation was based on an assumption of variable returns to scale so that a branch under evaluation is not penalized for the scale at which is operates and over which it has no control. The existence of VRS in branches activities was formally tested using the Kolmogorov-Smirnov test. The empirical results were presented via two broad segmentation categories, one on the basis of size (capital used) and the other on the basis of location (urban versus rural).

Four main reasons motivated the analysis: the absence of prior research on branch banking efficiency in Greece using in the output side of DEA the difference between average values of loans and deposits; the importance of returns to scale in the branch network for bank management decisions; the investigation of importance of bank branch characteristics and location to branch performance in a country-wide evaluation; and the identification of the most important contributor of the proposed input savings.

This study has led to some interesting results concerning the relative efficiency of branches examined here. These results are summarized below.

The results of the analysis on the basis of size considering two ratios as the number of transactions per personnel and operating expenses per transaction show that larger branches process more transactions per personnel than smaller branches, and branch size may have influence on the supplies used per transaction. Larger branches have higher efficiency and profits; and this can be an indication for the existence of economies of scale in branches' activities. Moreover, the results of the analysis examining the relation between DEA efficiency scores and size show that there is a gradual increase in average efficiency with size, as well as in percentage of efficient branches, though some of the inefficiencies identified with DEA may be due to scale economies related to personnel and supply usage. The null hypotheses of statistical significant differences between the three different size groups and the two performance indicators used here (i.e. DEA scores and profit index) are not rejected.

In the light of the results of the analysis on the basis of location, despite the fact that urban branches are superior on their DEA efficiency scores as compared to the rural branches location does not seem to play a differentiating role since no statistical association was verified linking that branch characteristic to efficiency.

The results of the analysis on examining the nature of returns to scale of the branches indicate that there is a potential for some branches to accommodate and manage higher levels of business volumes; e.g. a possible increase in the scale of operations of branches that are inefficient will lead to increased levels of volume of financial activities with a rate higher than that used to increase the input level.

This study also examined which input variables played the greatest role in generating relative operating efficiency scores by using the slack values; the most important contributor of the proposed input savings is the personnel expenses. The results of the analysis of input inefficiencies yielded by the DEA model indicate that the small sized branches have the highest possibility for reducing input resources. Moreover, there are significant differences between urban and rural branches and small and large sized branches in operating expenses category. The improvement of operation of inefficient branches could reduce their actual costs to a considerable degree of about 29%.

Directions for further research, if the appropriate data are found, are the examination of efficiency of branches over successive periods and the investigation of the effect on branch efficiency of other local variables such as population and regional GDP.

REFERENCES

Aigner, D., Lovell, C.A.K. and Schmidt, P. (1977), "Formulation and estimation of stochastic frontier productions models", *Journal of Econometrics,* 6, 21-37.

Al-Faraj, T.N., Alidi, A.S. and Bu-Bshait, K.A. (1993), "Evaluation of bank branches by means of Data Envelopment Analysis", *International Journal of Operations and Production Management,* 13(9), 45-53.

Athanassopoulos, A.D. (1997), "Service quality and operating efficiency synergies for management control in the provision of financial services: evidence from Greek bank branches", *European Journal of Operational Research,* 98, 300-313.

Athanassopoulos, A.D. (1998), "Nonparametric frontier models for assessing the market and cost efficiency of large-scale bank branch networks", *Journal of Money and Credit Banking,* 30, 172-192.

Athanassopoulos, A.D. and Ballantine, A. (1995), "Ratio and frontier analysis for corporate performance: evidence from the grocery industry in the UK", *Journal of the Operational Research Society,* 46(4), 427-440.

Athanassopoulos, A.D. and Giokas, D. (2000), "The use of Data Envelopment Analysis in Banking Institutions: evidence from the Commercial Bank of Greece", *Interfaces,* 30(2), 81-95.

Avkiran, N.K. (1999), "An application reference for data envelopment analysis in branch banking: helping the novice researcher", *International Journal of Bank Marketing,* 17(5), 206-220.

Bala, K. and Cook, W.D. (2003), "Performance measurement with classification information: An enhanced additive DEA model", *Omega International Journal of Management Science,* 31(6), 439-450.

Bank of Greece (2006), Summary of the Annual Report 2005, Greek Central Bank, April.

Banker, R.D. (1996), "Hypothesis tests using data envelopment analysis", *The Journal of Productivity Analysis,* 7, 139-159.

Banker, R.D., Charnes, A. and Cooper, W.W. (1984), "Models for estimating technical and scale efficiencies in Data Envelopment Analysis", *Management Science,* 30(9), 1078-1092.

Berger, A.N., Leusner, J. and Mingo, J. (1997), "The efficiency of bank branches", *Journal of Monetary Economics,* 40, 141-162.

Berger, A.N. and Mester, L.J. (1997), "Inside the black box: what explains differences with efficiency of financial institutions", *Journal of Banking and Finance,* 21, 895–947.

Camanho, A.S. and Dyson, R.G. (1999), "Efficiency, size, benchmarks and targets for bank branches: an application of data envelopment analysis", *Journal of the Operational Research Society,* 50, 903–915.

Camanho, A.S. and Dyson, R.G. (2005), "Cost efficiency measurement with price uncertainty: a DEA application to bank branch assessments", *European Journal of Operational Research,* 161(2), 432-446.

Charnes, A., Cooper, W. Lewin, A. and Seiford, L. (1994), Data Envelopment Analysis: Theory, Methodology, and Application", Kluwer Academic Publishers, Dordrecht.

Charnes, A., Cooper, W.W. and Rhodes, E. (1978), "Measuring the efficiency of Decision Making Units", *European Journal of Operational Research,* 2, 429-444.

Cook, W.D. and Hababou, M. (2001), "Sales performance measurement in bank branches", *Omega International Journal of Management Science*, 29, 299-307.

Cook, W.D., Hababou, M. and Tuenter, H.J. (2000), "Multicomponent efficiency measurement and shared inputs in data envelopment analysis: an application to sales and service performance in bank branches", *Journal of Productivity Analysis,* 14, 209-224.

Dekker, D. and Post, T. (2001), "A Quasi-Concave DEA model with an application for bank branch performance evaluation", *European Journal of Operational Research*, 132(2), 296-311.

Drake, L. and Howcroft, B. (1994), "Relative efficiency in the branch network of a UK bank: an empirical study", *Omega International Journal of Management Science,* 22(1), 83-90.

Emel, A.B., Oral, M., Reisman, A. and Yolalan, R. (2003), "A credit scoring approach for the commercial banking sector", *Socio-Economic Planning Sciences,* 37, 103-123.

Ferrier, G. and Lovell, K. (1990), "Measuring cost efficiency in banking: econometric and linear programming evidence", *Journal of Econometrics,* 46(1/2), 229-245.

Foster, G. (1986), Financial Statements Analysis, 2nd edn. Prentice Hall, Englewood, Cliffs N.Y.

Giokas, D. (1991), "Bank branch operating efficiency: a comparative application of DEA and the Loglinear Model", Omega International Journal of Management Science, 19(6), 549-557.

Giokas, D.I. (2008a), "Assessing the efficiency in operations of a large Greek bank branch network adopting different economic behaviors", *Economic Modelling,* 25, 559 -574.

Giokas, D.I. (2008b), "Cost efficiency impact of bank branch characteristics and location. An illustrative application to Greek bank branches", *Managerial Finance,* 34(3), 172-185.

Golany, B. and Storbeck, J.E. (1999), "A data envelopment analysis of the operational efficiency of bank branches", *Interfaces,* 29(3), 14-26.

Haag, S.E. and Jaska, P.V. (1995), "Interpreting inefficiency ratings: An application of bank branch operating efficiencies", *Managerial and Decision Economics,* 16(1), 7-15.

Hartman, T.E., Storbeck, J.E. and Byrnes, P. (2001), "Allocative efficiency in branch banking", *European Journal of Operational Research,* 134, 232-242.

Kantor, J. and Maital, S. (1999), "Measuring efficiency by product group: Integrating DEA with activity-based accounting in a large mideast bank", *Interfaces,* 29(3), 27-36.

Kosmidou, K., Pasiouras, F., Doumpos, M. and Zopounidis, C. (2004), "Foreign versus domestic banks' performance in the UK: a multicriteria approach", *Computational Management Science,* 1(3-4), 329-343

Kumbhakar, S.C. and Lovel, C.A.K. (2000), Stochastic Frontier Analysis, Cambridge University Press.

Lawder, K. (1989), "Ratios 101: back to the basics of financial analysis", *Business Credit,* 28-30 June.

Lovell, C.A.K. and Pastor, J.T. (1997), "Target setting: An application to a bank branch network", *European Journal of Operational Research,* 98, 290-299.

Oral, M. and Yolalan, R. (1990), "An empirical study on measuring operating efficiency and profitability of bank branches", *European Journal of Operational Research,* 46, 282-294.

Paradi, J.C., Mette, A. and Simak, P. (2004a), "Using DEA and worst practice DEA in credit risk evaluation", *Journal of Productivity Analysis,* 21(2), 153-165.

Paradi, C.J. and Schaffnit, C. (2004), "Commercial branch performance evaluation and results communication in a Canadian bank - a DEA application", *European Journal of Operational Research,* 156, 719-735.

Paradi, J.C., Vela, S. and Yang, Z. (2004b), "Assessing bank and bank branch performance - Modeling considerations and approaches", in: W.W. Cooper, L.M. Seiford and J. Zhu (eds.), *Handbook on Data Envelopment Analysis,* Kluwer Academic Publishers; 2004. p. 349-400.

Parkan, C. (1987), "Measuring the efficiency of service operations: an application to bank branches", *Engineering Costs and Production Economics,* 12, 237-242.

Pasiouras, F. and Zopounidis, C. (2008), "Consolidation in the Greek banking industry: which banks are acquired?", *Managerial Finance,* 34(3), 198-213.

Pastor, J.T., Lovell K.C.A. and Tulkens, H. (2006), "Evaluating the financial performance of bank branches", *Annals of Operational Research,* 145, 321-337.

Portela, M.C.A.S., Borges, P.C. and Thanassoulis, E. (2003), "Finding closest targets in non-oriented DEA models: The case of convex and non-convex Technologies", *Journal of Productivity Analysis,* 19(2/3), 251-269.

Portela, M.C.A.S. and Thanassoulis, E. (2005), "Profitability of a sample of Portuguese bank branches and its decomposition into technical and allocative components", *European Journal of Operational Research,* 162(3), 850-866.

Portela, M.C.A.S. and Thanassoulis, E. (2007), "Comparative efficiency analysis of Portuguese bank branches", *European Journal of Operational Research,* 177, 1275-1288.

Portela, M.C.A.S., Thanassoulis, E. and Simpson, G.P.M. (2004), "Negative data in DEA: A directional distance approach applied to bank branches", *Journal of the Operational Research Society,* 55, 1111-1121.

Resti, A. (1997), "Evaluating the cost-efficiency of the Italian banking system: what can be learned from the joint application of parametric and nonparametric techniques", *Journal of Banking and Finance,* 21, 221-250.

Schaffnit, C., Rosen, D. and Paradi, J.C. (1997), "Best practice analysis of bank branches: an application of DEA in a large Canadian bank", *European Journal of Operational Research*, 98, 269-289.

Sherman, H.D. and Gold, F. (1985), "Bank branch operating efficiency: evaluation with Data Envelopment Analysis", *Journal of Banking and Finance,* 9, 297-315.

Sherman, H.D. and Ladino, G. (1995), "Managing bank productivity using data envelopment analysis", *Interfaces,* 25(2), 60-73.

Soteriou, A. and Zenios, S. (1999), "Using data envelopment analysis for costing bank products", *European Journal of Operational Research,* 114, 234-248.

Soteriou, A.C., Zenios, C.V., Agathocleous, K. and Zenios, S.A. (1999), "Benchmarks of the efficiency of bank branches", *Interfaces,* 29(3), 37-51.

Sowlati, T. and Paradi, J.C. (2004), "Establishing the "Practical Frontier" in Data Envelopment Analysis", *Omega International Journal of Management Science,* 32, 261-272.

Stanton, K.R. (2002), "Trends in relationship lending and factors affecting relationship lending efficiency", *Journal of Banking and Finance,* 26, 127-152.

Thanassoulis, E. (2001), Introduction to the Theory and Application of Data Envelopment Analysis: A Foundation Text with Integrated Software, Kluwer Academic Publishers.

Tulkens, H. (1993), "On FDH efficiency analysis: some methodological issues and applications to retail banking, courts, and urban transit", *Journal of Productivity Analysis,* 4, 183-210.

Vassiloglou, M. and Giokas, D. (1990), "A study of the relative efficiency of bank branches: an application of Data Envelopment Analysis", *Journal of Operational Research Society,* 41(7), 591-597.

Zenios, C.V., Zenios, S.A., Agathocleous, K. and Soteriou, A.C. (1999), "Benchmarks of the efficiency of bank branches", *Interfaces,* 29(3), 37-51.

Zopounidis, C., Despotis, D. and Stavropoulou, E. (1995), "Multiattribute evaluation of Greek banking performance", *Applied Stochastic Models and Analysis,* 11(1), 97-107.

In: Computational Techniques in Economics and Finance ISBN: 978-1-61324-558-3
Editor: Constantine Zopounidis

Chapter 13

A COMPARATIVE FINANCIAL ASSESSMENT OF PRODUCING AND MARKETING COOPERATIVES IN RUSSIA AND GREECE

***N. Pashkova*[1], *G. Baourakis*[1], *C. Zopounidis*[2] and *D. Alexakis*[2]**

[1] Department of Business Economics and Management, Mediterranean Agronomic Institute of Chania, P.O. Box 85, 73 100 Chania, Crete, Greece.
[2] Financial Engineering Laboratory, Technical University of Crete, University Campus, 73100 Chania, Crete, Greece.

ABSTRACT

Cooperatives are considered as a form of business able to survive for many years, due to equal market opportunities and lower production costs for all their members. The main purpose of this research is to estimate the viability of a cooperative union under competitive conditions in the agricultural sector and to evaluate the financial aspects of its activities. Two countries, Russia and Greece, were selected for this study. Their development is still a controversial issue for agri-managers and financiers. The comparative analysis was carried out based on the data for four consecutive years (from 2003 to 2006). For the purpose of this study, ten cooperatives from the largest Greek island, Crete, and ten cooperatives from one of the biggest agricultural areas in Russia, the Krasnodar region, were chosen. Factor analysis and a multicriteria method (PROMETHEE II) were used to analyze the data. The aim was to determine the problems that exist within the cooperative unions and to compare them with each other.

Keywords: Producing and marketing cooperatives, financial ratio analysis, PROMETHEE, factor analysis.

1. INTRODUCTION

Over the past thirty years, the agricultural sector has undergone tremendous structural changes, which have greatly impacted on farmers and communities in rural areas. Globalization, internalization, the market concentration on industry and services plus a growing occupation and dependence on technology and biotechnology has changed the economic and social face of agriculture. It is placing an ever increasing pressure on farmers, influencing their prospects for success or failure. All these changes provoke the barest necessity for the creation of new institutes adapted to such an extent to the market conditions that they are able to establish a new level of economic relationship. At present, auspicious conditions for the agricultural cooperative movement have been created. The majority of countries have obtained a high level of efficient agriculture through such co-operations.

The reasons that encourage an individual to be socially and economically integrated were presented by Van Dijk (1997). These are based on the following needs:

- Accessing the market;
- Countervailing power against markets with a monopolistic position;
- Reaching efficiency through economies of scale;
- Reducing the price risk;
- Preserving employment and raising the income of members and their regions.

Cooperative structures are better adapted for market conditions than other organizational forms of business, since they are based on the economic mechanism that allows one to adjust his production activity better to deal with the changing market conditions and provide members with social security. These circumstances make it necessary to explore existing experience, future tendencies, determination of perspectives and methods of development. Therefore, a complex investigation of the problems concerning cooperatives' creation and organization of their production activity, are gaining in theoretical and practical importance (Ibragimova, 2007).

Nowadays, many economists and financial analysts have long been preoccupied by the performance evaluation of agricultural enterprises (Getzlogiannis, 1997). Researchers have paid much attention to different kinds of cooperatives. Almost every country in the world possesses cooperative organizations (Van Dijk, et al.,1996). Gert Van Dijk raised some questions in his book "Seizing Control: The International Market Power of Cooperatives". He interviewed leading agricultural economists and business professors from Europe and the United States to find out what kind of changes have a place within world food and agribusiness markets, and how regional and national cooperatives can find the opportunities to work within these markets. Apart from this he discussed problems of membership within the cooperatives, boards, and management, as farmers attempt to move closer to consumers through value-added processing (Van Dijk, et al., 1996). A number of studies have attempted to document equity redemption policies of cooperatives (Brown, et al., 1977; Conley, et al., 1980) and evaluate the impact of mandatory equity redemption on cooperative financial strength (Cook, 1981).

Several researches similar to this paper were carried out concerning the ranking of the marketing producing cooperatives of Crete. Zopounidis et al. (2006) analyzed the weak points in the financial condition of Cretan cooperative organizations and discussed ways to overcome the existing problems. The classification of 12 out of the 16 unions of Crete was made for the year 2002. The study concluded that the high loan burdening, low liquidity, and ineffective operations are some of their main problems.

Baourakis et al. (2002) also analyzed the financial performance of Cretan cooperatives and juice producing companies. They concluded that despite the high quality standards of Greek products, Greek agricultural firms are faced with high fluctuations in demand, low-selling prices, and a total absence of recognizable brand names. Furthermore, the absence of competitive market strategies (i.e., product differentiation, market segmentation, specialization, and diversification) prevents increases in profit margins and expansions in demand.

The current research was undertaken in order to examine the organizational function and economic status of the agricultural unions of Crete and the cooperatives in Russia. Apart from this, the idea was to locate the existing problems of agricultural enterprises, functioning under similar economic and social conditions and to define the reason for their appearance. This study is organized as follows: after the introductory part, both Russian and Greek producing and marketing cooperatives will be presented in two sections with a brief overview of the economic situation of both the countries where these cooperatives operate. This will be followed by the methodological framework which will be thoroughly presented in section 3. The subsequent section will present the results of the research, from which relevant conclusions will be made. Finally, an attempt will be made to shed light on the current existing problems in the producing and marketing cooperatives, proposing possible solutions and making suggestions for future empirical research.

2. Producing and Marketing Cooperatives in Russia and Greece: Current Situation and Description

2.1. Cooperatives in Russia

The agricultural sector is a very significant one in the Russian Federation, not only for the economy of the country, but also for society. According to the Russian Federal Statistic Service (ROSSTAT) data, in 2007 the share of agricultural production in the GDP reached 4.4%. But as a whole, according to the expert estimations, the agricultural producing sector constituted 8.5% of GDP.

More than 7 million people are employed in this sector (almost 11% of the entire economy's employees) while 3.4% of basic industry funds are concentrated here. Table 1 below shows the main indicators of the agricultural sector of Russia and their share in the whole country's economy.

As displayed in table 1, the agricultural sector constitutes 4.4% of GDP of Russia, which shows that it is significant for the economy; the government has to pay more attention to its development and especially on the individual farmers, who nowadays remain without the necessary significant support.

Table 1. Agriculture in the Russian economy, 2006

	Value	Share in economy,%
GDP, agriculture, million EUR	29634.3	4.4
The rural population (as of 1 January), ('000)	38 649	27
Employed in agriculture (excluding those employed in non-commodity sector) ('000)	7 106	10.6
Basic industry funds, million EUR	41200	3.4
Government expenses in agriculture, million EUR	1260	1.03

Source: Gordeev, 2007.

The cooperative sector is a very important segment of the Russian agricultural complex. In the Russian Federation, about 22 000 agricultural cooperatives are currently functioning. The incentives for cooperation are derived from consolidated means of production, the joining of different stages of technological processes, innovative techniques and increasing production. As a result, connections between branches are optimized, large scale trading business develops, transitional costs diminish and the borrowing power increases. During the last six years, with the help of cooperatives, the production of wheat has increased 2.3 times, sunflower seeds 1.5 times and potato 1.4 times, while the production of livestock and poultry has doubled, with milk production increasing 1.8 times. The contribution of cooperatives in the production of the most important plants is presented in table 2 below.

Table 2. Share of cooperatives in gross agricultural production

Wheat	27.2%
Sunflower	42%
Potato	31%
Sugar-beet	43%
Vegetables	15%

Source: Romanova, 2006.

The data in table 2 prove not only that producing cooperatives have helped to overcome a crisis after the agrarian reform, but that they are also beneficial for development. That is why nowadays cooperative enterprises in Russia have obtained the largest share from other organizational forms of business. Cooperatives are mostly concentrated in the Privolzhsky (3945 cooperatives - 40% of the total number of Russian cooperatives) and the Central regions (3053 cooperatives - 31% accordingly).

During the last few years there has been a tendency for cooperation to resort to the creation of large-scale producing cooperatives by transforming agricultural enterprises registered as some other form of business. Usually, there are two types of formation. First there is the creation of agricultural artels, based on joint stock companies and other collective farms, since they have, in their establishment, some cooperative characteristics. The second type is a transformation of unprofitable and insolvent enterprises that service cooperatives or other agricultural producers.

In the Russian Federation, many small enterprises, which constitute approximately 60% of gross production, are at risk of becoming bankrupt if they do not merge with cooperatives. Russia is especially willing to cross the threshold and become a member of the WTO. A significantly large number of small companies may halt activity.

The Krasnodar region was chosen for this research because it is one of the largest agricultural producing regions in Russia. According to data from the Russian agency "Expert", in 2006, the Krasnodar region was listed as one of the 6 regions with the highest investment potential and the lowest risk. Gross Regional Product (GRP) in 2006 was 14 248.6 million EUR. The Krasnodar region ranks in10th place among other Russian regions and is the leader of the Southern Federal region. The growth rate during the last six years has been approximately 106% (Administration of Krasnodar Region, 2009).

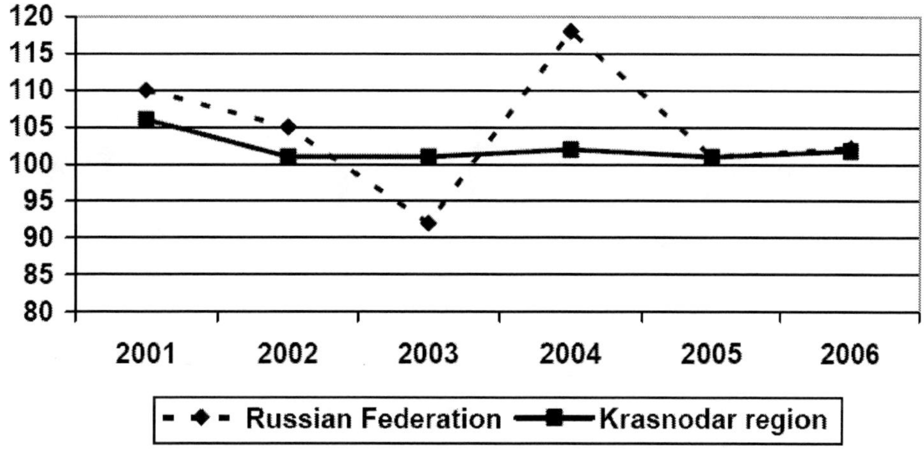

Source: Krasnodarstat, 2007.

Figure 1. Growth rate of agricultural production from 2001-2006.

The population of the region is 5.1 million, with 47% living in a rural area. Agriculture is a priority component part of the economy in the region. The share of agriculture from total gross regional production is greater than 13%.

2.2. Greek Cooperatives

At present, in the EU about 19.4% of the population is employed in the agricultural sector. This value is close to the Greek index, which is about 20.1% (Portugal – 12.2%, Spain – 9.2%, Italy – 9.1%, France – 6.7%, Denmark – 5%, Holland – 3.7%, Germany – 3.3%)(Ptashek, 1998).

The majority of the farmers are self-employed (56%) or family workers (16.5%), whilst 27.5% have employee status with full-time work dominating (80.5%). Among the workforce 93.4% has a low or intermediate education level. The majority of enterprises are small-scale. The agricultural sector accounts for 14.2% of total EU manufacturing output, with €675 billion worth of production. Of this output, 38.5% is generated by the co-operative sector. The 2004 EU enlargement meant an increase of 30% in agricultural land, while production expanded by about 15% for most products (COGECA, 2005).

From the International Cooperative Alliance's (ICA) annual report which describes not only the cooperative movement at the global level, but also at the regional level, it is obvious that cooperative organizations are maintaining a strong position both in the market and European society.

In total, there are, at present more than 267 000 cooperatives operating in the EU, 46 000 of which are agricultural cooperatives, with more than 5.4 million members. In the individual EU countries, the members and shares vary widely, as can be seen in figure 2.

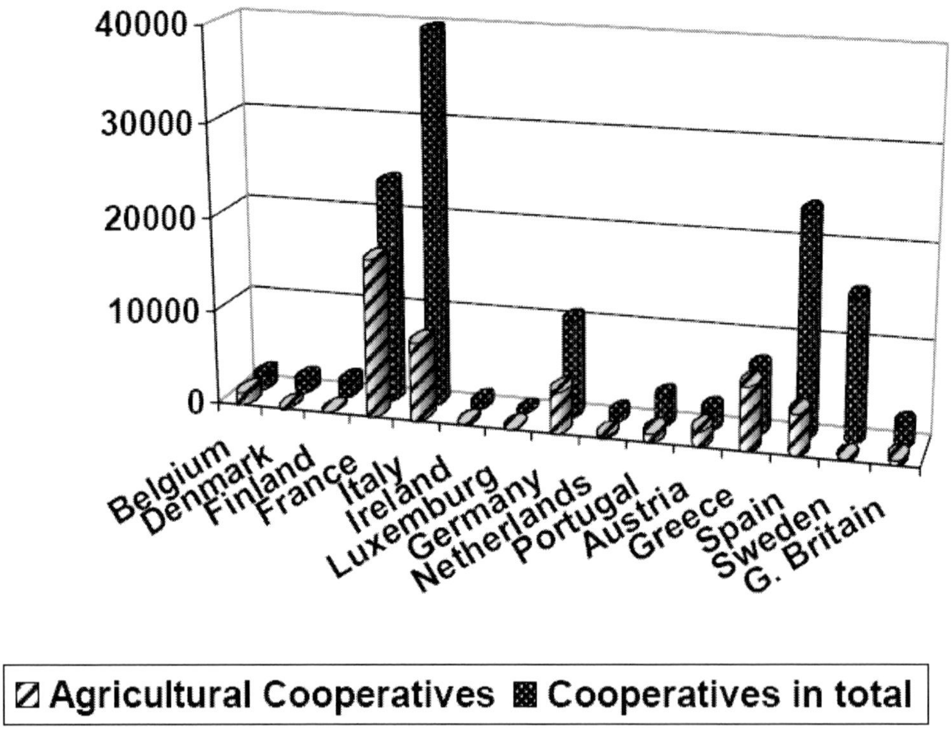

Source: B. Bouchkova, 2002.

Figure 2. Number of cooperatives and their members in the EU, 1996-1999.

At present, there are about 7 000 agricultural cooperatives in Greece. The relative numbers for the Greek agricultural industry compared with 14 other EU countries are not only indicative but also worrying. The number of farmers working in agriculture is 3 times that of those working in the same sector in the EU. In addition, the membership of the local co-ops in Greece is equal to the average number of the European market states' co-ops (Baourakis, et al., 2002). Greek agriculture in general has been declining, but is still continuing to occupy an important position in the economy, although its contribution is diminishing. Between the early 1990s and 2004, the share of agriculture in GDP declined from 14% to 7% and the share of farm employment from total employment declined from 22% to 15%.

Today, cooperatives are formed in a particular structure, consisting of three levels. The majority of them mainly belong to the first level of the structure. There are local cooperatives functioning in a rural surrounding, dealing mostly with the supply of farm inputs and processing. Cooperatives in Greece employ approximately 800 000 members. The cooperatives of the first level can be distinguished as multi-purpose cooperatives with varied kinds of activities.

The second level of cooperative structure in Greece consists of cooperative unions and is comprised of approximately 130 unions within the country, which are founded and functioning in each region. Together local and regional cooperatives constitute the third level, where the central unions are functioning. At this level, there are 10 unions concentrating on the marketing of one particular product (wine, olive oil, citrus fruits). For instance, the central co-operative union is "Elaiourgiki", the Union of Citriculturists of Crete, and the consortium which constitutes KSOS (a syndicate of co-operative organizations for grapes) (Zopounidis, et al., 2006).

Nowadays, agricultural cooperatives and their activity have become a significant determining factor for the agricultural development of all countries and each region individually, due to their large share and total amount of production in each country. Crete constitutes 7.4% of agricultural land in Greece and specializes in traditional cultivations such as olive and viticulture. Crete's share of national production in olive oil is 46% (in 2004), while approximately 10% of Greek fruit and vegetables originate from Crete. The region has a comparative advantage in the production of out-of-season vegetables and flowers due to its favorable climatic conditions (ABG, 2005). Besides this, about 50% of the population is employed in the agricultural sector. The employment of people by prefecture is depicted in table 3.

Table 3. Urban-rural population in Crete, 2001

Crete, prefectures	Urban population (%)	Rural Population (%)
Region of Crete	57.98	42.02
Heraklion Prefecture	64.50	35.50
Lassithi Prefecture	49.74	50.26
Rethimnon Prefecture	38.44	61.56
Chania Prefecture	60.11	39.89

Source: NSSG, 2001.

Due to the significant share of the rural population, agricultural cooperatives in Crete constitute a significant share of all agricultural cooperatives in Greece. There are about 650 cooperatives in Crete out of a total of 7 000 in Greece. In Crete, there are currently 14 operating unions, compared to the 17 existing unions up to 2002. Negative economic developments forced four unions in the region of Chania to merge and form a new one three years ago (OECD, 2005). In this research, attention was paid to the unions of agricultural cooperatives: their viability, problems and diminishing profitability.

3. Methodological Framework

The research used a sample of the 10 largest agricultural producing cooperatives located in the Krasnodar region and 10 agricultural unions located in Crete. The common characteristic for these two groups of enterprises is that they all belong to the same industrial sector and are located in the same geographical region, which means that market conditions, the legal framework and government programs share similarities within each group. The sample selection was also made based on the idea that the application of the methodology suggested in the current work can be applied to different business forms that function more or less in the same economic and business environment and face almost the same levels of financial risk and market uncertainty.

In order to examine the financial activity of producing cooperatives in the Krasnodar region, their financial statements (balance sheets and profit and loss accounts) for 4 years (2003 to 2006) were examined. All data for the current research were provided by the Administration of the Krasnodar region, Department of Agriculture and Producing Industry. According to the law, cooperative enterprises are not obliged to publish their financial statements. Due to the available information, all cooperatives are of approximately a similar size in terms of total assets and sales and all of them are profitable.

For the same period (2003 to 2006), the financial data for 10 Cretan cooperatives was gathered through personal interviews with the managers of these enterprises. The same sampling was used in similar studies with regard to the financial performance of cooperatives (Zopounidis, et al., 2006; Kalogeras, et al., 2004).

All the cooperatives located in Russia were established around the 1930s as collective farms and were later transformed into cooperatives. Therefore, most of them have a policy based on old principles of running business, but at the same time, the management of these enterprises is experienced enough to adapt to the changes of the political and economic situation. Cretan cooperatives have also been functioning for a long time, and are thus encountering the same problems: unqualified staff, weak management systems and vintage principles of running a business. These are the common characteristics that drive the cooperatives to unprofitable results.

A number of ratios have been found to be useful indicators of the financial performance and risk-bearing ability of the cooperatives under examination. These ratios could be grouped into three categories: profitability, solvency, and managerial performance, estimated with the help of financial analysis and then though the multicriteria decision-making methods.

3.1. The PROMETHEE Method

The evaluation of the financial performance for all cooperatives was made via the PROMETHEE II. The multicriteria method PROMETHEE II (Preference Ranking Organization METHod for Enrichment Evaluation; Brans, et al., (1986)) is an appropriate method for the kind of problems where several often conflicting multiple criteria must be taken into consideration. This method is based on the theory of outranking relations which constitutes a particular methodological current of multicriteria analysis. All the techniques based on the theory of outranking relations operate in two stages. In the first stage the development of an outranking relation between the examined alternative activities is pursued. In the second stage the exploitation of the outranking relation is fulfilled so that the result of evaluating alternative activities can be exported in a desirable form (classification, hierarchy, choice) (Doumpos, et al., 2004; Zopounidis, et al., 2004).

The resulting outranking relation allows the estimation of the strength of outranking of an alternative activity x_i against another alternative activity x_j. Each criterion is given a weight p

depending on its importance. The weight increases with the importance of the criterion. The criteria's weights constitute the basis for the assessment of the degree of preference for alternative x_i over alternative x_j (Kalogeras, et al., 2004).

The preference function can take various forms, depending on the judgment policy of the decision maker. In PROMETHEE six types of preference functions are used to assess the differences between the alternatives in the evaluation criteria (Brans et al., 1986). In this study the Gaussian function is used:

$$P_k(\boldsymbol{x}_i, \boldsymbol{x}_j) = 1 - exp\left(-\frac{(x_{ik} - x_{jk})^2}{2\sigma_k^2}\right)$$

where x_{ik}, x_{jk} are the descriptions of the alternatives on criterion k and σ_k a user-defined parameter.

The partial preference index evaluation $P_k\ (x_i, x_j)$ ranges between 0 and 1. The higher it is (e.g. when $P_k\ (x_i, x_j) \approx 1$), the stronger is the preference for activity x_i over activity x_j on criterion k. The partial preference indices are aggregated into a global preference index $\Pi(x_i,x_j)$ as follows:

$$\Pi(\boldsymbol{x}_i, \boldsymbol{x}_j) = \frac{\sum_{k=1}^{n} W_k P_k(\boldsymbol{x}_i, \boldsymbol{x}_j)}{\sum_{k=1}^{n} W_k}$$

where:

n is the number of criteria and W_k is the weight of criterion k.

Similarly to the partial indices, the global preference index ranges in [0;1] and represents the overall degree of preference for x_i over x_j.

The results of all the pair-wise comparisons are then used to assess the overall performance of each alternative x_i as follows:

$$\Phi(\boldsymbol{x}_i) = \sum_{j=1}^{m} \Pi(\boldsymbol{x}_i, \boldsymbol{x}_j) - \sum_{j=1}^{m} \Pi(\boldsymbol{x}_i, \boldsymbol{x}_j)$$

where:

m is the number of alternatives in the sample.

This net flow score ranges in [-m+1, m-1]. The case $\Phi(x_i) \approx m+1$ indicates that alternative x_i is strongly preferred over all the other m-1 alternatives, whereas $\Phi(x_i) \approx -m+1$indicates that each of the other m-1 alternatives are strongly preferred over x_i. This methodology helps to estimate the viability of cooperatives and to give a rational evaluation of their financial activity (through the financial ratios).

3.2. Case Study

In the current study, the following multicriteria problem was considered: 11 out of 15 criteria were chosen using factor analysis. These were considered as useful indicators of the financial performance of the cooperatives under investigation. The criteria and ratios for their calculation are presented in table 4.

The evaluation of the financial performance of agricultural producing cooperatives was made with the help of the PROMETHEE II method, because several conflicting criteria had to be taken into consideration. For the purposes of this study, the Gaussian preference function was used for all financial ratios. The use of the Gaussian form requires only the specification of one parameter. This function is a generalization of the other five forms, while the fact that it does not have discontinuities contributes to the stability and the robustness of the obtained results (Brans, et al., 1986).

Table 4. Financial ratios used in the evaluation of agricultural producing cooperatives

1. Net profit margin	NET PROFIT/SALES
2. Return on equity (ROE)	NET PROFIT/OWNER'S EQUITY
3. Total Assets turnover ratio	SALES/TOTAL ASSETS
4. Fixed Assets turnover ratio	SALES/FIXED ASSETS
5. Current ratio	CURRENT ASSETS/CURRENT LIABILITIES
6. Inventories turnover ratio	SALES/INVENTORIES
7. Accounts receivable turnover	SALES/RECIEVABLES
8. Turnover ratio of working capital	SALES/ (CURRENT ASSETS-CURRENT LIABILITIES)
9. Gearing	LONG-TERM LIABILITIES /(EQUITY+LONG-TERM LIABILITIES)
10. Ability of loaning indicator	EQUITY CAPITAL/TOTAL LIABILITIES
11. Debt ratio	TOTAL LIABILITIES/TOTAL ASSETS

Then, by using the PROMETHEE II methodology the ranking for two groups of cooperatives was obtained. The ranking is determined on the basis of the net flows obtained through the PROMETHEE II method (high net flow corresponds to high financial performance and vice versa).

In order to determine the weights of the selected financial ratios, 500 different scenarios were examined to discern the significance of the selected ratios tested (Baourakis, et al., 2002).

3.3. Discussion and Results

The corresponding results obtained by examining the two groups of agricultural producing cooperatives and the unions of cooperatives are summarized in tables 5 and 6 below.

3.3.1. Evaluation of the Financial Performance of the Agricultural Cooperatives in Russia

All of the Russian cooperatives included in the study are diversified enterprises, combining not only livestock, but also different kinds of crop production. The most common grain crops produced by the cooperatives are: cereals, winter crops, barley, corn, soy bean, pea, sun-flower and sugar-beet in a negligible quantity. The stock-raising branch consists mostly from the milk stock and pig-bearing in agricultural cooperatives. Moreover, almost all of them have at least a small processing plant producing final products, although none of them can be considered a marketing cooperative.

Taking into consideration 11 ratios obtained from Factor Analysis, an assessment procedure through the PROMETHEE II method was carried out. The corresponding results obtained by examining the agricultural producing cooperatives in Krasnodar Region are summarized in this section. The data for the cooperatives in Russia were grouped in table 5 below, which illustrates the Promethee net flows for each observed year (from 2003 to 2006), while the average results were calculated for the whole period.

Table 5. Ranking of agricultural producing cooperatives in Russia

COOPERATIVE	2003	2004	2005	2006	AVERAGE	RANKING
Rodina	1.88	0.43	-1.26	-0.37	0.26	4
Kalininskiy	-0.94	0.87	2.01	1.64	0.78	3
Kaukas	-0.27	0.20	-0.13	1.48	-0.01	6
Noviy Put	0.76	1.77	2.03	0.10	1.34	1
Druzba	-1.61	-1.70	-0.44	-0.52	-1.15	9
Kolos	-2.07	-1.54	-1.48	-2.06	-1.84	10
Mayak Revoluzii	-0.21	-1.32	-1.27	-0.43	-0.62	8
Bolshevic	1.45	0.98	1.09	1.17	1.34	2
Nasha Rodina	0.73	0.37	0.17	-0.30	0.03	5
Krasnaya Zvezda	0.27	-0.06	-0.72	-0.70	-0.14	7

In 2003 the agricultural cooperative "Rodina" ranked 1st, in spite of its significant long-term indebtedness by the end of the year. This enterprise is one the biggest cooperatives in terms of property, but the assets turnover coefficient constituted only 0.61 for this year which means that the management of the organization is not efficient enough; still the received profit came to almost 3 000 Euro. "Krasnaya Zvezda" earned the smallest net income; despite this fact it was ranked 5th, as well as "Mayak Revoluzii", which is in 6th place.

By the end of 2004 the situation had changed, as it is visible from table 5. In the first position is the agricultural cooperative "Noviy Put". The major specialization of this enterprise is livestock breeding (milk, livestock and pig-breeding). The agricultural cooperative "Druzba" ranked last, due to the negative profit it received. As a whole, ranking for this year can be considered well-grounded, because the biggest cooperatives with the largest assets, insignificant current liabilities, no backlog in payments, as well as high (but not very large) income, were ranked first.

By the end of 2005 the agricultural cooperative "Noviy Put" retained the leading position in the list and showed better indexes than the previous year. Based on the financial statements, it can be concluded that the management of this enterprise worked better, thanks to the net income increase of about 400 000 EUR, taking into consideration the fact that current liabilities grew insignificantly. The agricultural cooperative "Kalininskiy" ranked 2nd. It is the second largest enterprise in terms of assets.

Ranking changed by the end of 2006. Instead of keeping the 1st position, "Nasha Rodina" descended to 5st place, most probably due to the changes in the cooperatives: capital equity was increased and new loans were taken out for the purchase of modern equipment. "Krasnaya Zvezda" made a small profit in 2006 but finished this year with a negative result. Being familiar with the detailed reports for each year, it is necessary to construct the whole picture reflecting the results to understand the existing problems better.

The "Noviy Put" cooperative ranked 1st out of all the cooperatives. This company is of medium size, compared to the other cooperatives listed in table 5 and it does not make a very high profit level, but due to its policies, organization of management structure and proper use of raw materials, it has been expanding rapidly. Its main activity is grain crop and livestock production.

The cooperative "Bolshevic" ranked in 2nd place, producing grain crop, sunflower-seed oil, meat and milk. Like "Noviy Put", this agricultural company does not have huge assets, but it makes a net profit, thereby indicating the effective use of its assets. At the same time, at the end of the list are companies which have more assets but whose output is ineffective. In last position came the "Krasnaya Zvezda" cooperative, which, in 2006, closed its fiscal year with a net loss.

In general, the conclusion can be made that despite efforts, financial management as well as accounting are weak points for most cooperatives. Sometimes wrong resource allocation, use of loans and human resources management are causing many problems for the organization. Apart from this, old equipment and an absence of modern technologies do not let them grow and develop. In addition to all this, the government still does not desire to distinguish cooperatives from other forms of small business and to subsidize them in a specific way.

3.3.2. Financial Assessment and Description of Cretan Cooperative Unions

Agricultural cooperative unions are the economic mainstay of Cretan agriculture. Despite their inefficiency, due to marketing cooperatives, Crete is one of Greece's leading regions in the production of olives and olive oil, grapes, citrus fruits, and the carob bean, which are mostly exported to the mainland. Vegetables, fruits, nuts, and some barley and oats are grown for domestic consumption. One fifth of the island's land is entirely unproductive, and nomadic grazing of sheep and goats is widespread.

Table 6 illustrates the average ranking of the Cretan agricultural producing cooperatives, obtained from PROMETHEE II.

The agricultural union of Sitia whose focal points are in the fields of olive oil and wine was ranked 1st. In 2003 its sales level was high compared to other cooperatives, which helped it to use its productive capacities to full measure. The agricultural union of Iraklio was ranked 10th. This agri-union is one of the largest agricultural cooperative unions of Greece, with 167 1st level cooperatives and over 47.000 farmer members. It is a diversified cooperative, specializing in olives, olive oil and vine production. Nowadays the union handles 70% of table grape production, 40% of wine and 50% of olive oil produced in the prefecture of Iraklio. Having a big amount of fixed assets and the biggest number of current assets due to bad management, they find themselves ranking in last place.

Table 6. Ranking of the agricultural unions in Crete

COOPERATIVE	2003	2004	2005	2006	AVERAGE	RANKING
Agricultural union of Apokorona	-0.80	-0.36	-0.31	-0.08	-1.82	10
Agricultural union of Iraklio	-1.22	-1.23	-0.52	-0.88	-1.13	8
Agricultural union of Lasithi	1.21	1.71	1.41	0.64	1.22	2
Agricultural union of Milopotamos	-0.42	-0.36	0.23	-0.52	0.70	3
Agricultural union of Rethimno	-0.60	-1.11	-1.32	-1.48	-1.33	9
Agricultural union of Sitia	1.97	1.11	-0.86	1.01	0.07	6
Agricultural union ASEAR	0.20	-0.47	0.56	1.15	1.73	1
Agricultural union of Ierapetra	-0.40	0.11	-0.30	-0.76	-0.10	7
Agricultural union of Selino	-0.22	-0.32	0.04	1.59	0.39	4
Agricultural union of Monofatsio	0.28	0.92	1.06	-0.67	0.26	5

The agricultural union of Lasithi went up to 1st place in one year (in 2003 it was ranked 2nd). The cooperative concentrates mostly on olive oil production and during the current year the sales of this product were high enough to gain a good profit for this enterprise. In second place came the union of Sitia. The agricultural union of Iraklio earned 43 073 EUR during the current year, but still the management of this enterprise is ineffective.

The 9th place in the rankings belongs to the agricultural union of Rethimno, despite the fact that, within the region of Rethimno, the union processes about 1/10 of the total production of olive oil. The union, due to a significant increase in inventories, in addition to ineffective policy, closed the fiscal year with a negative profit. In 2nd place was ranked the agricultural union of Monofatsio. Compared to the previous year, the managers of the enterprise not only paid off some of the debts, but also added new equipment to their facilities and increased current assets.

In 2006 the agricultural union of Selino managed to be ranked 1st. As a whole the cooperative obtained good results from the financial activity, e.g. current ratio equal to 1.57, which means that the company is able to pay off its debts immediately. The agricultural unions of Rethimno and Iraklio are still sharing the last positions; this fact can be explained by the weak organization within the enterprises, because in terms of assets and owner equity, both of them are theoretically big and rich enough to be able to compete with other cooperatives. But afresh they were ranked 9th and 10th.

The results of the analysis indicate that the best agricultural union was ASEAR. This is a limited company located in the Rethimno prefecture. This cooperative was established in 1981. It can now be considered to be a rather large company with a capital of more than 1 500 000 EUR, producing mostly forage and birdseed. The cooperative of Sitia, which specializes in vine and olive oil production, earned a good profit last year, but since 2004 and 2005 it has incurred financial losses and was thus ranked in 6th place, while the agricultural union of Lasithi ranked 3rd. Astonishingly, the cooperative unions representing big prefectures, such as Iraklio, Rethimno and Ierapetra, ranked last.

Actually all the cooperatives are facing similar problems. The most common problem is weak financial management; as a result there are several structural weakness in the cooperative organizations, incorrect resource allocation, and wrong attitude towards debts.

The long-term obligations can not be covered. In combination with a drastic decrease in sales and low level of assets, cooperatives in Crete are not able to meet competition in the agri-market.

Conclusions

The financial performance of cooperative enterprises operating in two different agro-food markets in Russia and Greece was examined empirically in the current research. The purpose of this study was to rank the two groups of cooperatives and to explain the possible reasons for the existing ranking. Moreover, the aim was to locate the existing problems of agricultural enterprises functioning under similar economic and social conditions. Apart from this, the idea was to verify the weaknesses and strengths within each group and to find possible solutions to overcome the troubles that exist in the cooperatives' operating activities.

One of the biggest problems incurred for all enterprises in the agricultural sector is weak management, which also causes several difficulties in the production and financial activity of the cooperatives. Because of managerial incompetence, cooperatives are facing ineffective resource allocation in their use, high loan burdening and low liquidity levels. Some problems in marketing are common for both groups, such as the absence of certain market niches, most of which are not recognizable by their brand names.

In agreement with past research results, for the purposes of securing their financial health and competitiveness, agribusiness firms should restructure their operation in such a way as to achieve, on a strategic level, flexible decision-making mechanisms with effective financial management. This was suggested more specifically for the firms of the Greek agro-food stuff sector. The Greek cooperative enterprises showed themselves as inflexible enterprises due to the heavy loans, which causes them to charge higher prices to farmers.

To overcome prevailing difficulties, changes should be initiated from the higher managerial levels of organization. The differing responsibilities of the board of directors and managers must be clearly understood and carried out. Directors represent members and are legally responsible for the performance and conduct of the co-op. The key to the success of any cooperative is the effective organization of human resources. From the previous analysis it was found that cooperatives would benefit from the merger of unions. Membership in provincial and national associations can keep the new co-operative abreast of what others around the country are doing. These associations can be sources of education and training programs, as well as legislative and public relations support activities. They can also help to identify sources of special expertise. More specifically, for Russian cooperatives, one additional problem which can be mentioned is the weak legal framework and absence of significant government support for cooperation. Based on international experience, to create favorable conditions for the effective functioning of the public, private and cooperative sector, the legislation for government support of small business undertakings should be improved in both countries. Nowadays, the development of cooperative enterprises is very important, because they are becoming an immensely significant player not only within each country, but also at the global level.

REFERENCES

ABG (2005). Annual Report, Athens.

Administration of Krasnodar Region. (2009). www.admkrai.kuban.ru

Baourakis G., Doumpos M., Kalogeras N., Zopounidis C. (2002). Chania, Greece. Multicriteria Analysis and Assessment of Financial Viability of Agribusinesses: The Case of Marketing Co-operatives and Juice-Producing Companies. *Agribusiness, 18, 4, 543–558.*

Baourakis G., Kalogeras N., Zopounidis C., Van Dijk G. (2002). Chania, Greece. Assessing The Financial Performance of Marketing Co-operatives and Investor Owned Firms: A Multicriteria Methodology. *Supply Chain and Finance, 2, 29-47.*

Bouchkova B. (2002). Prague, Czech Republic. Agricultural Cooperatives: Perspectives for the 21-st Century. *Agricultural Economics, 48, 4, 166–170.*

Brans J.P., Vincke Ph., Mareschal B. (1986). Belgium. How to Select and Rank Projects: The Promethee Method. *European Journal of Operational Research, 24, 228-238.*

Brown P., Volking F. (1977). Washington. Equity Redemption Practices of Agricultural Cooperatives. Research Report (41).

Conley A., Dennis A., Lewis K (1980). Evaluating Financial Obstacles to Equity Redemption in Cooperatives: Program compared to Number Program cooperatives. *Agricultural Finance Review, 40, 51-60.*

Cook M. (1981). Increased Institutional Pressure for Mandatory Equity Redemption in Farmer Cooperatives. *Cooperative Accountant 29, 3-22.*

Doumpos M., Zopounidis K. (2004). Athens, Greece. Decision-making using multicriteria. An introduction to basic notions, methodology and applications. *New Technology Publications.*

General Confederation of Agricultural Co-operatives in the European Union (COGEGA) (2005). Agricultural cooperatives in Europe. Issues and trends.

Getzlogianis A. (1997). Economic and Financial Performance of Cooperatives and Investor Owned Firms: An Empirical Study.

Gordeev A. (2007). Moscow. Minister of Agricultural Sector RF Materials from the Government's Session.

Ibragimova G. (2007). Izhevsk, Russia. Formation and Development of Consumer Cooperatives in the Agrarian Sector of Regional Economy.

International Cooperative Alliance (ICA). (1995). *Statement on the Cooperative Identity.* www.ica.coop/coop/principles

Kalogeras N., Baourakis G., Zopounidis C., Van Dijk G. (2004). Evaluating the Financial Performance of Agri-food Firms: a Multicriteria Decision-Aid Approach. *Journal of Food Engineering, 1-7.*

National Statistical Service of Greece (2008). Greece in figures.

Organization for Economic Co-operation and Development (OECD) (2005). Greece. Place-Based Policies for Rural Development Crete (case study).

Greece. Market Shares of Farm Cooperatives in Greece, Before and After Accession to the EC. *Journal of Rural Cooperation, 1, 17-30.*

Ptashek Y. (1998). Poland. Poland: Problems in Agrarian Policy in Terms of new Conditions. *Problems of Theory and Practice in Management, 2, 23-28.*

Regional Statistical Service of Russia (2007). Krasnodar, Russia. Krasnodarstat.

Romanova U. (2006). Moscow, Russia. Development of Agricultural Cooperation in Russia. *Agricultural Producing Complex, Economics, Management, 6, 16-18.*

Van Dijk G. (1997). Holland Implementing the Sixth Reason for Co-operation: New Generation Cooperatives in Agribusiness.

Van Dijk G, Egerstrom L. Bos P. (1996). Seizing Control: The International Market Power of Cooperatives.

Vincke Ph. (1992). Chichester. Multicriteria Decision-Aid. *Wiley & Sons.*

Zopounidis C., Shiniotakis N., Baourakis G. (2006). Chania, Greece. Financial Analysis and Economic Aspects of the Agricultural Unions of Crete. *Agricultural Economic Review, 2006, 7, 2, 66-74.*

INDEX

D

E

F

G

H

T

U

V

W

Y